CHILDREN OF ABRAHAM
AN INTRODUCTION TO ISLAM FOR JEWS

THE HARRIET AND ROBERT HEILBRUNN INSTITUTE
FOR INTERNATIONAL INTERRELIGIOUS UNDERSTANDING
OF THE AMERICAN JEWISH COMMITTEE

Founded in 1998, the Institute encourages interreligious dialogue throughout the world through exchanges among seminaries, colleges, universities, and learned societies. It has developed strong cooperative ties to the Vatican, the World Council of Churches in Geneva, the Organization for Security and Cooperation in Europe, the Ibn Khaldún Society, and ecumenical organizations in Europe, Africa, Asia, and South America.

PUBLICATIONS

Children of Abraham:
An Introduction to Islam for Jews
by Khalid Durán, with Abdelwahab Hechiche

Children of Abraham:
An Introduction to Judaism for Muslims
by Reuven Firestone

CHILDREN OF ABRAHAM
AN INTRODUCTION TO ISLAM FOR JEWS

Khalid Durán
with Abdelwahab Hechiche

Dr. Stephen Steinlight
Executive Editor

Rabbi A. James Rudin
Senior Adviser on Interreligious Affairs

A publication of
THE HARRIET AND ROBERT HEILBRUNN INSTITUTE
FOR INTERNATIONAL INTERRELIGIOUS UNDERSTANDING
OF THE AMERICAN JEWISH COMMITTEE

In association with
KTAV PUBLISHING HOUSE, INC.

The author gratefully acknowledges the permission of Professor Mourad Wahba, Cairo, Dr. H. J. Brandt, Hamburg, and the Swedish newspaper *Dagens Nyheter* to reprint material in chapters 2 and 13.

Library of Congress Cataloging-in-Publication Data

Durán, Khalid.
  Children of Abraham: an introduction to Islam for Jews / Khalid Durán with
Abdelwahab Hechiche ; Stephen Steinlight, executive editor ; A. James Rudin, senior
interreligious adviser.
    p. cm.
  "An imprint of the American Jewish Committee."
  ISBN 0-88125-723-0-- ISBN 0-88125-724-9 (pbk)
  1. Islam. 2. Islam--Relations--Judaism. 3. Judaism--Relations--Islam. Hechiche,
Abdelwahab. II Steinlight, Stephen. III. Rudin, A. James (Arnold James), 1934-IV.
American Jewish Committee. V. Title.

BP163 .D87   2001
297'.024'296--dc21

                                                                    2001029

Distributed by
Ktav Publishing House, Inc.
900 Jefferson Street
Hoboken, NJ 07030
201-963-9524 FAX 201-963-0102
Web www.ktav.com
Email orders@ktav.com

Contents

Foreword

Why publish this book and its companion volume, Reuven Firestone's *Children of Abraham: An Introduction to Judaism for Muslims*, and why publish them now? The appearance of these works by Khalid Durán and Reuven Firestone responds to a significant period in the 1500-year relationship between Islam and Judaism. This period is fraught with danger and laden with opportunity. We at the American Jewish Committee are drawn to this task precisely because of the "civilizational" storm now looming and because of the enormous importance of what is at stake. We cannot and will not stand idle in the face of this great challenge. In a shrinking world with boundaries between the local and the global disappearing, there is an obligation to enhance mutual understanding and reduce mutual ignorance and suspicion.

These first two volumes of a series we have called the *Children of Abraham* will, we earnestly hope, render an important service to Jews and to Muslims by reminding us of uplifting, revivifying, and unifying seminal truths.

First and foremost, they tell us about the striking theological and moral resemblance between Judaism and Islam. Indeed, no two other major religions on earth are closer to each other. Of the three great monotheistic faiths, Judaism and Islam are most akin; both literally descend from

Abraham, our common biological and spiritual father. Knowledge of that connection has been largely lost among most Jews and Muslims, a casualty of the enmity of recent times.

The books also remind us of the long, rich, and often mutually nourishing historical relations between Jews and Muslims in many lands and the extraordinary gifts to humankind that Muslim-Jewish interaction generated in advancing knowledge and culture. True, as these volumes show, that history is complex; it did not always rise to the level of the earthly paradise some imagine to have existed in the Golden Age of Moorish Spain, but, even in its less glorious moments, it was generally far less fraught than Jewish-Christian history.

Finally, given the understandable contemporary preoccupation with the threat of Muslim fundamentalism (generally referred to among experts as Islamism), the *Children of Abraham* underscores the wide gap between the great universal religion of Islam and the totalitarian political ideology of Islamism.

These volumes of the *Children of Abraham* are groundbreaking in a number of ways.

Professor Firestone's work offers a unique encounter with Judaism designed specifically for Muslims. A respected scholar of Islam and a rabbi, he presents Judaism with a Muslim sensibility and frame of reference in mind, and his work thus establishes unprecedented intimacy between Jewish and Muslim consciousness and worldviews. Indeed, it represents the first work of its kind to offer a comprehensive introduction to Judaism with a special emphasis on issues of particular concern to Muslims. It explores with sensitivity and candor such difficult subjects as the "parting of the ways" between Abraham and his two sons Isaac and Ishmael, the role of the Jewish tribes of Medina in opposing the prophet Muhammad, the Zionist movement, and the emergence of the State of Israel.

Professor Durán's work, conceptualized in consultation with Professor Abdelwahab Hechiche, also breaks new ground in its ambitious introduction to Islam for Jews. A renowned Muslim scholar, he presents the majesty of the Muslim religion and Islamic history and culture. But he neither ignores nor rationalizes their more problematic aspects. His book offers a forthright and tough-minded treatment of Muslim fundamentalism and also offers a candid analysis of the situation of women in Muslim belief and practice, as well as an unsentimental assessment of the historical treatment of minorities within Islamic societies. Professor Durán's book is finally also a *cri de coeur* against intolerance, chauvinism, and religious triumphalism, as well as a passionate argument in favor of mutual respect and reconciliation between Muslims and Jews.

The American Jewish Committee's major project in Muslim-Jewish relations—the present volumes and those to follow, including a book on the two religions aimed at high school students as well as translations into Arabic of all the volumes—would never, could never have been undertaken except for the extraordinary vision and generosity of Harriet and Robert Heilbrunn. Their devotion to interreligious understanding, and particularly to the improvement of Muslim-Jewish relations, is being advanced through the pioneering work of the Harriet and Robert Heilbrunn Institute for International Interreligious Understanding of the American Jewish Committee, founded through their support. Their commitment has been the indispensable cornerstone of this agenda within the American Jewish Committee.

Several of my colleagues at the American Jewish Committee have participated in this ambitious undertaking. I would particularly like to acknowledge the efforts of Dr. Stephen Steinlight and Rabbi A. James Rudin, as well as Shula Bahat, Ralph Grunewald, Robert Rosenbaum, Linda Krieg, Mel Leifer, Yehudit Barsky, Larry Grossman, Aleida Rodriguez, and Brenda Rudzin. Moreover, Bernie Scharfstein of Ktav Publishing, as always, has been a wonderful partner.

The late and beloved Cardinal O'Connor of New York once said: "No organization I know in this city, in this country, in this world, has done more to improve Christian-Jewish relations than the American Jewish Committee."

Let us hope that, with the far-reaching initiatives made possible by Harriet and Robert Heilbrunn, the same will one day be said by religious leaders of our desire to forge an era of enhanced understanding and strengthened ties between Muslims and Jews around the world.

David A. Harris
Executive Director
The American Jewish Committee
February 1, 2001

Preface by Martin E. Marty

For Muslims and Jews in the United States this is a time of reconnoitering, of anxious probing, cautious testing. One of intense mutual curiosity mingled with deep apprehension. For the huge Christian majority, the moment constitutes a unique vantage point from which to observe the incipient American encounter of two communities laden with the heavy weight of historical antagonism and the baggage of suspicion stemming from conflicts in faraway lands. For Americans outside the fascinating and traditionally fractious Abrahamic family of Jews, Christians, and Muslims— whether they belong to other faiths or to none—it is a time to watch how Jews and Muslims begin to interrelate and speculate how their embryonic relationship will ultimately impact the greater national life.

In some respects these are gloomy times for Jewish-Muslim relations. The conflict in the Middle East between Arabs, chiefly Muslim, and Israelis, chiefly Jewish, has heightened precisely when, for the first time, these two sets of "Children of Abraham" live together in America in substantial numbers and have an opportunity to interrelate. The conflict casts a long shadow and inevitably clouds mutual perceptions, especially those of American Jews and Arab Americans. How far it conditions the outlook of the largest segment of American Muslims, those who emigrated from the subcontinent (India, Pakistan, and Bangladesh), is harder to gauge.

In other respects the times are, at least, relatively hopeful: some American Muslims and some American Jews have begun to build positive relationships. These twin books are one of the more formal and visible signs of the good intentions shown among a small but growing set of thinkers and leaders within both peoples, and the "ordinary folk," often neighbors, are also showing affirmative signs. They want to get along, keep foreign feuds and ancient rivalries outside the American equation, minimize conflict among each other in the United States, learn about each other, and make contributions together to a national life that had been so often identified simply with Christianity.

These books are not only signs of the intention to do so, but helpful and encouraging evidences that the learning can go on, indeed, that it is going on.

By and large, American religious leadership is not only adjusting intellectually to the new terrain, but it is also beginning to traverse it. The phrase "Judeo-Christian," which only recently became the semiofficial usage to characterize America's religious culture—and represented an advance over an older Christian triumphalism embodied in language that described America as a "Christian nation"—is, in turn, losing its capacity to encompass a far more diverse and complicated religious landscape.

In community after community formal dialogue goes on and "trialogue" becomes increasingly common. I was involved in a recent Muslim-Christian encounter in Houston, where the basketball star Hakim Olajuwon, a knowledgeable Muslim, hosted a presentation by a scholar of Islam and me. There was an overflow audience. The atmosphere was cordial. The questions were challenging. There was no superficial "feel good" interfaith blather about how "nice" everyone was. Instead, people spoke frankly, and thus there was a genuine chance that progress might result.

In interfaith meetings in Detroit and Milwaukee, I saw Christians and Jews now in open relation to Muslims. Many of the Christians and Jews were surprised to learn of the varieties of Islam and of the differences within the Muslim community. Too often Muslims are perceived as a monolithic bloc who agree not only on Qur'ân—which they do—but also on politics and economics—which they do not—or, as their enemies charge, as united in common support of terrorism.

As Khalid Durán's book convincingly demonstrates, it is Islamic nations and governments that are most threatened by radical Islamists. He also shows a very different and very accurate picture of an infinitely more expansive and inspiring Islam than one learns of in the popular media or in the folklore of the suspicious. As his book underscores, a great many non-Muslims in America and elsewhere confuse the political ideologies of the radical Islamic fundamentalists with the religion of Islam. His book permits us to encounter Islam the way most Muslims understand it—not as it is understood by the radical extremists whose perverted concept of Islam is widely reported in the media, causing widespread hostility toward and fear of Islam.

Jews in the United States, loyal to Israel though they may be, are also hardly monolithic in their attitudes. Nor do they line up automatically in defense of policies many Muslims regard as not only anti-Arab but also as anti-Islamic. On the contrary, American Jews have multiple agendas, including the need for the Jewish community to live in harmony with the Islamic children of Abraham as they have done in recent decades with their Christian counterparts. Indeed, Jewish organizations such as the American Jewish Committee, sponsor of these books, largely pioneered the field of human relations in the United States, working to foster democratic pluralism and mutual respect and understanding among religious, racial, and ethnic groups. It has also gone on record as strongly opposing discrimination against Arab Americans.

Both books of the *Children of Abraham* are serious, friendly, accurate, and helpful presentations of the history and practices of the two faiths. It is my earnest hope that they get used in schools, synagogues, mosques, and churches, as clear and fair-minded introductions to subjects too often still treated prejudicially. I end this Foreword with words of applause. These books will greatly benefit our nation, one in which Muslims and Jews share space and place, time and energies, policies and hope. They are a timely, thoughtful response to an urgent need.

Martin E. Marty
Fairfax M. Cone Distinguished Service Professor Emeritus
The University of Chicago

Author's Preface

This book owes much to many people, and most of all to Leonard Swidler of the Global Dialogue Institute at the Religion Department of Temple University in Philadelphia. Leonard and his wife, Arlene, founded the *Journal of Ecumenical Studies*, which grew from an inter-Christian concern to a Jewish-Christian link to a Jewish-Christian-Muslim forum. For many years, Leonard had been on the lookout for Muslims as partners in dialogue, and in 1984 he invited me to Philadelphia for a symposium with the late Wilfred Cantwell Smith, another champion of interfaith understanding.[1] Together with the late Rabbi Marc Tannenbaum, we then founded the International Scholars Annual Trialogue (ISAT) as a permanent body of nine Jewish, nine Christian, and nine Muslim university professors, all with leadership functions in their religious communities. We made plans for a 1992 meeting in Sarajevo. Chief Imam Hâfiz Kâmil Silajdzic, a protagonist of interfaith dialogue, was still alive. But, alas, the situation in the former Yugoslavia already had become too dangerous. Instead of Sarajevo, we convened in Graz, Austria. The following year, we met in Jerusalem, thanks largely to the organizational help rendered by Dr. Stephen Steinlight, then

---

[1] Smith was the author of an epoch-making study entitled *Islam in Modern History* (Princeton, N.J.: Princeton University Press, 1957).

vice president of the National Conference of Christians and Jews, now with the American Jewish Committee. In 2000, ISAT convened for the first time in a predominantly Muslim country, Indonesia, at the invitation of President `Abdu-r-Rahmân Wâhid, himself a religious scholar with a commitment to interreligious understanding.

After such a protracted involvement in interfaith dialogue, I was delighted when Rabbi A. James Rudin and Dr. Stephen Steinlight of the American Jewish Committee approached me with a request to write an introduction to Islam for Jews. One of the principles of interreligious dialogue is to accept the "other" as he understands himself, and not as we are used to seeing him or wish to conceive of him. For example, one of the things that most offended and infuriated Jews in recent memory was the equation of Zionism with racism at the United Nations, because Jews believe that their religion is opposed to racism. Muslims are similarly incensed by the association of Islam with fanaticism and holy war in the Western media, because Muslims believe theirs to be a religion of peace. In line with our commitment to interreligious dialogue, we believe that we ought to understand Judaism the way Jews understand and explain it.[2] I was exhilarated by this request by Jews to explain Islam to them the way we understand it as Muslims.

The purpose of this book is not to propagate Islam or to vindicate Muslim positions. I gladly took this opportunity to present basic Islamic teachings as understood by Muslims, as well as to provide insight into Muslim feeling and thinking.

---

[2] See Leonard Swidler, "The Dialogue Decalogue—Ground Rules for Interreligious, Interideological Dialogue," *Journal of Ecumenical Studies* 20:1 (Winter 1983).

Writing an introduction to Islam is an exacting task because the subject is vast and there are so many possible ways of approaching it. I count no less than one hundred introductions to Islam written in English alone. More than half cling to a fairly fixed pattern, while others follow various methodologies that serve limited purposes.

The special challenge in writing this book was that it had to be a response to a request from Jews who want Islam to be explained to them by Muslims, not by Jews or Christians, as is mostly the case. It was to be a general introduction to the religion, history, and culture of Islam, but it also had to be topical, and not limited to a given epoch or a particular part of the Muslim world. As such it had to be selective, with a focus on major themes that are of special interest to both Jews and Muslims. It had to delineate the concerns of today's Muslims and their Jewish partners in dialogue. Theretore it could not be as comprehensive as some other introductions. Many details in those studies are omitted here in order to make the book accessible to a larger audience and to devote space to newer issues, as well as to address the particular concerns of Jewish readers.

Obviously, I hope that this book will contribute to better Jewish-Muslim understanding. More concretely, I should like to see an end to the ambivalence that characterizes relations between the two communities. Bringing about a revolutionary change may not be possible because of the family relationship. Arabs and Jews are cousins not only in a metaphorical sense. If they were less closely related (linguistically, religiously, etc.), things might be easier. I believe, however, that uneasy family relationships can be vastly improved upon if both sides make a concerted effort to understand each other. A little empathy can lead to a great deal of sympathy.

A number of readers can be expected to be primarily interested in what I have to say about Jewish-Muslim relations. It would not be surprising if some read only Part III of the book. Therefore I should like to emphasize that for me this is but one of several important aspects. I was asked to write an introduction to Islam, not a comprehensive study on the relationship of Jews and Muslims. Several such studies do in fact exist, some of them dealing with history, some with contemporary affairs. The well-known writings of Bernard Lewis deal with both. For me, tackling this subject served the purpose of explaining Islam. The Jewish connection is an important factor in understanding the Islamic religion and the uneven relationship between the adherents of these closely related faiths. In fact, I consider it a major shortcoming of many other introductions to Islam that they fail to pay sufficient attention to the remarkable affinity between Islam and Judaism. Religions do not appear out of nowhere, and Islam defines itself as the religion of Abraham.

I am eminently conscious of introducing an intricate subject matter. It would be vast enough if I confined myself just to the teachings—that is, Islam in theory. Another ambitious project would be to discuss Islam in history or Islam in practice. In each of these cases, a single volume would hardly do justice to the topic, because I am talking about more than a billion people, spread out today over the entire globe with all its languages and races, as well as a history of fourteen centuries. The subject matter requires a combination of elements from various disciplines, such as anthropology, history, political science, sociology, and theology. This imposed restrictions at every step in order not to overemphasize this or that aspect. For instance, the section on sûfism may appear quite detailed to an uninitiated reader, whereas a specialist might accuse me of gross generalization. Deciding what is more important and what less has been the toughest challenge in writing this book. Fully conscious of these limitations, I have called it an *Introduction to Islam*. The aspects presented are of special importance to me, and I am convinced that they are the most significant elements for the reader to know and reflect upon.

While the principal intent of this book is to facilitate Jewish understanding of Islam, I am likewise keen on making it possible for Muslims to identify with the text as well as to find it enlightening. There are certain unwritten codes of *adâb* (etiquette) among Muslims regarding what to say and what not to say about religion.[3] Many Muslims are upset not only by analytical writings about Muhammad, but likewise by irreverent treatments of Jesus and other prophets in books and films. The many Muslims who do not fast during the month of Ramadân usually take care not to drink, eat, or smoke in public—not out of fear or hypocrisy, but as a matter of solidarity with the others who abstain.

The same applies to statements about Islam. As far as the critical study of religious sources is concerned, Muslim schol-

---

[3] See Akbar S. Ahmed, *Living Islam: From Samarkand to Stornoway* (New York: Facts on File, 1994), p. 115.

ars preceded the rest of the world by centuries, but much of that work remained private, within the narrow precincts of the academy, because of the overriding concern not to injure the feelings of others, usually the majority. One example: Medieval Muslim philosophers such as Ibn Tufail in Spain were of the opinion that independent human reasoning could arrive at conclusions similar to those provided us by revelations from on high. In other words, a revelation like the Qur'ân could very well be the product of Muhammad's mind alongside the message conveyed by an angel. Such philosophers saw the divinity of the revelation in the act of creation and its potentialities, the fact that the human mind can reach such heights that it becomes difficult to know what has its source in the heavens and what has its source on earth.

This view was widely shared by educated contemporaries of these philosophers. And yet, such thoughts were always clad in parables, so as not to give offense to dogmatists who felt more comfortable with the angel than with the human mind, and who would find Ibn Tufail's line of reasoning profoundly disturbing if not outright blasphemous. Today, opinions are divided. Many say that this glossing over sensitive issues is a major difference between East and West, and that it should be respected as part of a cultural identity distinct from the irreverent American one.

Just as many Muslims, however, believe it is wrong to refrain from a forthright critique of religious views. They insist that it is time to break with many a taboo and welcome critical analyses. Westerners, after all, underwent a process of emancipation from medieval etiquette hundreds of years ago. There is nothing wrong with emulating this progression, more and more Muslims say; in fact, many argue that this attitudinal change must take place sooner rather than later because we are living all together in one shrunken world.

Encouraging this process is a profound change in the social circumstances of Muslims in many countries. In the United States, for example, the vast majority of Muslims belong to the educated class. Many of them, if not most, would be exasperated by the use of parables or playing to the galleries of the dogmatists. A new generation is eager for the Islam in which they believe to be presented the way they know it and see it, rather than as a polished façade hiding ugly faces. The important thing is to delineate both the ideal and the reality honestly, rather than project unsavory practices at the expense of lofty ideals or present ethereal ideals as if problematic actualities did not exist. For instance, virtually all Muslims believe it would be desirable for all their coreligionists to be united, Sunnis and Shi'is. That is the ideal. The reality is that in several places they fight each other with planes and tanks, knives and sticks.

I had to keep both aspects in view and try to do justice to them. This cannot be done in a schematic manner, however, because sometimes there is more beauty and sometimes more ugliness, sometimes the ideal is stronger and sometimes the reality bleaker. Sometimes it is not so clear what really is the ideal, and even the reality cannot always be easily gauged.

Another difficulty is the enormous variety of viewpoints among Muslims with regard to their own religion. There are several books entitled *Understanding Islam,* and the authors all understand it quite differently. Some of the disparity has to do with the different stages of Muhammad's career as a prophet. Initially his chief concern was with the hereafter. He was deeply worried about his people, whom he saw as destined for hellfire because of their sinful conduct. Muhammad started as a warner, more concerned with the Day of Judgment than anything else. Toward the end of his life, he was a judge, a military commander, a statesman, and, above all, a social reformer. Believers tend to be more attracted to one or another aspect of his personality and experience than to the remainder, and this results in different views of Islam from person to person.

The ethnic, religious, and cultural background of a people also rarely fails to condition its way of understanding and living Islam. Most of the Muslims of South Asia think that they have completely broken with their pre-Islamic past; many insist on being Middle Easterners rather than South Asians. To other Muslims, however, the South Asians appear more like Hindus than Muslims. Much of their Hindu or Buddhist past has been subsumed into their Islam, and few are aware of the full extent of the commingling. Some who are aware of it think they must combat the pre-Islamic influences; others are proud of the Indian heritage and feel that it enriches their Islam.

Rabbi Dr. Lionel Blue of London's Leo Baeck College wrote one of the most delightful introductions to Judaism.[4] He skillfully analyzed the differences between Jews and Christians with regard to religious concepts and attitudes. Reading Blue's book as a Muslim, one is struck by the applicability of his method to recognizing the differences between

---

[4] See Lionel Blue, *To Heaven with Scribes and Pharisees* (London: Hodder, 1985).

Arab and South Asian Islam. Wherever Blue says "Jew," it is tempting to put "Arab," and wherever he says "Christian," it is tempting to put "South Asian." The differences Blue notes between Jews and Christians, adherents of separate and distinct religions, are no greater than those dividing Muslims within the vastness of the Islamic patrimony.

Many Muslims understandably dislike seeing their religion put under the varied disciplinary microscopes of the intellectuals and dissected. Of course, there is but one Islam. But where do we get it? It is there in the book, the Qur'ân, but the moment two human beings read or hear the book, there is bound to be a difference in understanding, sometimes slight and almost imperceptible, sometimes very profound. Soon there will be a billion and a half Muslim interpreters of Islam.

In 1998 an intellectual event of historic proportions took place whose significance has yet to be appreciated outside the Arabic-speaking world. *Ash-Sharq Al-Awsat*, an international Arabic newspaper, published a series of articles on Islam (some one hundred contributions in all) by a large number of authors. This remarkable debate went on for several months. The very title of the series was extraordinary: "What Kind of Islam Do We Want?" A decade earlier this debate would have been considered too daring because the opinions expressed were so diverse and free of traditional constraints. The title itself would have been impermissible because it means challenging a view that many hold as a dogma: There is but one Islam, clear and evident for everyone to see, and there can be no two opinions about it!

Writing this introduction, the task was to differentiate in order not to present a monolithic picture that does not comport with reality. At the same time I had to take care not to differentiate to the extent that the reader would feel unable to form any coherent picture at all because of a superabundance of images.[5]

The best general introduction to Islam written in the second half of the twentieth century is *Islam* by Fadlu-r-Rahmân (Fazlur Rahman; d. 1988), a Pakistani scholar. Before spending the last twenty years of his life teaching at the University of Chicago, he played a major role in the intellectual ferment of his country.[6] Significantly, his critical interpretation was strongly influenced by the groundbreaking *Vorlesungen über den Islam* ("Lectures on Islam") by Ignaz Goldziher, a Jewish scholar of Islam (Islamologist) from Hungary.

Fadlu-r-Rahmân was a rather circumspect Muslim thinker who held an important public function, director of the government's Islamic Research Institute, in a starkly conservative society. And yet, his *Islam* caused an uproar among segments of traditionalist Muslims who regarded it as foreign-inspired, if not subversive. Since then a new generation of Islamic scholars has emerged who reject the apologetic trend that dominated Islamic thought for so long. After a period of mostly defensive writings, it is natural that current studies by

---

[5] That this problem is universal is apparent from the following statement by Shaul Stampfer: "The topic of a Jewish view on anything is very problematic. The Judaism of the Bible is not identical to the Judaism of the Rabbis. There is the Judaism of the Hassidim that is not identical to the Judaism of the Mitnagdim. Issues that trouble Jews, rather than approaches, are shared by Jews." In his "Jewish Traditions and the Quest for an Ideal Society," *From the Martin Buber House*, no. 22 (Heppenheim, Germany: International Council of Christians and Jews, Winter 1994–95), p. 21.

[6] See Fazlur Rahman, *Islam* (Chicago: University of Chicago Press, 1966).

critical Islamic scholars should bend the other way.

Avoiding both pitfalls is all the more important in a contemporary introduction to Islam. As alluded to above, I felt that I should not disappoint the ever-growing number of open-minded Muslims for fear of offending the dogmatists. Yet it is not so much a matter of attempting to strike a balance as to remain independent in my judgments and conclusions and not succumb to trendy notions, as far as possible. Whether I have succeeded in accomplishing this is for the reader to judge.

Finally, there is a basic methodological question that is almost impossible to resolve in an introductory treatment—namely, whether to treat the subject matter in a more abstract, theoretical style or a more anecdotal one. I opted for the illustrative method and have provided concrete examples throughout. After all, the purpose is not to turn the reader into an expert on Islam but to facilitate access to the subject matter for the nonspecialist. That is one of the reasons why there are few footnotes in this book. Since I rely largely on original sources, most of the notes would have had to refer to materials written in Arabic, French, Persian, Turkish, and Urdu, and this would have raised insuperable linguistic barriers for the great majority of our readers.

A TECHNICALITY

The spelling of Arabic and other Muslim names remains a vexing problem. There exist a dozen different spellings of ʿOmar (e.g., Omar, Omer, Umar, Umer, Oumar, Oumer, ʿUmar, Ömer). Spellings of the name Husain range from

Hossein (Iran) via Hüseyin (Turkey) to Hoosen (South Africa). In Arabic letters the spelling is always the same, but there are various transcriptions, academic and popular, and they differ from country to country. Muslims themselves often do not recognize their names in the different spellings in Roman letters. Thus Benazir, the name of a former prime minister of Pakistan, is spelled wrong in most Arabic newspapers. Arab journalists see it written in Roman characters and do not recognize the Arabic original (*bî nazîr*).

Wahid can be Waahid or Waheed, two different names in Arabic. In this book I write Wâhid for Waahid, and Wahîd for Waheed. I selected the spelling that appears most helpful because even nonspecialists are served better with a correct pronunciation.

Muslim names are mostly Arabic, but there are slight differences in pronunciation between Arabs, Turks, Persians, Pakistanis, Bangladeshis, Indonesians, and others, as well as between Arabs and Arabs. I chose standard Arabic. Thus I write Fadlu-r-Rahmân, though on his Pakistani passport the name was spelled Fazlur Rahman, and that is how it appeared in his books. Muslim is a more academic usage than Moslem and has far wider general contemporary currency; as is the case with Muhammad rather than Mohammed, though Americans are prone to mispronounce it in any case. In order to facilitate understanding, I have sometimes appended the more popular spelling to the more academic one, for instance `Abdu-n-Nâsir (Abdel Nasser), `Othmân (Osman), Qur'ân (Koran), Rushdî (Rushdie).

Iran is one of the few countries in which a systematic transcription of names (based on French spelling) is followed with some consistency. For this reason I write Khomeini instead of Khumainî, and Mojahedin-e Khalq instead of Mujâhidîn.

ACKNOWLEDGMENTS

I am indebted to my Tunisian colleague Abdelwahab Hiba Hechiche, professor of political science at the University of Southern Florida in Tampa, for his preparatory work. I consider him not only a companion on the road but a coauthor.

Several persons have been very helpful in reading the manuscript, offering advice and making suggestions or inspiring the author with their writings. First and foremost among them are my colleagues Abidin Bozdag, Tirmiziou Diallo, `Azîz Gardîzî, Farîba Hashtrûdî (Hachtroudi), Muhammad Hûrânî, Khamîs Al-Jirbî, `Abdu-r-Rahmân Al-Khasâsî (Abderrahmane Lakhsassi), `Omar Al-Qarrâ'î (Elgarraie) and Maimûna Shaikh (Meimouna Seck). I am grateful to Wajdî Al-Khatîb and `Abdu-n-Nâfi` Qâsim for their moral support and to Shîma Khân and Halîma Kraus for their technical assistance.

Most of all I should like to thank Dr. Stephen Steinlight for his contribution to this work and to Muslim-Jewish understanding. Not only is this book his brainchild—he conceived of the idea and outline—it also is his product in many ways. He was a demanding and sensitive editor who always kept me mindful of the uninitiated reader whose understanding should not be blocked by my arcane musings. Equally, he urged me to anticipate the prejudices of the reader so they would not defeat me. When he urged upon me to have the book translated into Arabic, and I was lucky to win Abdelghani Benbrahim for the job, the enterprise turned into an even larger project, with Stephen Steinlight as its director. Sometimes I felt overawed, flanked by these two masters, Benbrahim of Arabic and Steinlight of English, but it was a great experience, and I am glad I did not miss out on it. Dr. Steinlight chaired a panel at the 1997 convention of the Ibn Khaldún Society in Washington, D.C., which for many of us, his Muslim colleagues and friends, became an unforgettable event. We never published the proceedings of that meeting; instead, we are presenting this book to the public.

K. D.

Part I
The Faith and Its History

We believe in God and the revelation given to us and to Abraham, Ishmael, Isaac, Jacob, the Tribes, to Moses, Jesus and that given to all prophets from their Lord. We make no distinction between them and bow to God in submission [*islâm*] (Sûra 2:136).[1]

<hr />

[1] Quotations from the Qur'ân in this book are taken from the forthcoming translation produced by the CMA (Congregation of Muslim Americans) Translation Committee under the editorship of Latifa Jackson and Khalid Durán.

1

The Prophet

ARABIA BEFORE MUHAMMAD

Under Roman rule, the province of Arabia included southern Syria, present-day Jordan, the Negev, and the northwest of what is today Saudi Arabia. The center of the Arabian Peninsula consisted of vast deserts, and its inhospitable nature kept invaders away and made central Arabia a refuge for people from neighboring countries, especially religious dissidents. Since few people dared to travel in such a wilderness, it became a land of mystery. The Romans called the south of the peninsula "Fortunate Arabia" (*Arabia Felix*) because it had some very fertile regions, and several of its states and legendary kingdoms, such as Sheba, Ma'in, and Hadramaut, were well known. This was the land that produced the incense so coveted by the ancient powers. Frankincense and myrrh were used by the Egyptians for embalming and by the Romans for funerals. As is mentioned in Leviticus (2:14–16), the Israelites used frankincense as an essential part of the first fruits offering and to accompany the bread offering in the Temple.

In the centuries preceding the common era, the Arabs were nomads with a typical tribal society. Desertification left them no other choice but to become Bedouins' (nomads), and the introduction of the camel in about 600 B.C.E. made them highly mobile. Given Arabia's long coastline, many Arabs turned to seafaring, which took them as far as China, where they founded Macao as a trading post. Several cities in Indonesia and in East Africa were originally settlements of Arab traders, and the stories of *Sindbad the Sailor* reflect an ancient tradition. These two factors, the unrivaled mobility of the Bedouins and the widespread network of Arab traders in Southeast Asia, later contributed to the rapid spread of Islam from one end of the "known world" to the other.

Today some Muslims are fond of claiming that Arabic was the original language of mankind. It may, in fact, be close to the original Semitic language that was the mother of Aramaic, Hebrew, Phoenician, Syriac, and other Semitic tongues. Many of the peoples in the areas surrounding the Arabian Peninsula are said to have migrated there from Arabia over the course of thousands of years. The spread of the desert forced one group after the other to move to more fertile regions. In recorded history, Arab tribes claimed descent from two ancestors, the northern ones from `Adnân, the southern from Qahtân. Both are said to have been descendants of Ibrâhîm (Abraham) through his son Ismâ`îl (Ishmael).

Most Arab households possessed their own individual idols. In the north, tribes and clans would put their idols in the central sanctuary at Mecca, until it was home to some 360 statuettes and pictures. Though worshipers of numerous idols, Arabs did have a notion of a Supreme God as the

Creator, called Al-Lâh (Al-ilâh), "The God" or "The One God." One of the major female deities was Al-Lât.

The temple at Mecca was called the Ka`ba (Kaaba), which means "cube." Muslims believe that Abraham and Ishmael rebuilt it on the ruins of the oldest temple dedicated to the worship of the One God. Noteworthy is the form in which it was restored to monotheism. The ritual performed in the sanctuary bears a certain resemblance to that of the Holy of Holies in the Temple in Jerusalem: the Ka`ba is but an empty room, to be entered only twice a year for a cleansing ceremony by the highest authority.

In pre-Islamic Arabia there were several Ka`bas, a fact suggesting that this kind of temple, as an aid in contemplating God not as an idol but as an abstraction, is based on an ancient tradition of pilgrimage to holy shrines.

Muhammad's tribe, the Quraish, made themselves custodians of the Ka`ba in Mecca only about a hundred years before his birth. Conducting an annual fair and festival at the sanctuary, which obliged the warring tribes to keep peace every year for a few months, the Quraish became sedentary. Mecca was ideally situated halfway between the north and the south of the peninsula. Moving merchandise between Yemen and Syria, the Quraish became mercantile aristocrats. The idol worship at the Ka`ba with the annual pilgrimage season and its fair was a major source of income for them. Therefore, when Muhammad began preaching monotheism, they saw their vested interests threatened.

In the fifth and sixth centuries, much of southern Arabia

was occupied by Abyssinia (Ethiopia) and sometimes by Persia. The three great powers of the time were Byzantium, Ethiopia, and Persia. The Gulf was then really a Persian Gulf because the eastern coast of Arabia was occupied by the Persians and so was Mesopotamia, now called Iraq. During Muhammad's lifetime the Persians sacked Jerusalem, which resulted in a prophecy in the Qur'ân, in the chapter entitled "The Byzantines," to the effect that soon Byzantium would defeat Persia:

> The Byzantines have been defeated not far from here. Within a few years of this defeat, however, they will be victorious again. It is all up to God, as it has been in the past. The Believers will be able to rejoice and thank God for his help. He gives victory to whom He pleases (Sûra 30:1–6).

This quotation indicates Muhammad's identification with Christians and Jews as monotheists struggling against idol worship. The Persians had their own prophet, Zoroaster (d. 1800 B.C.E.), though over the centuries his religion had been compromised by superstitious beliefs. Neither Jews nor Christians recognized that the original Zoroastrianism was akin to the faith of Abraham. The way Persians practiced their religion in the sixth century made them seem to be fire worshipers. In reality, it was not the fire that was worshiped but the purity it symbolized. Zoroastrians keep an eternal flame in their temples that burns away all impurity. Some historians of religion believe that many notions we are familiar with from Judaism, Christianity, and Islam had precursors in Zoroastrianism, in particular the concept of heaven and hell, the Day of Judgment, and the angels. It is an old dispute whether the word *dîn* ("law," "religion") is Semitic and was adopted by the Persians, or whether it was originally Zoroastrian and found its way into Arabic and Hebrew.

Egypt was a province of Byzantium, but the Copts (Egyptians) and the Greeks followed different forms of Christianity. At times the imperial church of Greek Orthodoxy oppressed the Coptic Church. The Ethiopians adhered to the Coptic Church, under which Abyssinia became a superpower that frequently intervened in Arabia, contending with Persia for dominance in the region. In Yemen the Himyarite dynasty adopted Judaism, which was introduced to the region by a group of Jewish immigrants who intermarried with the local population. The Yemenite kings may have chosen Judaism as a dividing line between southern Arabia and imperial Abyssinia. There was much conflict between Jews and Christians in the region. Najran, an area to the south of Mecca, was then northern Yemen; today it is southern Saudi Arabia. The population was largely Christian but was ruled by Jews. All of them were Arabs, and the Arab Jews persecuted the Arab Christians. It has sometimes been said that this was a unique case in history where Jews persecuted Christians rather than the reverse.[1]

---

[1] See Raphael Patai, *The Seed of Abraham: Jews and Arabs in Contact and Conflict* (Salt Lake City: University of Utah Press, 1988).

REVELATION AND MISSION

Muhammad was born in the "Year of the Elephant," so called because at that very time an Ethiopian army withdrew without attacking Mecca when one of its war elephants, so legend has it, bowed down upon seeing the Ka`ba. Apparently the Ethiopians were stricken by some natural calamity. These events are recounted in Sûra (chapter) 105 of the Qur'ân, entitled *Al-Fîl*, "The Elephant."

Muhammad was born into one of Mecca's important clans, the Hâshim. Orphaned at an early age, he was raised in poverty along with his uncle's many children. Diligence and intelligence made him rise quickly from camel driver to businessman with a reputation for managerial efficiency and honesty. Employed by a rich widow, he led her caravans in the summer to Syria and in the winter to Yemen, as was the custom with the Quraish, the tribe of merchants to which he belonged.

To become acquainted with Jewish and Christian beliefs and traditions was practically unavoidable. In those days Manichaeism, founded by Mani in the third century, was still a force on the religious scene, and a handful of the Meccan merchant aristocracy were adherents. The term *zindîq* (from "gnostic") was sometimes used for the followers of Mani. Due to its geographic location midway between two dozen political and religious forces, Mecca had become something of an intellectual crossroads just as much as a junction for trade. Today we would call such an entity an independent, neutral, nonaligned Third World state, and a "tiger" to boot.

At age twenty-five Muhammad married his employer, Khadîja, who was then forty. Despite the age difference, they remained happily married until her death twenty-five years later. Khadîja's role can hardly be overstated. Some ten years after their marriage, Muhammad began to spend extended periods in the wilderness meditating. When, at age forty, he had his first revelations, accompanied by a state of trance, his wife comforted him, insisting that what happened to him was a call to prophethood. In his vision he saw the angel Gabriel, who ordered him to read. For a moment Muhammad felt helpless because he was illiterate, but suddenly he could in the sense that there was a text that he was made to recite:

Read!
In the name of your Lord who created,
who created man from a clot of blood.
Read!
Your Lord is the most generous,
He taught to write with the pen,
Taught man what he did not know (Sûra 96:1–5).

Muhammad was so shaken by this experience that when he reached home, Khadîja had to wrap her shivering husband in a blanket. Later she took him to a cousin of hers who was a Christian, and this man told Muhammad that he was a prophet and his appearance had been foretold by both Moses and Jesus. Moses had announced the coming of a prophet "from among your brethren," the Ishmaelites, and Ishmael, the "wild ass" in the desert, was Muhammad's ancestor. Jesus had told his followers that he still had many more things to tell them, more than they could then bear, and that teaching them what remained to be learned would be the task of the Holy Spirit (Paraclete).

Thus a Christian was the first person to tell Muhammad that he was a prophet, the announced messenger of God for whom his people had been waiting. Waraqa, Khadîja's cousin, was not the last Christian to interpret Jesus' prophecy in this manner. Throughout history, many Christians have accepted Islam by putting their trust in Muhammad rather than in an unfathomable Holy Spirit. Initially at least, Muhammad saw himself as part of the Judeo-Christian patrimony.

Muhammad's climbing a mountain on the outskirts of Mecca and meditating there in a cave for days on end until the angel appeared to him is reminiscent of Moses on Mount Sinai. Solitary meditation was not an uncommon practice at that time. As was mentioned earlier, Arabia used to be a favorite refuge for hermits. Some of them were "religious dropouts" from adjacent lands where different sects of Christians were locked in bitter feuds; others were indigenous seekers after truth, like Muhammad himself. They were collectively known as *hunafâ'* (singular *hanîf*). In later Muslim parlance this term became a collective name for nondenominational monotheists, the Abrahamic prototype in Muhammad's imagery. Abraham was a *hanîf*, says the Qur'ân. Today Hanîf is a Muslim given name, like Ibrâhîm (Abraham), Ismâ`îl (Ishmael), and Ishâq (Isaac).

Choosing a religious career did not make Muhammad rich; on the contrary, he ended up as poor as he had been in childhood. Khadîja did not complain, even though in previous marriages she had been wealthy.

The excerpt that follows is taken from *The Book of the Prophet's Ancestors: A Genealogy of the Best in God's Creation* by a sixteenth-century Syrian writer. Typical of this biographical genre, it mixes historiography with popular piety. Produced as a piece of decorative art, the text had to be succinct, forcing the author to be selective, and the resultant shorthand shows what is most essential in Muslim eyes, how the Believers love to see Muhammad. The author was neither an eminent thinker nor a great scholar; he was a well-educated librarian who reproduced the image of the Prophet that is commonly depicted in sermons. Whether accurate or inaccurate, this is the picture most Sunni Muslims have of Muhammad. The genealogy at the beginning is of special interest in that it connects the forebears of Arab tribal tradition with the biblical ancestors of mankind. After the connecting link the names are no longer Arabic, but Hebrew or other:

Muhammad, son of `Abdullâh Ibn `Abdi-l-Muttalib Ibn Hâshim Ibn `Abd Manâf Ibn Qusayy Ibn Kilâb Ibn Murra Ibn Ka`b Ibn Lu'ayy Ibn Ghâlib Ibn Fihr (known as Quraish) Ibn Mâlik Ibn An-Nadr Ibn Kinâna Ibn Khuzaima Ibn Mudrika Ibn Ilyâs Ibn Mudar Ibn Nizâr Ibn Ma`add Ibn `Adnân Ibn Udad Ibn Al-Muqawwim Ibn Al-Yas`a Ibn Al-Humaisa` Ibn Nibt Ibn Salâmân Ibn Hamal Ibn Kedar Ibn Ishmael Ibn Abraham Ibn Terah

Ibn Nahor Ibn Serug Ibn Reu Ibn Peleg Ibn Eber Ibn
Salah Ibn Arphaxad Ibn Sem Ibn Noah Ibn Lamech Ibn
Methuselah Ibn Enoch Ibn Jared Ibn Mahalalel Ibn
Kenan Ibn Enosh Ibn Seth Ibn Adam, whom God may
bless.

God's Messenger (peace and the blessings of God be
upon him) was born in the Year of the Elephant, on a
Monday. His father died when he was only two months
old, though it is also said that his father died before he
was born. He was reared among the tribe of Banî Sa`d
for four years until his mother took him to Medina,
where he lived among his maternal relatives. While
returning to Mecca she died, and he was taken to his
grandfather, 'Abdu-l-Muttalib. When the Blessed One
was eight years old, the grandfather died, entrusting the
orphan to the care of his son, Abû Tâlib. At the age of
twelve, the Blessed One had already been to Syria with
his uncle Abû Tâlib, and when he was twenty-five he
went there again, this time on business, working for
Khadîja. When the Ka`ba was reconstructed, there
erupted a dispute about how to complete it. The controversy lasted for two months. Finally, the Quraish
accepted the young man's Solomonic judgment on
rebuilding the Ka`ba and how to place the Black Stone
back into its wall. At that time he was thirty-five years
old. When he was forty, he was sent as a prophet to both
kinds of creatures, the humans and the jinn [*jinni*, spir-
its]. His uncle, Abû Tâlib, died when the Prophet (peace
be upon him) was about fifty. Three days later the

Prophet's wife, Khadîja, also died. God's Messenger called this the Year of Sorrow, because Abû Tâlib had protected him against those who wished to harm him, and Khadîja had believed in him when he took refuge at home. She kept on reassuring him, against all odds, by telling him, "Your are God's Messenger."

On a moonlit night the Blessed One rode on Burâq [the celestial mare] to Jerusalem, from where he ascended physically and fully awake to the heavens. He returned to Mecca but later migrated from there, accompanied by his friend Abû Bakr, leaving behind on his bed `Alî —with whom God may be pleased —to whom he assigned the task of returning whatever belongings of others were in his possession, to pay off debts and later join him. At the time of his emigration he was fifty-three years old. He entered Medina on Monday, the twelfth of Rabî` Al-Awwal. This became the first day of the new era.

The Prophet's coming to Medina led to a change in the direction of prayer. Henceforth the believers prayed no longer toward Jerusalem but toward the Holy House in Mecca. The Blessed One died in Medina after he had stayed there for ten years and two months. The years in Medina combined with the preceding thirteen years in Mecca, constitute the prophetic phase of his life. He died on Monday, the first of Rabî` Al-Awwal, in the year 64 of the Elephant, and eleven years after his emigration. At the time of his death he was sixty-three [lunar] years and three months old. He was buried in `A'isha's house, may

God be pleased with her. Gabriel led God's angels in prayer for his soul, followed by the Prophet's family. After Muhammad's clan, the Hâshim, had prayed for him, the Muhâjirûn [Muslims from Mecca] and Ansâr [Muslims from Medina] entered, followed by crowds of people whom no one led in prayer, then the women and the children. It was like the Day of Resurrection. May peace and God's blessings be upon him.[2]

Shortly before his death, the Prophet delivered a last sermon, standing on Mount Mercy (*jabalu r-rahma*), a hill near Mecca. This Farewell Sermon sums up an important part of his teachings:

People! Just as you take this month, this day, this city to be sacred, so regard the life and property of every Muslim as a sacred trust. Return the goods entrusted to you to their rightful owners. Hurt no one so that no one may hurt you. Keep in mind that you will definitely meet your Lord, and that He will take you to account for what you have done.

God has forbidden you to take interest; therefore, all interest obligations shall henceforth be forgiven. Your capital, however, is yours to keep. You will neither

---

[2] M. Sâdiq Fahmî Al-Mâlih's edition of Yûsuf Ibn Hasan Ibn `Abdi-l-Hâdî Al-Hanbalî, *The Book of the Prophet's Ancestors* (Damascus, 1904). The seventeenth-century original version was based on an older text by an unnamed author. The text, so far available only as a work of art (calligraphy), has recently been translated into French, to be published in 2001: Khalid Durán, *Le Livre des Ancêtres du Prophète Béni: L'arbre généalogique du meilleur homme du monde*. An English rendering by the Translation Committee of the Congregation of Muslim Americans is in preparation.

inflict nor suffer inequity. God has ruled that there shall be no interest, and that all interest due `Abbâs Ibn `Abdi-l-Muttalib [the Prophet's uncle] is to be waived.

Every right arising out of homicide in pre-Islamic days is henceforth waived. The first such right I waive is that arising from the murder of Rabiya Ibnu l-Hârith [a relative of the Prophet].

People! The unbelievers tamper with the calendar in order to make permissible what God has prohibited, and to forbid what God has allowed you to do. Beware of Satan, for the safety of your faith. He has lost all hope ever to lead you astray in big things, so be sure not to follow him in small things.

People! It is true that you have certain rights with regard to your women, but they also have rights over you. If they abide by your right, they are entitled to be fed and clothed in kindness. Do treat your women well and be kind to them, for they are your partners and committed helpers. It is your right that they do not make friends with anyone you do not approve of, as well as never commit adultery.

Listen to me carefully, people! Worship God, say your five daily prayers, fast during the month of Ramadân, give your wealth in *zakâ* [charity], and perform the *hajj* [pilgrimage] if you can afford it.

All mankind is from Adam and Eve. An Arab is not superior to a non-Arab, nor a non-Arab superior to an Arab. A white person is not superior to a black, and a black person is not superior to a white, except by piety and good action. Learn that every Muslim is a brother to another Muslim, and that Muslims constitute one brotherhood. A Muslim has no right over something that belongs to another Muslim unless it was given freely and willingly. Therefore, be not unjust to yourselves.

Remember, one day you will appear before God and answer for what you have done. So take care not to stray from the path of righteousness after I am gone.

People! No prophet will come after me and no new faith will be born. Reflect and try to understand what I am telling you! I leave behind me two things: the Qur'ân and my Sunna [example]. If you follow these, you will never go astray.

All those who listen to me should pass my words on to others, and those to others again. May the last ones understand my words better than those who listen to me right here. Be my witness, God, that I have conveyed Your message to Your people.

FROM *ISLÂM* TO ISLAM

When Muhammad set out on his mission, his intent was not to found a new religion. He was driven by the desire to bring the Peoples of the Book (primarily Jews and Christians) back to the original faith of Abraham. He had learned that the various types of Christianity and sects of Judaism all sprang from the same source. Since they had come to differ among themselves, he regarded it as his task to reestablish the original Abrahamic religion:

They say: "Be Jews or Christians if you want to do the right thing." Tell them: No! I follow the religion of Abraham, the true one. He did not join gods with the One God. You People of the Book! Why do you fight over Abraham? He was first, before the Torah and the Gospel were revealed. Don't you understand? (Sûra 2:135, 3:65).

Muhammad's primordial intention was not to create yet another community of faith in addition to the existing Christian churches and Jewish sects. His original mission was to bring all of them together on a common platform: the reconstituted Abrahamic original. Since he wanted to make them convert, or rather reconvert, to the religion of Abraham, the prototypical Abrahamic religion had to be reconstructed. That reconstruction became the religion of *islâm*, at least in its ideal sense, as enshrined in the revelation of the Qur'ân.

This explanation may astonish those who associate the word *islâm* with the religion of Islam as we know it today, with the world community of Islam as a political and social phenomenon with a history of fourteen centuries. Let us momentarily set aside this conception of Islam and bear in mind that the word *islâm* means "submission to the will of God." It is related to *salâm*, which is the same as the Hebrew *shalom*, meaning "peace," with the underlying connotation of soundness and wholesomeness. In the Qur'ân we read:

This was the legacy that Abraham left to his sons, and so did Jacob: "My sons! God has chosen the faith for

you, therefore die not except in the faith of *islâm*" (Sûra
2:132).

One who practices *islam* is a *muslim*, that is, a person who
surrenders to the will of God. According to the Qur'ân "It is
the cult of your father, Abraham. He was the one who named
you Muslims" (Sûra 22:78). It is in this sense that we have to
understand the verses of the Qur'ân that speak of *islâm* as a
precondition for salvation: "Whoso desires another religion
than *islâm*, it shall not be accepted of him" (Sûra 3:85); "With
God the religion is *islâm*" (Sûra 3:19). The reference here is to
islâm in its theological meaning, not to Islam in the sociologi-
cal sense as the communal base of the caliphal empire.

Many mystics and reformers stress the literal meaning of
the word *islâm* over and against its communal one, thus distinguishing the present-day community of followers of Islam
from the ideal notion underlying the term *islâm*. No Jew or
Christian could possibly object to *islâm* in the sense of peace-
fulness and submission to God. In this ideal sense of the
word, *islâm* remains a goal for all alike: Jews, Christians,
Muslims. Some Muslims hold that today's followers of Islam
are often as remote from the ideal meaning of *islâm* as are
Jews and Christians, while many Jews and Christians are
quite close to *islâm*.

Scholars have often sought to determine whether Islam is
closer to Judaism or to Christianity, or, as some put it,
whether the Qur'ân has taken more from the Hebrew Bible or
the New Testament. Those asking the question usually fail to
consider that in the sixth and seventh centuries, and particu-

larly in Arabia, Christianity was still fairly close to Judaism, despite the conflict between them in Southern Arabia. Many Christians were of Jewish origin, for which reason we speak of Judeo-Christians. Having said as much, the relationship between Judaism and Islam is extraordinarily close, stronger than between any other two religions. Muslims rarely deny this link, and many regard Christianity as the odd man out in the Abraham family, on the grounds that the Holy Trinity is a break with the monotheism that Jews and Muslims share.

When the Najran Christians sent a delegation to Muhammad in Medina, they were well received. He offered them his mosque to hold their service. His relations with Christian Ethiopia were equally good. When the persecution of his followers in Mecca became unbearable, he sent them to Ethiopia. The negus, as the Ethiopian king was called, believed their insistence on kinship with Christianity and protected them.

Islam and Christianity are kindred spirits in their revolt against the overly ritualistic strand of Judaism, though the same pedantic formalism soon surfaced in both of them. Pristine Christianity was a revolt from within Judaism, and so was Islam. It is clear that Muhammad was immersed in Jewish materials (the stories of Joseph in Egypt and the Exodus are reproduced in the Qur'ân, while *sharî`a*, the term for Islamic law, is an Arabic rendering of *halakhah*). Some polemicists have called Islam a Christian heresy. By the same token it could be called a Jewish heresy, just as Christianity began as a Jewish heresy. We are fortunate to live in a time when the term *heresy* no longer has a solely negative connotation.

Christian critics have sometimes alleged that Muhammad misunderstood the Trinity as consisting of Father, Mother, and Son. In doing so they ignore the history of Christian doctrine. The ancient notion of Trinity, found in many cultures, took a while to find its way into Christianity, and it existed in several other versions before it crystallized as a dogma in its present form. It also has to be borne in mind that the New Testament had not yet stabilized in Muhammad's time; apocryphal gospels were still in circulation, especially in Arabia, where so many "heretical" elements had found a safe haven. Muhammad was not disputing with the Vatican but with the Christians of seventh-century Arabia. The idea that the Trinity represented the Holy Family was one of the versions in vogue, as reflected in the Qur'ân's rejection of the Trinity. Other "heretics" rejected the idea of Jesus as God (Son of God) altogether. Muhammad found their view more convincing, as we read in the one of the verses of the Qur'ân most often cited in Muslim prayers:

Say: He, God, is One.
God is Unique.
Neither does He give birth, nor was He born,
and nobody is like Him (Sûra 112).

There is no denying the fact that the central dogmas of the major Christian denominations are distasteful to Muslims, and some of the rituals, such as the Eucharist, appear revolting to them. In an age of interreligious dialogue, this poses a problem. No matter how sincerely a Muslim may wish to regard his Christian neighbors as fellow believers with whom to join in prayer, such teachings as original sin and redemption through the sacrificed blood of God incarnate in his Son remain profoundly offensive to Muslims.

Important in the present context is that this rejection applies to the non-Jewish elements in the church, dogmas that were not part of original Christianity but won acceptance in the course of its adaptation to non-Jewish traditions. In the Muslim perspective these elements are tantamount to a reparganization of Christianity, even though they have rarely failed to distinguish between symbolism and real polytheism. Upon his victorious return to Mecca the Prophet had 360 idols to smash. When one of his Companions, who helped in the iconoclasm, threw down a little wooden cross, the Prophet picked it up, put it in his pocket, and said, "Not this one."

2

The Caliphate

Within just two generations Muslims created a mighty empire of enormous extent, comprising numerous races and nations. Even after it was divided, first into a western caliphate (Córdoba) and an eastern caliphate (Baghdad), and later into some two dozen sultanates and principalities, the world community of Islam still preserved its imperial glory. For centuries most of these powerful states dealt with external threats fairly successfully, overcoming repeated challenges by the Crusaders and the devastating Mongol invasions. The greater threat, right from the start, came from within.

After the Prophet's death in 632, there was dissension that later degenerated into civil war. It began with a dispute as to who should lead the community. Muhammad did not designate a successor, but just before his death he appointed Abû Bakr, his closest Companion, to lead the prayers. Abû Bakr then became the successor, or "Deputy [caliph] of God's Messenger." Before his death in 634, Abû Bakr designated `Omar as his successor. Before his assassination in 644 at the hands of a disgruntled slave, `Omar designated a council of six members for the selection of the third caliph. They selected 'Othmân, who was assassinated by rebels accusing him of nepotism. In 656 'Alî, Muhammad's son-in-law, was finally made caliph. Some had wanted him to succeed the Prophet right away and regarded the first three caliphs as usurpers. But even now the choice of 'Alî was fiercely contested. The governor of Syria, Mu'âwiya, appointed himself caliph, and 'Alî was soon assassinated by some of his more radical followers, who were disappointed by his readiness to compromise.

Mu'âwiya was not a Companion of Muhammad's, and therefore Muslims regard his regime as the end of the caliphate of the Râshidûn, the "Rightly Guided Caliphs."

These conflicts were not just about personalities but reflected differing visions of the community and its leadership. The majority chose as leaders Companions of the Prophet who were closest to him and belonged to his tribe, the Quraish. Others felt that this criterion was inadequate, that leadership should rest within Muhammad's family. They added the notion of divine grace as a condition of leadership, and they believed it was an inherent characteristic of the Prophet's family. The believers in a charismatic leadership became known as Shi'is because they constituted the *shî'a* (party) of 'Alî, Muhammad's cousin, who also was his son-in-law.

Others adopted a more democratic attitude and argued that anyone should be given a chance, no matter whether he belonged to the Prophet's family, his tribe, or the Arab race. Their slogan was *wa lau kâna 'abdan habashîyan* ("Even if he were an African slave"). The dissenters gained adherents among the masses of non-Arabs who had joined Islam. Called *khawârij* ("outsiders, secessionists"), they held sway especially over North Africa and threatened the caliphate even in Syria and Iraq. At times, `Alî's partisans (*shî`at `Alî*) likewise dominated among the non-Arab converts and even ruled over Egypt.

The Khawârij and the Shi`is have sometimes been called the Left and the Right of early Islam. Both were defeated, not intellectually, but militarily. The Shi`is only established their hold over Iran in the sixteenth century. The ruling Turkish dynasty of the time needed Shi`ism to distinguish itself from rival Turks next door, the Sunni Ottomans. The Iranians, then predominantly Sunni, were ordered to become Shi`is, and ever since Iran has been the only country where Shi`ism is the official denomination or "religion of the state."

In the course of time each of these early factions developed a separate theology, drifting apart in matters of ritual and law as well as communal structure. What at one time were political parties turned into religious sects.

The Shi`is turned Muhammad's relatives into a holy family, the "People of the House" (*ahlu-l-bait*). The hand, one of humanity's oldest religious symbols, came to be called *Yad Fâtima* ("Fâtima's hand"), with the five fingers symbolizing Muhammad, Fâtima (his daughter), `Alî (her husband), and Hasan and Husain (their sons). Shi`ism stimulated the allegorical interpretation of the Scripture. For instance, where the Qur'ân speaks of the marvels of creation and mentions the two oceans and the treasures that can be found therein, Shi`i preachers explain these words as a reference to `Alî and

Fâtima as the two oceans and their children as the treasures.

Some Shi`is went so far as to say that the revelation was meant for `Alî, but when the angel could not find him on that day, it was given to Muhammad instead. Other Muslims were horrified by such concoctions and began to call themselves Sunnis, in order to emphasize that they followed the Sunna (example, practice) of Muhammad. Today Sunni is sometimes rendered as "orthodox," a somewhat polemical term.

Another difference of opinion regards the story about the Twelfth Imâm. The Shi`is opposed the caliphate, which they regarded as a usurpation of power by outsiders (not belonging to the People of the House), and created a rival institution called the imamate. In Sunni Islam, *imâm* means "prayer leader," the one religiously "in front." The Qur'ân reminds us that the Lord said to Abraham: "I will make you an *imâm* to the nations" (Sûra 2:124).

Among Shi`is, however, the word *imâm* acquired the meaning of supreme spiritual guide. Historically the imâms, direct descendants of Muhammad through `Alî and Fâtima, used to be rivals of the caliphs. Some Shi`is acknowledge a chain of seven imâms, but the majority, known as the Twelver Shi`is, look back to twelve imâms. The Twelfth Imâm is said to have disappeared as a child from a house in Baghdad. According to Shi`i teachings, he lives in hiding (occultation), waiting to return toward the end of time as the Promised Messiah, to usher in an age of righteousness.

During Ayatollah Khomeini's lifetime, some Shi`is hailed him as the returned Twelfth Imam. Since his death in 1989

Khomeini has come to be called the precursor of the Promised Messiah. Most Sunni Muslims are totally unaware of these beliefs, and those who know them find them an embarrassment.

Many Muslims are reluctant to acknowledge these differences and insist that the sectarian variations are not serious because they are political in origin and essence, not religious. They insist that the division into Sunni and Shi'i Muslims should not be likened to the split of Christians into Catholics and Protestants.

This argument is untenable. Although the split was caused by the struggle over Muhammad's succession, it developed into a religious schism within a short time. There are only a few holidays that separate Catholics and Protestants, or that they celebrate differently. With Sunnis and Shi'is, it is as if some of their celebrations were directed against each other, especially `Âshûrâ', the tenth of the Islamic month of Muharram (the day on which Husain, the Prophet's grandson, was martyred at Karbalâ' in Iraq).

For Shi'is,`Âshûrâ' is a day of mourning, but in the Maghreb countries it has a different meaning, connected to the deliverance of the Children of Israel from Egypt. It is a day of special prayers but also of rejoicing, with music bands in the streets and much merrymaking.

If an uninformed Iranian were flown to Morocco on an `Âshûrâ' day, he would explode with rage over such frivolous behavior and would regard everyone there as a satanic enemy of Islam. Conversely, a Moroccan taken to Iran on `Âshûrâ' might refuse to accept people there as Muslims.

There are so many seemingly irreconcilable differences between Sunnis and Shi`is, it is remarkable that they have managed to coexist for so long. In some ways it is easier for Jews and Muslims to live together amicably.

The conflict between Sunnism and Shi`ism resembles that between Judaism and Christianity. Just as Christians have held Jews responsible for the killing of Christ, Shi`is hold Sunnis responsible for the killing of `Alî and his sons, Hasan and Husain. Shi`i processions marking these tragic events are similar to the cult of crucifixion. There is a resemblance between the controversial *Passionsspiele* (passion play) in Oberammergau and the *ta`zîya* (procession of mourners) tradition in Iran. The resemblance is even closer between the processions in Seville during the *Semana Santa* (Easter Week) and those in Lucknow, India, during the month of Muharram. Both feature self-flagellation, a practice that Sunni Muslims, like Protestant Christians, abhor.

For Sunnis, one of the most bewildering aspects of Shi`ism is the existence of a religious hierarchy that resembles the priesthood in other religions. In most countries of Sunni Islam there is a body of religious leaders that seems to run counter to the ideal of Islam as a churchless society, but none of it can compare with the clergy in Iran, which has a clearly defined and powerful hierarchy as well as a vast organization. Nonetheless, some traces of the original anticlerical ethos survive, because the Shi`i hierarchy resembles a university system more than it does the Catholic Church. A senior clergyman, a university graduate entitled to teach, is called a *mujtahid*. The next rank up, *hojjato-l-eslam* (*hujjatu-l-islâm* in

Arabic), may be likened to one who holds a Ph.D. Then there is the ayatollah, comparable to a full university professor. Finally there are a few grand ayatollahs (*ayatullâh `uzma*), and at the very top, one or several *marja`-e taqlîd* ("the one who sets the norms to be followed"), the guiding light of the time, the supreme one among the good exemplars.

The title *ayatollah* seems strange to other Muslims, most Sunnis having never heard of it before the emergence of Khomeini. In Arabic *ayatullâh* means a "sign of God," and the Qur'ân uses it mostly with reference to the marvels of creation. Niagara Falls, for instance, could be called an *ayatullâh*. As a title for a senior cleric in Iranian Shi`ism it is of fairly recent origin. An eighteenth-century king desperately in need of money did what many European monarchs had done before him; he invented extravagant titles, both worldly and religious, and sold them. "Ayatollah" was one of the most expensive. The title is not used elsewhere even among Shi`i scholars; it is peculiarly Iranian.

Khomeini was one of the lowest ranking of the forty ayatollahs of the day when he was threatened with execution because of his opposition to the shah's reforms in 1963. The highest religious authority of the time, the *marja`-e taqlîd*, Grand Ayatollah Kâzim Sharî`at-Madârî, then promoted Khomeini to the rank of grand ayatollah, because the Iranian constitution did not allow the execution of a grand ayatollah. In this way Khomeini's life was spared and he went into exile, first to Turkey, then Iraq. Once in power he had his benefactor arrested and publicly humiliated. Sharî`at-Madârî, the real grand ayatollah, died under house arrest.

Throughout history numerous attempts have been made, from both sides, to bridge the gulf between Sunnis and Shi`is, itself an indication of the seriousness of the schism. The Mu`tazila, a movement of rational theologians in ninth-century Iraq, worked hard to overcome the division, and so did some remarkable leaders of thought in nineteenth-century India, Sayyid Ahmad Khân (Sunni) and Sayyid Amîr `Alî (Shi`i), who initiated a kind of ecumenical movement in Islam. It was continued at Al-Azhar, Cairo's famous seminary, with numerous conferences on *taqrîb* (rapprochement), all to no avail. Friction never ceased, and most of the time Muslims fought more among themselves than against non-Muslims. The frequent unrest in many Muslim countries is by no means a novelty of the twentieth or twenty-first century. Ancient conflicts are still being fought out as if they had occurred only yesterday.

Khomeini was a Shi`i cleric who owed his Islamism ("fundamentalism") to Sunni ideologues like Pakistan's Abû-l-A`lâ Maudûdî and Egypt's Sayyid Qutb. Ambitious to become a world leader of revolutionary Islamism, Khomeini made some concessions to Muslim unity. Overall, however, his sectarian background only worsened the divisions. In many countries, Sunni-Shi`i bloodshed has been an annual occurrence for centuries, taking place mostly during Muharram, a holy month for Shi`is when they hold processions to mourn their saints slain by Sunni Muslims. Since 1980 this conflict has escalated into frequent massacres and simmering civil war, especially in Afghanistan and Pakistan. Karachi, Pakistan's megapolis of 14 million, has seen more death and destruction than Beirut, but this fact has barely been reported in the world media.

In many places Iranian activism has been counterproductive. Rather than win the population over to the cause of Khomeinism, it has generally caused Sunnis to turn more anti-Shi`i. Some of the most murderous movements today, such as Pakistan's Sipâh-e Sahâba ("Soldiers of the Prophet's Companions"), are not directed against the West and America, but against the Shi`is. Because Shi`is curse `Omar, the second caliph, in some of their rituals, extremist Sunnis have started to celebrate a Yawm `Omar ("Omar's Day"). In the year 2000 Pakistan's military government deployed the army in full force to prevent Sunni-Shi`i clashes on such occasions, but several massacres took place nonetheless.

Sunni Islamists (fundamentalists) are divided on this matter. Many have a liking for Khomeinist Iran because of its anti-Americanism, and yet they do not identify with it because of the sectarian differences (Sunni vs. Shi`i). Others are opposed to Iran because of the Khomeinist claim to Islamist leadership. Tehran maintains its own network of extremists and terrorists separate from the network of Sunni Islamists. Non-Iranians who join the special network are like converts to Khomeini's brand of Shi`ism or at least are prepared to shut their eyes to what Sunnis regard as Shi`i "distortions" of Islam. These hardliners follow instructions from Tehran in the belief that it is the only power that can seriously challenge the West. An example is the Kashmiri Zafar Bangash in Toronto, who edits the *Crescent International*, a fortnightly paper propagating Khomeinism. Bangash is a

Sunni Muslim following "the line of the Imam," that is, Khomeini.

Palestinian Islamists are split into the radical Hamas and the even more radical Islamic Jihâd of Palestine. Both receive Iranian support, but Jihâd more than Hamas. While Jihâd is fully on the Iranian side, some elements in Hamas are not so fond of Iran because of the Shi`i dimension.

For many years the Saudi fugitive Usâma Bin Lâdin (Osama Bin Laden) was very close to an Afghan leader Gulbuddîn Hikmatyâr, who found refuge in Iran after having been driven away by the Tâlibân, a neofundamentalist movement emanating from religious seminaries in Pakistan. To the surprise of some, Bin Lâdin did not follow Hikmatyâr but took the side of the anti-Iranian Tâlibân and stayed in Afghanistan. In Iran he would have been safer, but he would have had to obey commands by superiors. Bin Lâdin chose the path of adventure as a freelance terrorist. Given the fact that some of his associates are fanatically anti-Shi`i, the sectarian issue may have influenced his decision to steer clear of Iran.

Shi`ism is not more fundamentalist (Islamist) than Sunni Islam, nor is it inherently extremist or revolutionary. The crux of the matter is that some of its tenets appear so metaphorical that intellectuals feel impelled to look for new meanings, either within Islam or outside of it. A particularly striking example of this tendency can be found in India, where Muslims are a minority and Shi`is constitute a minority within the minority. And yet, more than 50 percent of the members of the Communist Party of India were at one time Shi`i Muslims. In the same vein, no Muslim nation has produced as many atheists, agnostics, and apostates as Iran. Shi`ism also gave birth to a very radical reform movement that ultimately turned into a new religion: Bahâ'ism.

It is sometimes said that Shi`i intellectuals are generally more given to free thought than their Sunni counterparts. This may be debatable, but Iranians have been leaders among Muslim philosophers and scientists (though many of those lived during the centuries when Iran was predominantly Sunni). The Iranian Revolution of 1979 might not have occurred without the innovative teachings of Ayatollah Mahmûd Taleghani and Professor `Alî Sharî`atî, enlightened thinkers who envisioned an Iran very different from Khomeini's "mullacracy" (mullas, or mullahs, are the preachers and teachers of religion, indistinguishable from the clergy in other religions).

Besides, there is an elaborate culture in Shi`ism that compensates for its doctrines. The largest number of Shi`is live in India and Pakistan. These two countries together have a Muslim population of 270 million, of whom some 60 million are Shi`is, as compared to 50 million Shi`is in Iran. In the month of Muharram, preachers entertain their audiences with artful speeches interspersed with recitals and poetry, moving them from laughter to tears and back. These are great annual events that even those who are less religious hate to miss. Sunnis and Shi`is sometimes watch the shows together on TV. Among the educated class, not many people take the contents seriously; it is more culture than faith. What counts is the rhetoric and performance. One might compare such events to Westerners watching a classical drama.

Just as people sometimes wonder how Nazism rose to power in Germany of all places, the land of *Dichter und Denker* ("poets and thinkers"), many Iranians and other Muslims have been asking the same question about Islamism. Why of all places did it achieve power in Iran? Within the Islamic universe, Iran, even more than Germany in the European context, used to be known as the land of poets and philosophers.

A SUCCESSFUL SYNTHESIS

The preceding section emphasized the profound differences between Sunnism and Shi`ism. There are, however, just as many commonalities that illustrate the family relationship. Some would say that despite everything there is more that binds the two groups than separates them. Viewpoints differ on this matter. The discussion in this section delineates a dilemma shared by both.

Like other religions, Islam became institutionalized as a multidimensional phenomenon. In addition to its primordial role as a belief in the Hereafter, it came to be known as a state deriving its authority from religion, as a moral teaching, a philosophy, a way of life, and many things more. Most of these manifold manifestations were combined into a framework that presented an almost monolithic appearance. However, one or another aspect would alternately predominate. Islam's dimension as a law code held sway for much of Muslim history, but mysticism too had its periods of supremacy, and sometimes it could be quite anarchic. During other phases a considerable degree of balance was attained.

Early Muslim history stood out for its "amazing cross-cultural absorptiveness" and its "peculiar capacity" to fuse heterogeneous elements into new creations without losing its Islamicity.[1] In the course of centuries Islam succeeded at "digesting" extraneous influences until they were no longer recognizable as such. Those ingredients invigorated the old Arab foundation and caused the growth of a splendid culture upheld by a divine vision.

Islamic culture, therefore, has been epitomized as "acceptance of opposed ideas and mediation between them, either in the form of a synthesis, or in assigning separate spheres to each and tolerating their co-existence."[2] While one scholar called this a characteristic feature of the Arabs, another regarded the ability to synthesize as typical of the Persians.[3] No wonder, then, that others hold it to be the unmistakable quality of Muslim civilization as a whole. Ghazâlî (d. 1111), one of the outstanding theologians of Muslim history, serves as an instance. He is said to illustrate an essential trait of Muslim individuality: the almost unlimited ability to amalgamate contradictions and to construct a harmonious whole.

Such examples encouraged later Muslim reformers to endorse the ideal of synthesis by making appeal to "classical" Islam's record of successful blending that engendered a culture *sui generis*. The incipient phase of Muslim culture, especially between 800 and 1000, culminated in the creativity of

---

[1] Gustave E. Von Grunebaum, *Modern Islam: The Search for Cultural Identity* (Los Angeles: University of California Press, 1962), p. 6.

[2] H. A. R. Gibb, "The University in the Arab World," in *The University Outside Europe*, ed. E. Bradby (New York: Oxford University Press, 1939), p. 231.

[3] See C. H. Becker, *Islamstudien* (Leipzig: Quelle & Meyer, 1939), p. 231.

the early Abbasid reign, when traditions, doctrines, and institutions were adopted almost naively. This stage came to an end as the awareness began to dawn that continuous cultural borrowing might endanger the individuality and coherence of Islam as a social phenomenon. Much of the ancient wisdom of the various races constituting the empire had by then been assimilated to Muhammad's teachings. The independent character of his message was safeguarded by a process of selecting as truly Islamic those elements that were felt to correspond to the image of the Prophet.

That this ideal of striking a balance became pivotal in Islamic thought is evident from the fact that in South Asia it was almost institutionalized. In Iran, too, the synthesizing tradition survived in some seminaries, even into the nineteenth century, perhaps more than among Sunni Muslims. Significantly, it is this tradition of reconciling religion and science, philosophy and mysticism, whence came the initiator of Muslim resurgence in the nineteenth century, Jamâluddîn Al-Afghânî.[4]

The synthesizing process was not a planned or systematic enterprise, however. Sunni Muslims generally take pride in theirs being a churchless community, a religion without a clergy, where every believer is his own priest. The disadvantage of this position is that the community cannot easily unite on questions of detail, and often not even on broad principles. There was no unanimity and there could be no binding decision because of the absence of a central religious authority

---

[4] See Majid Fakhry, *A History of Islamic Philosophy* (New York: Columbia University Press, 1970), p. 399.

comparable to the Vatican. The `ulamâ' (scholars of religious
law and theology), as representatives of the community, did
not reach such a consensus as an organized body, because
Islamic theory made no provision for a clerical apparatus.

The Islamic notion of *ijmâ`* ("consensus") may sound pro-
gressive and democratic, but in the absence of well-defined
mechanisms to arrive at such a consensus the process tends to
be anarchic. Whatever consensus there is in Muslim communities today is primarily the result of long-lasting feuds during which the upholders of contrary opinions became
exhausted or were overpowered. It would be an illusion to
speak of a popular will being the determining factor when in
reality it was mostly military backing for one position over
another that decided a religious or political dispute.

Ijmâ` used to be more like a struggle for survival of the
fittest elements of thought, and the result was an armistice
rather than a peace treaty. Usually the "consensus" was
arrived at after a free-for-all among the warring groups of
theologians. This phenomenon is perhaps best illustrated by
Ash`arism, a compromise school of theology. Ash`arism
became dominant in Sunni Islam after rival schools had
become too exhausted by a gory feud that lasted, with changing fortunes, for several centuries.

Since Islam, or at least the Sunni version, knows no church
in the Christian sense, functions such as determining dogma
have been exercised mostly by the state. Often caliphs decided the battle in favor of one or the other school. Generally this
would occur after a protracted dispute, so that the state
authorities could conveniently intervene on the side of the

faction that had turned out to be the most popular. For this reason some scholars are inclined to regard *ijmâ`* as something like a *vox populi*, a consensus of the entire community rather than of the canonical doctors only.

It is a moot point, too, whether this evolutionary process, with its endless ups and downs and long intervals of paralyzing suspension, was a blessing or a bane in the history of Muslim peoples. It has been projected as "the slowly accumulating pressure of opinion over a long time,"[5] the building up of a general will "by gradual stages over a period of many generations."[6] The question, however, is whether such a drawn-out conflictive process of selection and rejection by scholars—and the powers behind them—can provide a perspective for modern emulation. Results typically lie far ahead in a distant future and are necessarily just standstill compromises, "ascertained only in a vague and general way."[7] The suggestion to embody the principle of *ijmâ`* in the form of modern parliaments may not be a distortion of Islam, as some critics argue, but certainly it is an innovation.

Islamic revivalism or renewal is not new. Ideas of reform can be traced back to the seventeenth century, independent of Western influence. In the eighteenth century various parts of the Muslim world witnessed debates about such topics as how far should the Prophet's practice (Sunna) guide Islamic law? There was much dispute about the authenticity of the

[5] H. A. R. Gibb, *Modern Trends in Islam* (Chicago: University of Chicago Press, 1947), p. 11.
[6] Ibid., p. 15. See also Kenneth Cragg, *Counsels in Contemporary Islam* (Edinburgh: Edinburgh University Press, 1965), p. 74.
[7] Snouck Hurgronje, *Mohammedanism* (New York: G. P. Putnam's Sons, 1916), p. 84.

Hadîth (sayings of the Prophet) and their importance in determining the meaning of the divine text of the Qur'ân.

Such debates were particularly intense in India and Arabia. While in India the outcome was innovative theology, resembling a reformation, in Arabia the result was an anti-intellectual literalism that today we call fundamentalism. Paradoxical as it may seem, some of the nineteenth- and twentieth-century reform movements in the Muslim world were stimulated by the Arabian revivalism that is commonly known as *Wahhâbî* (after its founder, Muhammad Ibn`Abdi-l-Wahhâb). Its adherents call themselves Muwahhidûn (Unitarians) or Salafîs, wishing to follow the pious forebears (*as-salafu s-sâlih*). While the "fundamentalists" of the Wahhâbî School condemned every innovation as "satanic," reformists distinguished between good and bad innovations. The Wahhâbîs or Salafîs insisted on *taqlîd* (imitation), which means to emulate the example of the pious forebears. The reformists in India replaced *taqlîd* with *tatbîq*, which in their understanding of Arabic meant "synthesis." In other words, they wanted to draw on the entire intellectual history of Muslims, precisely what the Arabians wanted to discard (and did not hesitate to burn where they got a chance to do so). *Taqlîd* meant blind adherence to the teachings of classical law books and commentaries, *tatbîq* aimed at drawing inspiration from those sources in order to advance innovative thinking.

This conceptual pair is linked to an important disputation, known as the *ijtihâd* controversy. In the tenth century, traditionalist scholars argued that there had already been enough independent reasoning (*ijtihâd*) by the pious forebears. If new generations continued in this vein, there was a danger of straying from the path, because by now the age of the Prophet had become remote. For this reason, the Gate of Independent Reasoning (*bâbu l-ijtihâd*) must be closed. There was now to be nothing but *taqlîd*. In eighteenth-century India, the region's greatest Islamic scholar, Shâh Waliyullâh of Delhi, demanded that the *bâbu l-ijtihâd* be reopened and that *tatbîq* (synthesis or dialectical thought) take the place of *taqlîd* (imitation or blind adherence). Some joined him; others opposed him, and the controversy has been raging ever since.

The result of the many internal conflicts was a strengthening of autocracy, not only in the conduct of government but also in Muslim political thought. Mainstream (the Sunni majority) theologians and jurists often had no choice but to furnish a theoretical underpinning for the existing regime. Their theories of government were, more often than not, a rationale for the facts on the ground created by those with the greatest military power. Today some of their writings about statecraft appear quite hilarious because they were so neatly tailored to the needs of one warlord battling against another. For instance: The caliph should never be bald, stipulated the great Ibnu n-Nafîs, who lived at the court of a thick-haired ruler threatened by a bald-headed contender for power.

Other scholars articulated the genuine concerns of the community, highlighting the yearning for peace of a people suffering from protracted civil strife. Thus they devised the motto that it was preferable to live under any one ruler, even an arbitrary one, than to have a single day of civil war.

This was only one side of the story, however. Such philosophy did not preclude frequent revolts against unjust rulers, especially a sultan straying from the trodden path of Islamic orthodoxy. Recourse was found in the Prophet's saying that "the most virtuous *jihâd* [struggle for the cause of God] is to stand up to a tyrant" (literally, "to confront an unjust sultan with a word of truth"). There was no unanimity, however, as to what constituted a transgression serious enough to make revolt incumbent upon the believers.

In the twelfth and thirteenth centuries, and perhaps even more in the fourteenth, the Muslim world suffered enormous convulsions. Many of the lands of Islam came under the rule of *condottieri*, uncouth warlords, some of them scarcely Islamized. Many of them were illiterate "barbarians" from remote steppes or mountains. Other areas fell under the rule of Christian kings, some of them indistinguishable from the "barbarians." This was a situation for which the Muslims of those days had no legal provision, and the theologians had no answer right at hand. The responses of Muslim scholars were sometimes diametrically opposed. One of them would say, "Adjust yourself to the changed circumstances and make the best of it." Another would urge, "Leave this evil behind, abandon your ancestral home, and migrate to a land under Muslim rule. You might have a chance to come back as conquerors."

Both ethical paradigms, that of political quietism and that of revolutionary dissent, have evolved up to the present time. The tension between these two visions has resulted in two very different stereotypes of Muslim Easterners. On the one hand is the image of the passive endurer of all kinds of indignities, the notorious fatalist; on the other is the image of people living in perpetual rebellion, with one political upheaval following upon another.

Such issues have been of great concern to Muslim thinkers, whether Arabs or Persians, Sunnis or Shi'is. How to react to oppressive rule has been the subject of searching analyses over the centuries. Much intellectual labor has been expended in answering these universal questions in the context of Muslim historical development. It is evident that the intellectuals were not just drifting, and the sheer variety of their responses is impressive. Their delicate handling of complex issues will fascinate those who are familiar only with the crude outer crust of political life. What Westerners have sometimes labeled "Oriental Despotism" blinded them to the serious efforts by Muslim scholars to clarify the responsibilities of the citizenry vis-à-vis oppressive regimes. Generations have thought and written about the political ideas of Greeks and Romans, Persians and Indians; they have borrowed and incorporated from others and yet remained original in their Islamic contribution.

In the twentieth century, however, Muslims received little guidance from their traditional religious leadership. It is wrong to say, as some do, that the theologians at the famous seminaries have been utterly unresponsive to the challenges of Westernization. But it is accurate to point out that they have generally been unimaginative. Those few among the `ulamâ' of Egypt's Al-Azhar (a huge and ancient seminary sometimes likened to the Vatican) who ventured onto fresh ground were quickly expelled from the faculty. In the writings of the Azharites there is, to use a somewhat poignant formulation, "not the slightest sign or inkling of a restatement of the faith."[8] A development comparable to the Second Vatican Council is foreseeable neither in Cairo nor in Fez (Morocco), where another great seminary is situated, the Qarawiyîn.[9]

A complicating factor is that theological and philosophical questions can no longer be discussed within the Islamic framework alone, as was the privilege of the medieval thinkers. For them, as for European leaders of thought during the Reformation and the Enlightenment, there was no reference to outsiders; they merely had to make their intellect prevail against established norms. The foreign cultures that seduced Muslim thinkers under the Abbasids belonged either to the pre-Islamic past or to peoples whose political glory had come to an end. In the nineteenth and twentieth centuries, however, Muslims were in no such enviable position. They were faced with the formidable task of asserting their consciences in the tension between two disparate traditions: their own, being the weaker in terms of worldly power, and that of foreign nations with the political supremacy and technological advancement that allowed them to define the terms of debate.

Doctrinal issues, therefore, can no longer be considered on their own merits. It has become necessary to demonstrate

---

[8] Jean Lacoutre and Simone Lacoutre, *Egypt in Transition* (London: Criterion Books, 1958), p. 438.

[9] In June 2000, the director of the Dâru l-Hadîthi l-Hasanîya, an important institution of Islamic learning in Rabat, complained that "Islamic Studies at our universities lag behind the social reality." See `Omar `Abdu-s-Salâm, "Mudîr dâri l-hadîth . . . ," *Ash-Sharq Al-Awsat*, June 7, 2000, p. 14.

simultaneously that Muslim intellectual currents and social structures are not only as progressive as those of the West, but that one's own views are also more truly Islamic than those upheld by opponents at home. Some scholars believe that the necessity of fighting simultaneously on two fronts is the reason for the dearth of rigorous systematic thought. Instead of systematic thought, we have superficial slogans and angry polemics. Others speak of the Janus-faced character of Muslim reconstruction. On the one hand, they say, it stands in dire need of foreign inspiration in order to recover its former creativity. It therefore has to overcome the impermeability of its own society to the new. On the other hand, it also has to preserve the stimulating prestige of the past.

The pressure of rapid transition, a pressure coming from abroad, and the tension created by new paradigms result in acute vacillation. The multifarious expectations from and the demands on such a historically inspired synthesis are overwhelming. Intellectual life is kept in a state of hypertension that results in frequent shifts of loyalty, symptoms of the crisis of the intellectuals about which so much has been written.[10]

THE KEMALIST MODEL

The fertility of thought among Muslims in eighteenth-century India was followed by an intensive quest for reform in nineteenth-century Turkey, or what was then the Ottoman

---

[10] See Abdallah Laroui, *The Crisis of the Arab Intellectual* (Berkeley, University of California Press, 1976).

Empire. In the forefront were intellectuals from some Arab countries and, especially, from Bosnia. Mustafa Kemal, later known as Atatürk ("Father of Turks"), was the providential leader who saved Turkey from dismemberment by its many enemies. In 1923 he proclaimed the Turkish Republic, and in 1924 he abolished the caliphate.

Atatürk has sometimes been depicted as a one-track military mind who cut the Gordian knot by simply dismantling the religious institutions and putting Islamic activity under tight state control. In reality he immersed himself in the endless debates on reform— economic, political, social, and religious. It should disconcert contemporary Muslims that the debates in nineteenth-century Turkey were more profound and insightful than similar debates in today's Iran and some of the Arab countries, or, indeed, in Turkey itself. Atatürk's reforms were the result of a long quest and deep reflections. The terrain was well prepared for drastic measures that were to affect not only the new Turkey but much of the Muslim world.

Traditionalists, and fundamentalists even more so, hold against Atatürk that he exchanged the Arabic script for the Latin one. The critics show scant regard for the highly vocalized Turkish language with its sound system so fundamentally different from that of Arabic. Because Atatürk abolished the caliphate, he is also sometimes accused of apostasy. In reality the caliphate existed only on paper, and its abolition was merely an act of political realism. The Abbasid caliphate had come to an end centuries before with the destruction of Baghdad by the Mongols in 1258. Some descendants pretended to continue it in Egypt, and an Ottoman sultan claimed that while he was in Cairo, the last Abbasid had bestowed the caliphal power upon him. By the time of its abolition in 1924 the caliphate was once again little more than pretense.

Many Muslims never belonged to the Ottoman Empire in any case and did not acknowledge the Turkish sultan as their caliph. Moroccans, for instance, regarded their own sultan as a caliph. The Arabs who revolted against the Ottomans during World War I thought of the Sharîf Husain of Mecca as their caliph. The bulk of the British army fighting the Turks in Iraq and elsewhere were Muslims from India. Under these circumstances the Istanbul caliphate had become a farce, and Atatürk set out to put an end to all that was farcical.

The abolition of the caliphate certainly came as a shock to many because of its symbolic value. When the Moroccan freedom fighter `Abdu-l-Karîm Al-Khattâbî defeated a combined French-Spanish army in 1921, there was talk of proclaiming him as the new caliph. In 1926 King Fu'âd of Egypt aspired to initiate a new caliphate but did not succeed against competition from other contenders. It had become clear that there was no chance of achieving the consensus required to reestablish the caliphate.

Another response on the part of some Muslims was to declare the concept of a caliphate obsolete, proclaiming it an historical accident and Islamically unnecessary. First an Indian Muslim, Barkatullâh, expounded his refutation of the caliphate in a thesis written in France in 1925. A year later an Islamic scholar in Egypt, `Alî `Abdu-r-Râziq, wrote the same in Arabic, causing an uproar among his colleagues. He lost his post at Al-Azhar, but a majority of the educated class accepted his thesis as valid. Barkatullâh, `Abdu-r-Râziq, and other reformist thinkers argued that the Prophet had not aspired to found an empire. His call, they said, was purely religious, and he was reminded by God that he was not responsible for those who turn away (Sûra 6:66–67). Muhammad was told to tell his audience that he was not appointed as their guardian (Sûra 10:108, 25:43).

The concept of the caliphate as a political institution is not given in the revelation. The Qur'ân explains the term differently. Man is called "God's vicegerent [caliph] on earth." Man accepted the earth as a trust from God and now has to manage it to the best of his capacity. There is but one hint in the book that points to an understanding of *caliph* as judge or ruler: "David! We appointed you as a manager [caliph] on earth. Your job is to provide justice. You can't follow your whims" (Sûra 38:26).

The caliphate as a political institution began with Abû Bakr, the Prophet's Companion, who became his successor as head of the community. Later the caliphate turned into a monarchy, with the Omayyad and then the Abbasid dynasty. During the later phase of the Abbasids it was actually a kind of papacy. The caliphs had also adopted the title *sultân* (ruler), and several warlords appointed themselves sultans, letting the caliph continue as a religious leader. This system caused a division between the temporal power (the sultan) and spiritual office (the caliph). Religion and state may not have been separated, but they were administered separately. This history poses a challenge to Islamists, who insist that secularism is no concern of theirs because the conflict between church and state is a European/Christian phenomenon, alien to Islam.

When the Ottomans rose to power, they again assumed both titles, caliph and sultan, reuniting religion and state. At the same time there emerged a kind of Muslim clergy that bore some resemblance to the Byzantine imperial church on whose historic soil it sprouted, bringing about a contradiction in terms, since Sunni Islam has often taken pride in being a "churchless" religion. Having disbanded this "pseudo-clergy," Atatürk ought to have been acclaimed by the Islamists, who used to denounce the "clergy" in the thirties and forties, when most traditional scholars of Islam rejected the Islamists. However, instead of praising Atatürk, Islamists cursed him for allegedly having outlawed Islam. A major reason for their enmity was Atatürk's replacing of Islamic law, the sharî`a, with a civil code based on Belgian and Swiss law. This legal transition revolutionized, *inter alia*, the position of women, which for Islamists is the most disturbing issue.

Atatürk did not intend to abolish Islam but to reform it, in a rather drastic manner. He wanted the old imperial and decadent version to be replaced by a new, revolutionized one. The task of elaborating this modernized version was assigned to his one-time foreign minister, Fuat Köprülü, an outstanding Islamic scholar immersed in humanist sûfism (mysticism).[11] Neither Atatürk nor Köprülü lived long enough to accomplish the task, and the result is a void that has never been filled.

---

[11] One reason for his not having made a greater impact may have been his concentration on the study of literature, such as his pioneering book *Türk Edebiyatinda Ilk Mütasavviflar* ("Early Mystics in Turkish Literature"). Literature was, of course, an indispensable source for the reform enterprise.

Kemal Atatürk's followers call his reform program Kemalism and refer to themselves as Kemalists. In 1999 they suggested Atatürk as the "man of the century." Islamists would rather have him named the most destructive figure. They call him an agent of British imperialism even though he was the only leader in the Muslim world who emerged victorious against the British. Wishing to besmear his legacy, Islamists allege that Atatürk was of Jewish ancestry. (He was born into a Turkish Muslim family in Saloniki, now in Greece.) Such allegations are indicative of the anti-Semitism currently in vogue among a segment of Muslim Middle Easterners.

It turned out that the trend set by Atatürk was irreversible. With the end of colonialism, many of the newly independent states followed the Turkish example, more or less.[12] Nationalism took the place of the old Islamic identity for which the caliphate was the supreme symbol, at least in the territories under Ottoman control or influence (Central Asia, for instance).

---

[12] See, for instance, Sayyid Qudratullâh Fâtimî, Pakistan Movement & Kemalist Revolution (Lahore: Institute of Islamic Culture, 1977).

Part II
Present-Day Threats

As for those who cause dissension within their religion and break up into sects, don't bother about them. It is up to God to look into the matter. Eventually He will take them to task for what they did (Sûra 6:159).

3
Islam and Islamism

Any attempt at understanding Islamic developments today must proceed from the differentiation between Muslims and Islamists.

The division became manifest in the 1970s, when some Muslims began to call themselves Islamists to define their political identity. Their attitude was primarily a rejection of foreign influences, emphasizing the perniciousness and irrelevancy of "imported ideologies." This new identity was also a way of distinguishing themselves from fellow believers who were Muslims only in a cultural sense or who practiced Islam in their own individual way, as the vast majority do, with differences from country to country, and even region to region.

Some Western scholars are not happy with the use of the term *fundamentalist* to describe the tendencies of the radical activists lately so much in the news. The Islamists, too, object to being called fundamentalists because the term is of fairly recent coinage, with its origin in early twentieth-century Protestant America, whereas the group of Muslims subsumed under this rubric has antecedents in the nineteenth

51

and even eighteenth centuries. And yet, whether they like the term or not, their understanding of religion resembles that of fundamentalists in other religions.

This is not to say that Islamists are more religious or more genuinely Islamic than other Muslims. A common misunderstanding in the West is that the fundamentalists are the most faithful of all Muslims, the authentic upholders of tradition. This is not at all the case. The Islamists have a problem with many traditionalists, especially the sûfîs (mystics).

Priding themselves on having revived the golden age of early Islam in its pristine purity is a tall Islamist claim. There is in fact an appreciably modernist strand in this Islamic fundamentalism, inasmuch as it castigates superstitious practices and certain unsavory excesses of popular religion connected with saint worship and black magic. Movements known as fundamentalist advocate voluntarist ethics and combat fatalist quietism. They promote education, even for girls, and venture into new economic activities. Quite a number of them are characterized by a Calvinist tone. Islamists seek to dominate by employing the most advanced technologies, and in that sense they are modernists. But their model for the ideal society takes its inspiration from a romanticized seventh-century Arabia and an ahistorical view of religion and human development in general. It is an anachronistic mode of thinking in profound conflict with modern concepts of democracy, pluralism, and human rights.

Most so-called Muslim fundamentalists are self-described Islamists. This term has made significant headway in their publications, and few adherents regard *Islamist* only as a label; most choose it as a legitimate term. It is their way of reacting to "isms" that they consider to be foreign, such as liberalism and secularism, nationalism and socialism. "No Capitalism, No Communism; Islamism, Islamism!" runs the slogan. (This is a rather late version of a fascist slogan from the 1930s that found its way to General Peron's Argentina in the 1940s: "Ni Capitalista, Ni Comunista; Peronista, Peronista!")

Islamism is a form of late twentieth-century totalitarianism. It follows in the wake of fascism and communism, has been influenced by them, and seeks to refine their methods of domination. Islamists mold tradition to serve their political ends, causing them to clash with traditionalist Muslims who resist the manipulation of religion for power politics. Islamism "is not a reaction of people feeling a loss of religious meaning, but a reaction to a sense of loss in the political sphere; it is a quest for power, an attempt to conquer the state, not to regain independence for religion, least of all individual faith."[1]

Islamists are more political than religious in outlook, despite their pious rhetoric. They claim to be vanguard Muslims, integrating faith and politics, but their cardinal concern is the achievement of political power. Since Islamists resent being ruled by non-Islamists (whether non-Muslims or non-Islamist Muslims) or by women, it is difficult to call them anything but supremacists. Like most totalitarian ideologies, Islamism is a form of utopianism, and like others in actual practice it results, unsurprisingly, mostly in dystopian societies.

---

[1] Muhammad Tózí, "The State: Muslim Perceptions and Islamist Objectives," *TransState Islam* (Washington, D.C.), Spring 1997, p. 18.

Because traditionally Muslim political power claimed to be derived from the Qur'ân, religion and politics were interwoven. In modern times this merging has prompted Islamists to coin the slogan "Islam Is Religion and State" (*al-islâm dîn wa daula*). The perceived fusion of the spiritual and the temporal is a concern not only of the Islamists but also of many traditionalists. Reformists, too, generally share this holistic view of Islam, contrasting it directly with the Christian dictum, "Render unto Caesar what is Caesar's, and unto God what is God's."

Few Muslims would deny that political commitment is part of Islamic ethics, but most disagree with the Islamist insistence that there exists a clearly defined Islamic system different from all other political systems. Islamists refuse to accept a secular state that puts a member of a non-Muslim minority on a par with a member of the Muslim majority, and women on a par with men. For the ordinary Muslim, the term *political Islam* (or Islamism) connotes an overemphasis on politics at the expense of the faith and ethics. To what do Islamists aspire, and what does their supremacism lead to? The three countries where they rule—Afghanistan, Iran, and Sudan—present a picture of oppression against all who are unwilling to toe the party line, not just non-Muslims and women but also Muslim men with divergent viewpoints.

Islamist ideology may be subdivided into some two dozen tendencies, and yet they share enough common characteristics to be classified as one political program or ideology. Islamism is not just an ideological allegiance or a vaguely defined trend, it is an organized force, based on well-structured cadre parties of an all-encompassing type with many-tiered systems of members and sympathizers, fronts, and networks. The perennial debate as to whether it is possible to classify some adherents of the Islamist movement as moderate and others as radical has yielded the conclusion that the differences are but minor. Islamist opinions differ with regard to methods and tactics, with means but not with ends. Some prefer an evolutionary approach whereas others opt for the revolutionary course. Some claim to be part of mainstream Islam but acknowledge that they stand little chance of gaining wide acceptance unless helped by extraordinary circumstances. Others are outright sectarian zealots who regard the mainstream as utterly corrupt. Because they say that other Muslims are Muslims no more, they are called *takfīrîs* ("excommunicators").

Ever since the term *Islamism* was coined in the 1970s, most Muslims have come to distinguish sharply between Islam and Islamism. They may do so by using terms other than *Islam* and *Islamism*, but the reference is always to the difference between the old religion and the new ideology. For most Muslims, the Islamists are a clearly distinct and recognizable species—but an outsider may not always be able to discern the borderlines, a significant problem in terms of the perception of Islam by non-Muslims fearful of fundamentalism.

Most Islamist organizations, though, go by the name Islamic, not Islamist, and Islamists call their worldwide network the Islamic movement, not the Islamist movement, although it is legitimate to translate the Arabic term *islâmî* as "Islamist" whenever we deal with this specific phenomenon.

FROM SELF-RIGHTEOUSNESS TO SUPREMACISM

The Sudanese followers of the Islamist leader Hasan At-Turâbî are especially fond of calling their totalitarian rule the "Project of Islamic Civilization." In the African context, this expression connotes "Islam's civilizing mission," an Islamic version of Kipling's "white man's burden." This "civilizational project" is based on (1) an unabashed supremacism, deriving from a self-righteous interpretation of religious texts; and (2) their insistence on authenticity, as illustrated by their rejection of secularism and the projection of the holistic nature of Islam. They act as if the holistic ideal were entirely absent in other segments of humanity.

Like most other peoples undergoing the transition to modernity, which requires change at an ever increasingly rapid pace, Muslims are faced with innumerable challenges. Prominent among the stumbling blocks on their path is their self-perception as a superior people. A contemporary Muslim scholar calls this view "narcissistic anthropology." Some Muslims scoff at the Jewish self-perception of being the chosen people. The proportion of people who think of themselves as chosen may actually be higher among Muslims than among Jews, whose supposedly chauvinistic pride has been historically counterbalanced by a universalistic ethics and outlook, but the term "chosen people" is not used. The Qur'ân speaks of Muslims as "the best community ever brought forth for the benefit of mankind" (Sûra 3:110). The language of Scripture is not meant to convey ethnic particularism, but it has long since acquired a communal connotation, as if any Muslim were better than a non-Muslim simply because he is a Muslim.

While the Qur'ân speaks of Muslims as the best people, it attaches an assignment to this distinction, as does the concept of chosenness in Judaism: "so that you may bear witness to mankind." In other words, for both Jews and Muslims, the idea of being elevated as a chosen people is conditional upon their being equal to the task, a task that is not always pleasant and is sometimes downright fatal. During the years of ethnic cleansing in Bosnia, there was no dearth of people who cried in despair, "Why did we have to be born as Muslims? If only we could be something else!" Some Jews undoubtedly thought the same during the long history of their religious martyrdom up to the Holocaust.

Current Islamist supremacism finds its strongest expression in militancy against America. "We have brought one superpower down [the Russians in Afghanistan], why not also bring down the remaining one?" After finishing off the last superpower, they reason, the world will be theirs. The notion of Islamism as a successor to the communist threat is not an invention of the "evil West"; it first surfaced in Khomeini's entourage. His admirers in Iran, Sudan, Afghanistan, Pakistan, and elsewhere rejoice over portrayals of Islam as the new danger to the West. Khomeinist publications speak of a New World in which the opposite poles are no longer Washington and Moscow, but Washington and Tehran. Like the communists before them, Islamists, especially of the Khomeinist brand, produce propaganda of every kind. Regular publications in all the major languages cater to all age groups, including comics to indoctrinate children. While some of it is fairly direct propaganda, such as *Al-`Âlam*, a newsmagazine in Arabic, other publications offer a more subtle, indirect propaganda, such as the monthly *Africa Events*, published in London.

Islamists infiltrate local political parties, such as Argentina's Peronists, and set up front organizations, such as the Islamic Scientific Academy (connected with Germany's University of Cologne) or London's Muslim Institute, whose hard-line "Muslim Parliament" supposedly represents most of the 2 million Muslims in Britain. (In reality it represents little more than the two hundred members of the "parliament.")

The moderate majority of Muslims are understandably unhappy with the notion of Islam taking the place of communism. The word *Islam*, they reason, is not different from *salâm*, which in Hebrew is pronounced *shalom*, "peace." Diaspora leaders like Bülent Özyol, the chairman of the Turkish Community Organization in Hamburg, Germany, fear that Islamist supremacism will cause a backlash against Muslims in the West.

CRAVING FOR AUTHENTICITY AND UNIQUENESS

Present-day Muslim apologists, especially the Islamists among them, are fond of emphasizing the otherness of Islam, in the sense of specialness or uniqueness. A certain singularity is indeed observable in Muslim political history, and it would not be entirely unjustified to speak of an Islamic political system, provided it is not understood as of scriptural origin, but as a system that evolved over the course of centuries. The irony is that Islamists claim to stand on the Scripture only, rejecting most of Muslim history as a deviation. The Qur'ân, however, does not describe political procedure in anything approaching the detail required to permit us to speak authoritatively of a peculiarly Islamic political system.

Some historical examples of a Muslim political system and the writings about them bear some uniqueness, despite the frequent inconclusiveness due to the divergences of opinion that hardened over the centuries. How far these historically established patterns are religiously binding upon the believer of today, and how far they are still relevant to the changing societies of our age, are very different questions.

A growing desire to come up with cultural and political structures and systems that are seen to be unique and indigenous is observable throughout the world. The longing to have authenticity expressed through Islam is shared by many Muslims, probably a majority. It is undoubtedly true that nowhere in the world is globalization discussed so heatedly as in Muslim countries. Hardly a day passes without an article in the major Arabic newspapers on the topic of `aulama ("globalization"), which most writers view as a threat to their cultural identity. This obsession with the threat posed by globalization was evidenced poignantly by a Moroccan girl student who wrote: "Authenticity without a future is preferable to a future without authenticity!"

Not many Muslims, however, go along with the Islamist methods of manifesting authenticity. During the Iranian Revolution a majority was persuaded to support the notion of *asâla* ("authenticity") as against *gharbzadegi* ("Westoxication," or being smitten with blind admiration for everything Western), but later most Iranians discovered that what the Islamists meant by these terms was by no means what the majority had in mind. An *Islamist* scholar from Sudan defended the draconian punishments stipulated by the sharî`a as an element of authenticity, but an *Islamic* scholar from the same country rebutted him by reasoning that these punishments had little to do with authenticity; rather they were a remnant from the childhood of humanity.

Islamist propaganda bases authenticity on the supposed oneness of the temporal and the spiritual. They would have us believe that their slogan "Islam Is Religion and State" has its origin in the primary sources, as if it had been coined by the Prophet himself. In reality the word used for "state" (*daula*) did not yet have this meaning in Muhammad's time. In those days it meant something like "rotation." Different forces would rule turn by turn: today it is somebody's turn to hold the reins of power, tomorrow it will be somebody else's. After the Omayyads, the Abbasids had their turn. People then took *daula* to mean the "rule" of the Abbasids and, finally, their "state."[2] Given this semantic shift, skeptics take the slogan "Islam Is Religion and State" as of fairly recent coinage, scarcely more than an Islamist response to secularist challenges.

It may be argued, however, that the slogan does go back to the fifteenth or even fourteenth century. Muslims became

---

[2] Ahmad Baidún, "The State: Muslim Perceptions and Islamist Objectives," *TransState Islam* (Washington, D.C.), Spring 1997, p. 21.

aware of challenges to their holistic worldview quite early, long before they were assailed by nineteenth-century secularism. The motto "Islam Is Religion and State" expresses the rejection of a separation of religious and worldly authority. The differentiation became obvious in Abbasid Baghdad when a warlord had himself proclaimed sultan, or worldly ruler, alongside the more or less powerless caliph, who was now largely relegated to the narrower confines of religious trappings. As mentioned earlier, the ensuing conflicts between the actual rulers (sultans) and their vindictive figureheads (caliphs) were not all that different from the warfare between medieval kings and popes. Islamist assertions that there are no parallels at all between developments in Christendom and the Muslim world are propagandistic rather than accurate.

4

Key Concepts Hijacked

SHARÎ`A

Islamist rhetoric centers on the key words *sharî`a, system, ideological state,* and *project.* Sharî`a is the ancient law that the Islamists regard as divine and want to substitute for man-made laws. Sometimes they speak of the sharî`a as an "Islamic system." But then they seem to conceive of the Islamic system as if it were a broader category under which the sharî`a is subsumed. Obsessed with the term *system,* they claim that there is an Islamic system for everything, from an Islamic economic system to an Islamic medical system.

Then there is the Islamist vision of the Islamic state, which the Islamists assert must be ideological; that is to say, its purpose is to enforce the Islamic system, starting with the sharî`a. Recently, Islamists have begun to speak of an "Islamic project," using the Arabic word *mashrû`* so often that one sometimes wonders whether to translate it as "project" or as something else. Apparently *mashrû`* ("project") has now taken the place of *nizâm* ("system") as their new magic term. It could, of course, be understood as the endeavor to establish the Islamic state, enforce the sharî`a, and implement the Islamic system.

Sharî`a designates Islamic law in the widest sense; it

includes what some Christians would call canon law as well as the guidelines regulating religious rituals. The sources of the sharî`a are (1) the Qur'ân; (2) the Sunna, which means the Prophet's words and actions; (3) *qiyâs*, meaning deductions by analogy in order to solve problems for which the first two sources do not provide the answer; and (4) *ijmâ`*, decisions based on scholarly consensus, ideally reflecting the views of the entire community.

The foregoing is the order of precedence in which the pious would list the sources, because Qur'ân and Sunna are holy. Yet in terms of sheer weight of influence, the order would be exactly the reverse, because only about eighty verses contain legal provisions, primarily family law and the law of inheritance. "The Qur'ân contains almost seven thousand verses. How many of them deal with issues of legal import, commandments and instructions that yield material for the sharî`a?" asks Naila Sîlînî, a Tunisian Qur'ân specialist. "Whatever their exact number, they are very few in proportion to the qur'ânic text as a whole."[1] Most of the verses deal with rituals, such as prayers, fasting, pilgrimage, hygiene, and correct behavior.

From these roots, the sharî`a developed into a massive collection of norms that govern the lives of the faithful. As comprehensive and impressive as it is in some respects, it is less of a law and less of a system than one might think. The corporal punishments for murder, robbery, theft, the drinking of alcohol, adultery, and indecency attract attention, while in

---

[1] Neila Silini, "Women Between Re-Islamization and Islamism," *TransState Islam* (Washington, D.C.), Spring 1997, p. 10.

some areas of public law one looks in vain for the comprehensive catalog of crimes and sanctions typical of other legal
codes. Because the development of the sharî`a stopped in the
tenth century, many violations of law with which we are
familiar today are not dealt with. The same applies to normative changes in response to certain offenses. In the course of
the centuries the application of the sharî`a in the judicial sys-
tems of Muslim societies was progressively reduced until little more remains of it in practice than family law.

In this context it may be helpful to look at the term *qânûn*,
or "secular" law, as it acquired importance in the Ottoman
Empire. The Turkish emperors recombined the function of
sultan and caliph, thus giving credence to the notion that
Islam was both religion and state. At the same time, however, they limited the scope of traditional Islamic law, the
sharî`a, by introducing additional laws and unabashedly call-
ing them *qânûn* (from the Latin "canon").

Süleyman the Magnificent, under whom the Ottoman
Empire reached its apex, was also called Süleymân-e Qânûnî
(Solomon the Lawgiver). In the sixteenth century he did the
opposite of what today's Islamists wish to do. They regard
the sharî`a as a God-given law, divine in origin, and demand
that it replace all man-made law (such as *qânûn*). From a historian's point of view this notion is untenable, because only a
minor portion of the sharî`a is based on the Qur'ân, the larg-
er part having been devised over the span of two and a half
centuries. The early Muslim jurists leaned heavily upon Arab,
Persian, Roman, and especially Jewish law (*halakhah*).

But now the term *sharî`a* is considered sacred, while *qânûn* is derided as a borrowed term and rejected out of hand as foreign. Few Muslims are aware of the fact that the Arabic word *sharî`a* ("trodden path, road" = "way to salvation") is itself merely the translation of the Hebrew *halakhah*.

Because the sharî`a was not codified in a standard version, it remained largely impenetrable to the nonspecialist, and its unfathomable character helped its proponents to mystify it. Thus we have now reached the current state of affairs, where a compendium few people really know is being propagated as an all-encompassing miracle system, "a blueprint that only needs to be taken out of the drawer," as the Islamists say. A former military dictator of Pakistan, General Diyâ' ul-Haqq, urged his Islamist ideologues over and over again to put the blueprint on the table, so that he could start implementing it. Except for a curtailing of the rights of women and minorities, nothing much came of this enactment, and in the end even the Islamist general despaired of ever getting a clear answer. His dream of becoming the one ruler to introduce the Islamic system remained unfulfilled, because there was no consensus as to what the sharî`a really is.

When *zakâ* (charity) was declared a tax, 1 million Shi`i Muslims converged on Islamabad in the largest protest demonstration ever seen in Pakistan's capital. Most demanded that *zakâ* be voluntary, while others bluntly declared that they would not pay *zakâ* to a state dominated by Sunni Muslims. In the end it became an additional tax for Sunnis, comparable to the church tax in some of the Northern

European countries, except that in Pakistan it is not customary to pay any taxes at all. This result caused great disillusionment, because Islamists had promised for many years
that *zakâ* would take the place of all "foreign taxes." There
would be only one tax, the *zakâ*, and that meant "Pay less, get
more!" Just as in Europe many people quit the church, aban-
doning Christianity in order not to pay the church tax, so in
Pakistan many Muslims tried to pass as members of non-
Muslim minorities. An added incentive for this apostasy is
the fact that only non-Muslims can get a license to purchase
alcohol.

In his Farewell Sermon on Mount Mercy, the Prophet
clearly prohibited *ribâ* (interest). But that was with reference
to the practice in Mecca to take 100 percent interest or more
on consumer loans. Would he have prohibited the taking of
interest between banks and the state or between economic
institutions? Would he have included in *ribâ* the interest
accruing from an individual's savings?

Much of the confusion is due to the reluctance of modern
scholars to subject the sharî`a to in-depth intellectual analysis.
First of all, there is an academic hurdle. The study of the
sharî`a does not fall into everyone's area of scholarly exper-
tise, and one is easily overcome by a sense of futility. To elu-
cidate this point we will hazard a loose but useful analogy:
The attitude of traditional scholars in dealing with the sharî`a
is somewhat akin to that of the Catholic Church, which sees
itself as in charge of interpreting the Bible. Not many
Muslims will appreciate this analogy because, as mentioned
earlier, Sunni Islam aspires to be a "churchless" faith. In real-

ity, however, it possesses something very much like a church in the form of bodies of religious scholars who teach Islam and, with rare exceptions, use the sharî`a as their focal point. In contrast, members of the modern educated class know little about the sharî`a; they derive their understanding of Islam mostly from an individualistic and selective reading of the Qur'ân. The outcome of these two very different approaches is a wide divergence of views, as if they were dealing with two different religions.

A second reason for the reluctance to deal with the sharî`a is that it is dangerous to be too specific in criticizing its concrete aspects. Islamist—and many traditionalists—interpret such critiques as attacks upon Islam per se. Many ordinary believers misunderstand the term *sharî`a*, taking it to be identical with ethics or right conduct. Ethics (*akhlâq*) is a separate discipline among the Islamic sciences, but on a popular level sharî`a means moral conduct. Criticism of the sharî`a, therefore, is profoundly disconcerting to most ordinary people. They may follow the sharî`a only very imperfectly, but they are prone to perceive licentiousness and rebellion against God and His Prophet behind any critique of it, and the Islamists have skillfully exploited this perception, especially in Sudan.

JÂHILÎYA

After the triumph of Islam over the pagans of Mecca in the year 630, Muslims referred to the preceding era as the *jâhilîya*, literally a "state of ignorance," with the connotation of "Dark

Age." Before Islam's triumph, Mecca had been ruled by a mercantile aristocracy which profited from an ancient temple that drew worshipers from all over Arabia. Muhammad's new faith was a revolt against idolatry as well as against the hypocrisy, materialism, and injustice that characterized this cynical ruling class.

The Prophet himself started to use the term *jâhilîya* for the barbarism he finally succeeded in supplanting. His followers developed this theme into a great historical divide, taking their cue from verses of the Qur'ân that hail the transition from darkness to light, from evil conduct to heavenly morality.

After the death of the Prophet, dissension within the community led to civil war. Some of those who had opposed Islam became leading figures in the new empire, and their more pious fellow citizens began complaining that the *jâhilîya* was surfacing again.

Negative references to prevailing conditions, comparing them to pre-Islamic times, can be traced throughout the history of Islam. In the twentieth century the *jâhilîya* analogy was popularized by Abû-l-A`la Maudûdî from Pakistan, whom we mentioned earlier as the chief ideologue of Islamism. According to him, millions live as if in pre-Islamic times (*jâhilîya*); they are Muslims in name only.

The Prophet Muhammad fought the *jâhilîya* from within for two decades, until he and his disciples emerged victorious and were able to cleanse Mecca. The course of this transformation provided Maudûdî and the Egyptian Islamist Sayyid Qutb of the Muslim Brotherhood Party with ideas for restoring Islamic correctness, as they understood it. In Egypt, younger extremists declared current society to be un-Islamic, urging "true believers" to abandon it and create alternative communities, sometimes in the desert, whence they would someday return to the urban centers and reestablish Islam in its "pristine purity"—by force. Their rejection of society prompted the security services to label them *Takfîr wa Hijra* ("excommunication and emigration"). The name stuck. Today it is still used for one of the dozens of "anarcho-Islamist" groups working underground in countries as diverse as France and Sudan.

Reacting to the zealousness of the Islamists, quite a few Muslims poke fun at their flamboyant rhetoric, including the allusions to the *jâhilîya*. In his controversial book *The Satanic Verses*, the Indian-born British novelist Salmân Rushdî was reflecting the attitudes of intellectuals who feel driven into an almost antireligious stance by the totalitarianism of ideologues like Maudûdî and Qutb. Rushdî, however, provoked special outrage when he used the word *jâhilîya* not for the pre-Islamic period, but as a name for the city of Mecca after the triumph of Islam, as if to suggest that nothing had changed and that the barbarism continued.

Rushdî's *Satanic Verses* is fundamentally at odds with the basic precept of Islam: that the Prophet supplanted the paganism of the Dark Age with a divine order of justice and probity. Many regard the freedom of expression Rushdî demanded as a typical manifestation of the neo-*jâhilîya* that they must counter. Islamists ridicule the concept of a New World Order by translating it as neo-*jâhilîya*.

JIHÂD

Muslims in general do not view jihâd as "holy war," but as a moral idea relating to the individual's fight against the evil within, as self-purification. This is called the "Greater Jihâd." The "Lesser Jihâd" denotes the Muslim's military obligation, strictly for the purpose of defending religion. Today the word *jihâd* is often used more loosely in the sense of "campaign." For instance, a literacy campaign is called a "jihâd for mass education," a malaria eradication campaign is a "jihâd against malaria," and so forth.

The leaders of some extremist groups, however, call the concept of Greater Jihâd nonsense, insisting that there is only one type of jihâd—the battle against infidels; and it is their use of the term that has become, in essence, the only one recognized in the West. This view was shared by `Abdullah `Azzâm (d. 1989), leader of the "Arab Afghans" (Arab Islamists fighting in Afghanistan) and mentor of Usâma Bin Lâdin. He was inspired by the writings of `Omar `Abdu-r-Rahmân, who was convicted of the World Trade Center bombing.

Another of Shaikh `Omar's disciples, `Abdu-s-Salâm Farag, wrote the treatise that motivated Sâdât's assassins in 1981. *The Neglected Duty* by Farag claims that jihâd, in the sense of holy war, is a religious obligation that Muslims have put aside to please the powerful West. We should admit straightforwardly, he wrote, that jihâd has always meant taking up arms against the infidels. Proceeding from a narrow reading of history, this "anarcho-Islamist" insisted that Islam spreads only by the sword, and that without jihâd it cannot prosper. Farag endeavored to place jihâd on the same obligatory level as the Five Pillars of Islam (see chapter 13), as if there were a sixth pillar. `Alî Bin Hâj, a leader of Algeria's Islamist insurgency, goes as far as to suggest that jihâd should be enumerated as the third pillar, before charity, fasting, and pilgrimage.[2] If his suggestion were known to a larger number of Muslims, it would cause outrage as frivolous tampering with the basics of Islam. Most children learn at the beginning of their instruction in religion that "Islam is built upon five," not upon six.

In support of the interpretation of jihâd as the internal struggle of the individual to achieve an ethical existence, other Muslims recall that upon returning from battle the Prophet once told his Companions that the Lesser Jihâd was over, and now it was time for the Greater Jihâd, meaning moral rearmament. Islamists like `Azzâm denounce this report as an invention, insisting that the Prophet never said any such thing.

Some Western scholars tend to agree that jihâd has always meant the caliphate's military effort to establish political supremacy. Conversion was not to be by coercion, but neither was the mission of Islam to be obstructed, not even indirectly. Jihâd facilitated the spread of Islam by making Muslims rule supreme. The interpretation of jihâd as primarily a moral effort, they argue, gained ground only after the loss of

---

[2] In a pamphlet available only in Arabic. See Ash-Shaikh Abû`Abdi-l-fattâh `Alî Bin Hâj, *Ghâyatu l-murâd fî qadâyâ al-jihâd* (Aachen, Germany: Al-jabhatu l-islâmîya li-l-inqâdh, 1994), p. 13. With a preface by Râbih Kabîr, representative of Algeria's Islamic Salvation Front (FIS) in Europe.

Muslim political power in the wake of Europe's imperialist expansion. Its internalization was the sad product of military defeat.

There is ample evidence that the interpretation of jihâd as moral exertion is much older than the age of Muslim political decline, but neither is the strictly militant view a recent invention; it has its roots in the history of the early caliphate. Both ideas have existed side by side for more than a thousand years and reflect a profound, continuing tension within Islam.

According to a recorded statement (Hadîth) of the Prophet, "The most virtuous jihâd is standing up to tyranny" (literally, to tell an unjust ruler a word of truth). Thus, jihâd, while understood by many Muslims as primarily an effort at self-purification, can also imply a political commitment—and one that is to be acted upon.

In the worldview of extremists like `Azzâm and his Arab Afghans, jihâd in the sense of holy war plays so pivotal a role that it appears to be their new religion. They talk about jihâd the way other Muslims talk about Islam or about Allah. The Arab press has come to speak of them as "jihâdists." Their attitude signals an escalation of extremism. First some extremists began to call themselves Islamists rather than Muslims, and now a new brand of even more radical militants have taken another step—from Islamism to Jihâdism.

5

Jihâdism

In the 1980s a new generation of Islamists came of age for
whom jihâd is not a matter of moral rearmament (as many
Muslims wish it to be understood) but purely of armed struggle. Their favorite form of self-purification is martyrdom,
preferably by sacrificing their lives for the cause in a suicide
commando attack. They have taken the twentieth-century
progression from Islam, the old religion, to Islamism, the new
ideology, several steps further. Now the Arab press refers to
them not just as mujâhidîn ("holy warriors") but as jihâdists.

In Egypt a jihâdist insurgency began simmering with
Sâdât's assassination in 1981, and since then more than
twelve hundred people have died. The mushrooming
Islamist associations were wielded together by the blind
`Omar `Abdu-r-Rahmân into a single Gamâ`a Islâmîya
("Islamic Community"). One important group, Al-Gihâd Al-
Islâmî ("The Islamic Holy War"), stayed outside his united
fold. (The word gihâd in the name is the same as jihâd, but
written to reflect the Egyptian pronunciation.) They reasoned
that a handicapped man could only be a spiritual mentor, not
the real leader. And yet the blind sheik's group became

Egypt's most important underground movement. By contrast, Gihâd suffered several factional splits.

Initially some Gihâd leaders were opposed to the killing of police officers, calling it counterproductive and un-Islamic; their priority was assassinating government ministers. By contrast, Gamâ`a's combatants did everything: they tried to assassinate President Mubârak, murdered petty officials and Christian shopkeepers, and slaughtered fifty-eight European tourists in Luxor in 1996. Gihâd criticized the killing of foreign tourists, which became a major weapon in Gamâ`a's war against the Egyptian government. Scaring tourists away caused hardships for tens of thousands of Egyptians, but they did not blame the government; they blamed the terrorists. The fugitive Saudi financier of Islamist terrorism, Usâma Bin Lâdin, prevailed upon the leaders of Gamâ`a and Gihâd to stop fighting the domestic enemy and concentrate on the Great Satan (the United States). Too many of their operatives had been neutralized by the Egyptian security services. Since 1998, when both Gamâ`a and Gihâd more or less ceased to operate in Egypt, the full force of their new activism, carried out by thousands of expatriates all across the globe, came to be directed against Americans.

Volunteers from the Arab world who joined the war against the communists in Afghanistan received military training in camps along the Pakistani border. In the nineties, a new generation of jihâdists emerged as sons began to step into the shoes of their mujâhidîn fathers. Some of these young men have an Arab father and an Afghan or Pakistani mother. They are obsessed with using their experience to topple governments back home and establish Islamic states. The Arab press calls them the "Arab Afghans," a term that makes rulers shiver with fear; they are also collectively referred to in the press as "the Monster" and "our Frankenstein."

When Dr. Aiman Az-Zawâhirî assumed the leadership of Gihâd abroad and the group came under the sway of Usâma Bin Lâdin, selective terrorism gave way to more murderous tactics. Its list of targets also became more ambitious than the Gamâ`a's had been. In 1998 there was a widespread restructuring of terrorist groups and changes in their leadership and tactics, including agreement to use the most violent means, even if they would cause the death of hundreds of bystanders. This unification of personnel, tactics, and objectives resulted in a significant radicalization of the terrorism carried out internationally by the jihâdists, as well as an increase in the number of incidents. Already in November of 1995, the bombing of the Egyptian embassy in Islamabad killed seventeen diplomats and several nontargeted watchmen—Afghans and Pakistanis. It was a rehearsal for the bombing of U.S. embassies in East Africa.

In February 1998, the exiled leaders of Gamâ`a and Gihâd announced what appeared to be a merger. This was made possible by their accepting Bin Lâdin as their supreme leader and joining Al-Qâ'ida ("The Base"), his very own "bureau," and the Global Islamic Front to Fight Jews and Crusaders, an umbrella organization founded under his command. The Egyptian jihâdists are important because of their large following at home and the presence of so many of them all around the world. Experienced in underground activities (some are experts in one or another technical field), they became the core of Bin Lâdin's new tribe, though his associates are of many nationalities.

The unification meant the ascendancy of Gihâd's secretary general, Zawâhirî, a medical doctor and Bin Lâdin's favorite among the Egyptian Islamists. Both are fugitives from their respective governments, Zawâhirî since 1985. His was an ascendancy over several rival leaders, including `Omar `Abdu-r-Rahmân, who was convicted for his involvement in the World Trade Center bombing. Imprisoned in the United States and suffering from depression because he was out of the limelight, the blind sheik ceded his role to the Saudi millionaire and his Egyptian right-hand man.

BIN LÂDIN: QUALIFICATIONS OF A CHARISMATIC LEADER

An important factor in the unification of jihâdism and its globalization was the leadership provided by Usâma Bin Lâdin, Aiman Az-Zawâhirî, and a dozen other activists. Some observers have argued that the struggle against Islamist extremism should not focus so heavily on the hunt for Bin Lâdin, since there are other important terrorist leaders in hiding. Such criticism underestimates the uniqueness of the Saudi rebel. Bin Lâdin is an extremely forceful leader who became a rallying point for several reasons:

1. His wealth allows him to purchase passports for his small army of technical experts and to bribe officials in many countries, as well as to avail himself of the most advanced technology. Egypt's minister of the interior, General Habîb

Al-`Adlî, has asserted that Bin Lâdin is the major source of funding for jihâdists in Egypt.[1]

2. His record of personal bravery and dedication is key to attracting and maintaining his hold on his followers. Bin Lâdin is one of the few Arab Afghans who actually fought in Afghanistan in more than just a symbolic fashion.

3. His intelligence and inventiveness are also critical to his success. Like many of the Arab Afghans, the Saudi jihâdist is also a messianic zealot. And yet he is a restrained person with a practical bent of mind. Efficient in running his construction companies, he applied his experience to the war. Taking a fleet of bulldozers to Afghanistan, he built underground fortifications the Russians were never able to fully destroy.

4. His leadership qualities have enabled him to make the right choice of lieutenants and avoid betrayal over a period of some twenty years. He has the gift of not antagonizing associates and the knack of gathering followers, making them coordinate at least some of their activities, no mean feat in the underground world of international terrorism. In March 2000, some jihâdists in Egypt asserted that the association with Bin Lâdin was their biggest mistake, and in consequence Zawâhirî resigned from the Gihâd leadership. But this incident did not seriously impair Bin Lâdin's capacity for action, and the number of his devotees only continued to increase.

5. His Arabian origin gives him a psychological advantage. Jihâdists believe that some of the worst people can be found in Saudi Arabia. And yet, once an Arabian is acknowledged

---

[1] See "Tasrîhâtî . . . ," *Rûzu l-Yûsuf*, no. 3686 (February 1, 1999), p. 12.

as a leader, a halo attaches to him with which others cannot easily compete. The House of Saud made full use of that fascination until Bin Lâdin directed the weapon against them. A businessman with no Islamic training, he acts as if he were a religious authority. It is doubtful that he could have succeeded in carrying this off were he not an Arabian.

6. His internationalism is also a major asset. Bin Lâdin has lived in several countries, and one of his wives is from the Philippines. The embassy bombings in East Africa and hints by his companions lend some credence to a highly confidential 1996 report by Philippine military intelligence that the culprits in the Oklahoma City bombing had an association with the Abû Sayyâf group of jihâdists in the southern Philippines. This would implicate Bin Lâdin in the bombing. U.S. authorities discarded the report as manipulative.

7. His pragmatism also brings great advantages. At the start of the Afghan adventure, he attached himself to Hikmatyâr, whom Pakistan's military intelligence (ISI) wanted to install as new ruler in Kabul. In 1996 the ISI launched the Tâlibân as Pakistan's stalking horse in Afghanistan. The Tâlibân looked more promising than Hikmatyâr, who promptly took refuge in Iran. Given the intimate relationship between Hikmatyâr and the Arab Afghans over a period of more than fifteen years, one would have expected Bin Lâdin to be an enemy of the Tâlibân. Moreover, the Tâlibân were initially financed by the Saudi government, as a counterweight to Hikmatyâr, who sided with Saddâm Husain in 1991. To find Bin Lâdin in Tâlibân territory as a brother for whom they were prepared to risk their lives was astounding,

all the more since the Tâlibân have no connection with the
international network of jihâdist parties, such as the Muslim
Brethren; in fact, the Tâlibân chased the jihâdists away.
Therefore the Islamists' international leadership cursed the
Tâlibân as an American creation. The Tâlibân had in fact
emerged from a religious establishment in Pakistan opposed
to the Islamists.[2] Their core consisted of Afghan orphans who
knew nothing of the world except what they were indoctri-
nated with in Pakistani refugee camps. Those were the men
Bin Lâdin needed because their example inspired. Thousands
of Pakistani teenagers ran away from home to join the jihâd
in Afghanistan. Bin Lâdin chose the winning side and helped
it on to further victories.

CAIRO PROCEEDINGS AGAINST THE "BALKAN ARABS"

In 1999 the Haekstep military camp near Cairo was the set-
ting for the prosecution of 107 persons accused of terrorism,
most of them members of Gihâd. The trial soon came to be
known as the Albania Returnees case, echoing the name of
the earlier Afghanistan Returnees case, which dragged on for
years.

In 1998, Albania handed over fourteen Egyptians to their
government. Others accused in the case were extradited from
Azerbaijan, Bulgaria, Canada, Ecuador, Kuwait, Pakistan,
South Africa, Uruguay, the United States, and the United

---

[2] See Ahmed Rashid, *Taliban: Militant Islam, Oil and Fundamentalism in Central Asia* (New Haven: Yale University Press, 2000).

Arab Emirates as well as several Arab states that did not want to be mentioned. Five were imprisoned in Britain, and another suspect was imprisoned in Austria. Sixty-one were tried in absentia, several of whom were known to be in Afghanistan, others in Yemen, while the whereabouts of some were unknown. Many of the accused had spent periods of time in Albania, Bosnia, or Bulgaria, and they were thus collectively referred to as "Balkan Arabs."

The principal accused, Ibrâhîm An-Najjâr, declared, "I support the Nairobi operation, because that embassy was the biggest spy center monitoring Islamist movements in the region. I am a Muslim and opposed to the Jews. I am with Usâma Bin Lâdin in whatever he does. The confrontation with America is a challenge, and Zawâhirî must not be left alone with this task. It is an obligation upon the entire Islamic nation."[3]

These remarks were typical of the declarations through which the jihâdists vented their fury over CIA participation in their arrests and interrogations. Three of them, including a Sudanese national, were allegedly kidnapped by the CIA in the Azeri capital, Baku. Whatever means of torture the Egyptian interrogators used was seen as beside the point: now it was all the fault of the CIA. The Serbs wiped out mujâhidîn, but the blame fell on the Americans who told the Kosovars not to cooperate with Arabs. In London, terrorism-suspect Ibrâhîm ʿIdarûs complained that he was in jail not because of Egyptian demands, but because of American pres-

---

[3] M. Salâh, "Misr: dammu-l-islâmbûlî ilâ lâ'ihati-l-muttahamîn," *Al-Hayât*, February 2, 1999, p. 5.

sure. In Cairo, the accused turned the proceedings into a propaganda demonstration against the United States and vowed
to continue their war. The slogans they chanted were directed not against the Egyptian government, but against the
Great Satan:

> *thaura thaura bi l-qur'ân didda l-yahûd wa l-amrîkân*
> Revolution with the Qur'ân against Jews and Americans!
> *thaura thaura islâmîya didd amrîka s-salîbîya*
> Islamic Revolution against Crusader America!
> *ya clinton, ya la`în ya saffâha l-muslimîn*
> Damn you, Clinton, you butcher of Muslims![4]

Nine of the accused received the death sentence, including
Zawâhirî, and eleven were sentenced to life imprisonment.
The eleven would have been sentenced to death as well had
the Egyptian authorities not had to assure the extraditing
countries that the accused would not be executed. Cairo was
hoping that more countries, especially Britain, would extra-
dite jihâdists, adding to the ever-growing list of "returnees
from everywhere," but those hopes did not materialize.
When Germany went so far as to grant asylum to another
Egyptian fugitive, Cairo felt free to go ahead with the execu-
tions, starting with Ibrâhîm An-Najjâr. Bin Lâdin was not for-
mally charged, but the Egyptian security service accused him
of seeking to create, with the help of Gihâd, a new funda-

---

[4] See M. Salâh, "Al-ahkâm fî qadíyati 'l-`â'idún min albâniya'," *Al-Hayât*, April 19,
1999, p. 5.

mentalist generation in Egypt, by recruiting members at the universities and in slum areas.

FROM THE HINDU KUSH TO LAKE VICTORIA

The globalization of the jihâdist movement has proceeded apace. In 1995, Zawâhirî went on a fund-raising tour of the United States, visiting mosques frequented by Egyptians and other Arabs. His disciple Abû Dhahab went to San Francisco to learn to fly in order to pass on his skills to fellow-jihâdists in the Jalalabad, Afghanistan. They intended to liberate Gihâd members by flying a hang glider from Cairo's Moqattam Hill to Turra Prison. Eventually the plan was dropped and Abû Dhahab returned to the United States, where he connected calls from around the world with members of the organization inside Egypt, thereby assisting in the preparation of terrorist attacks. He also furnished Zawâhirî with forged documents.[5] Another Gihâd activist, Abû-s-Sa`ûd, formerly an officer in Egypt's special forces, joined the U.S. army in 1987 and, while working as one of Bin Lâdin's operatives, became an instructor in Middle Eastern topography.[6]

The most adventurous of his operatives was `Alî Ar-Rashîdî, called Al-Banshîrî. The name derives from Afghanistan's Panj-Sher Valley region, where he fought the Russians at the side of the Tajik warlord Ahmad Shâh Mas`ûd. Banshîrî was last heard of when a boat capsized in

---

[5] See M. Ash-Shâfi`î, "Milafât at-tahqîq . . . " *Ash-Sharq Al-Awsat*, April 16, 1999, p. 7.
[6] See M. Salâh, "Al-qâhira . . . ," *Al-Hayât*, February 10, 1999, p. 7.

Lake Victoria. The military court sentenced him in absentia to life imprisonment, just in case the drowned man should surface on another continent.[7] The report of his death in Kenya ought to have drawn attention to the presence in East Africa of confidants of Bin Lâdin before the attacks on the U.S. embassies in Dar-es-Salaam and Nairobi.

Disinformation is a favorite Gihâd tactic. In 1996 they reported in some detail, including photos, on Zawâhirî's activities in Switzerland, while he was in a different corner of the world. During the 1998 court proceedings he was said to be hiding in Albania, confronted with a grim situation, according to his followers. But this seems to have been another piece of disinformation.

The disclosure that for some time Malaysia had been the matrix of Gihâd's international activities was a contributing factor to the downfall of Anwar Ibrâhîm, a powerful Islamist minister in Kuala Lumpur.[8] More startling was the scheme of smuggling Bin Lâdin into Egypt to undergo a cosmetic operation intended to make him unrecognizable.[9] Such medical arts were too sophisticated for the uncouth Tâlibân; the procedure necessitated pharaonic skills.

Confessions by Albania returnees confirm that Bin Lâdin is indeed the menace he is considered to be by U.S. experts on terrorism. An arrested collaborator of his claimed that the Saudi extremist was in possession of biological and chemical

[7] See "Laghzu wafâti l-banshîrî," *Al-Wasat*, no. 370, March 1, 1999, p. 29.
[8] See M. Salâh, ". . . mâlîziyâ mahattatun li-a`dâ'i l-'jihâd'," *Al-Hayât*, February 19, 1999, p. 5.
[9] See Khâlid Sharafuddîn, "Bin Lâdin tarâja` `an dukhûl misr . . . ," *Ash-Sharq Al-Awsat*, March 8, 1999, p. 8.

weapons. Some commentators hoped that this frightening information was merely another piece of disinformation or perhaps just the strutting bravado of an "Arab Afghan." Like most of the other accused, however, he acted as if he were intoxicated with a sense of the inevitable victory of his cause, and most observers were left with gnawing doubts.[10] While the Egyptian government claimed to have domestic terrorism under control, Cairo was bracing for more court proceedings on the pattern of the cases against the Afghanistan and Albania Returnees.

---

[10] The danger was confirmed by George J. Tenet in his testimony to the Senate Select Committee on Intelligence, "The Worldwide Threat in 2000: Global Realities of Our National Security," on February 2, 2000. See "Sunni Extremists," *Middle East Quarterly*, June 2000, pp. 89–90.

6

Too Many Imponderables for a Prognosis

Throughout the 1980s and 1990s there was considerable speculation about the future of Islamism and jihadism. The general assumption among Muslims used to be that the phenomenon would prove ephemeral. "Give them a chance and let them make fools of themselves; that is the only way to get rid of this nuisance" was an often-heard comment in the early seventies.

In Pakistan, the Islamists got their chance and ruled for thirteen years under both Diyâ ul-Haqq (1977–88) and his successor, Ghulâm Ishâq Khân (1988–90). The prediction came largely true, because in subsequent Pakistani elections the Islamists received barely 3 percent of the votes. It was a costly experiment, however, because the country sank into an economic abyss and social chaos, producing a situation that might be labeled semi–civil war. In Iran, the Khomeinists were unable to keep their promises and ended up with economic disaster. In Sudan, Islamist rule meant intensified war between north and south, involving several neighboring states. In these three cases Islamist dictatorship proved to be more repressive and brutal than anything experienced before—and the regimes the Islamists had replaced were by no means humane.

The problem with the general prognosis for the future of Islamism is that domestic developments are only partly determinative. There are a host of additional factors, and most are imponderables. Who would have imagined, in 1980, that in the nineties Malaysia would be financing Islamists worldwide and bailing out the Sudanese dictatorship? Or that China would become massively involved on the side of an isolated Sudan? Or that a Canadian company by the name of Talisman would try to play a larger-than-life role in the oil fields of southern Sudan, a literal slave state? Not even the fraternal relationship between Khartoum and Baghdad was foreseeable in 1980, because in Iraq Islamists used to be hunted down. The Muslim Brethren used to portray Saddâm Husain as the incarnation of the devil; yet in the nineties the Islamist regime in Khartoum owed its survival largely to Iraqi weapons and oil, which reached Sudan via Iran.

Among many such imponderables one occupies a place of central importance: the Arab-Israeli conflict. Islamism received a tremendous boost from the Arab defeat in the 1967 war with Israel. The "disaster," as Arabs call it, led many to believe that only Islam could help them. This situation led to the fashionable slogan "Islam Is the Solution," and many Arab nationalists jumped on the Islamist bandwagon. Twenty years later the tide began to ebb because of a host of setbacks. But this embryonic counterreaction was stillborn when one of the great revolutions of the twentieth century occurred: the fall of the Soviet Empire. Orphaned communists began to join the Islamists because they presented themselves as the only force left to challenge the West. Maoist intellectuals, such as Algeria's Rashîd Bin`Îsa or Pakistan's popular columnist Safdar Mîr, formerly an anti-Islamist polemicist, rallied to the cause of Khomeini and Islamist revolution. Those who were leftists only because of anti-Americanism now joined the Islamic movement. Their number included people in the West. For instance, a medical doctor in Oslo, formerly head of Norway's small Maoist party, converted to Khomeini's Islamism and built an Islamic Center in the heart of town (quite different from Oslo's fifteen or sixteen mosques, which are mostly ethnic, and none of which is run by Islamists). Kalîm Siddîqî, a leftist intellectual of Indian origin, created the Muslim Institute and Muslim Parliament in London. Eventually he became the major Khomeinist spokesman in the West. The Islamists benefited immensely from this influx of leftist and nationalist cadres.

After the demise of the Soviet Union in 1989, the Islamist regimes in Iran and Sudan began to profit from the availability of now-jobless Eastern European technical and military experts. The price of their services had once been prohibitive, but now they could be hired for much less, and a great many were. In short, Islamism became the successor to communism in more than one respect.

In the West a spate of books and articles defended the Islamists against the charge of being successors to the communists. American scholars accused the United States of indulging in an old pastime: the building up of an enemy image, the notion that the American psyche, as well as its military industrial complex, requires a global foe in order to prosper. It was argued that the idea of Islamism as a new threat to the West after the fall of communism was merely the invention of malicious minds, mostly based in Washington.

If one were to believe these theoreticians, one would have to conclude that the many people in the Muslim world with painful, hard-won first-hand experience of this "Green Peril" are suffering from hallucinations. Ultimately the jihâdists may not be up to the task and may fail to supplant the remaining superpower. The point, however, is that they do indeed aspire to be the Green Peril that will bring the West to its knees, and they have been more successful in this attempt than most Western decision-makers realize—or are ready to admit. The Green Peril is not a chimera.

Part III
Jews and Muslims

We [God] revealed the Torah, therein is guidance and light. Its standards were applied on the Jews by the prophets who submitted to God, the rabbis, and the doctors of the Law. To them was entrusted the protection of God's Book, and they were witnesses thereto (Sûra 5:44).

7

A Difficult Start

Fleeing persecution in his hometown of Mecca in 622, Muhammad settled in Yathrib, an oasis to the north of Mecca. Later it came to be known as *madînatu n-nabî* ("City of the Prophet"), shortened to Medina. Two pagan Arab tribes and three Jewish tribes were living there at that time. Tired of internecine tribal warfare, delegations from Yathrib had been entreating Muhammad for several years to move to their city and be their chief. They needed what today is called an ombudsman. Some had already converted to Islam; others did so upon the Prophet's arrival.

Since he was joined by a number of his followers from Mecca, Muhammad's community now consisted of two groups, the immigrants (*muhâjirûn*) and their local helpers (*ansâr*). Muhammad welded them into one brotherhood. Thus, Medina's population came to consist of three factions: Jews, Muslims, and pagans.

The Prophet strengthened the bonds of community by devising a pact intended to unite the different segments of the populace in common citizenship. This pact was called *sahîfa* and also *mîthâq*, meaning "charter." Some call the Charter of

Medina the first secular constitution because it united people
of different religions in common nationhood.

In discussing relations between followers of different religions, it has become customary to speak of tolerance, which
is to say that we are prepared to put up with one another. The
Charter of Medina went beyond tolerance and was more
demanding. It states:

> The Jews of Banî `Auf form one nation together with the
> Muslims. The Jews have their religion, their followers,
> and themselves, and so have the Muslims. One who
> transgresses and commits a crime does harm only to
> himself and to his family. The Jews shall be responsible
> for their financial affairs, and the Muslims for theirs.
> Together they shall fight those who wage war against
> the signatories of this pact. Their relations shall be guid-
> ed by mutual sympathy, wishing each other well, and
> by righteous conduct, not by sinfulness.

Giving practical shape to the general principles enshrined
in the Qur'ân, the Charter says: "The Jews shall follow their
religion, the Muslims theirs." Thus the Charter of Medina
favored pluralism. Two communities, Jews and Muslims,
agreed to form one nation under God, with the clear commitment that each would preserve its religious autonomy and
maintain its cultural identity. While accepting these differences, they formed one unit to face outside forces, whether
hostile to either or both of them.

Since the Arabian Jews professed Judaism, the Prophet
expected them to acknowledge his intent to (1) establish a
common platform for all monotheists by recreating the proto-

typical Abrahamic religion that would be acceptable to both Jews and Christians, and (2) convert idol worshipers to Abraham's faith in the One God.

This first attempt to find a common denominator did not work out as the Prophet had hoped. Conditioned by historical circumstances, the Arabian Jews of Medina had developed an overbearing attitude toward their non-Jewish environment. They scoffed at the Prophet's sermons, ridiculed the revelations he received, and referred to him haughtily as a Prophet of the Goyim (*ummiyîn* in Arabic). *Ummî* has the connotation of "illiterate" and became a term of pride among the non-Jews, so much so that Muslims venerate Muhammad as *an-nabiyu l-ummî*, "the prophet who could neither read nor write," but who enunciated what Muslims regard as the literary masterpiece of all times, the Qur'ân. Muhammad's reading ability was rudimentary, and he was able to write hardly more than his name, but that only enhances his prestige in Muslim eyes, because it makes the Qur'ân all the more a miracle: such a gem could not have come from an illiterate, therefore it is of divine origin.

Breaking the treaty they had concluded with Muhammad, the Medinese Jews aligned themselves with his enemies, the powerful rulers of Mecca, who were idol worshipers bent on crushing the nascent Muslim community. After repelling an attack by a tribal alliance led by the Meccans, the Muslims turned on the Jews of Medina, who had betrayed them. This tragic confrontation resulted in bloodshed and the expulsion of Jews from most of the Arabian Peninsula.[1]

---

[1] See Gordon D. Newby, *A History of the Jews of Arabia: From Ancient Times to Their Eclipse under Islam* (Columbia: University of South Carolina Press, 1988), p. 78.

Although at the time the Charter experiment resulted in failure, it nonetheless retained its model character and continues to be referred to by Muslims as an exemplary effort, an experiment in civic life that might succeed after many attempts. This fact has to be kept in mind as one looks at Jewish-Muslim relations in the wake of the disaster of Medina.

POLEMICS: ISLAM AND JEWISH TRADITION

Our knowledge about the first century of Muslim political expansion comes primarily from the earliest biography of Muhammad, *Sîrat Rasûli-llâh* ("The Biography of the Messenger of God") by Ibn Ishâq. This book was decisive in forming an image of the Prophet that contributed to the spread of Islam. It established Muhammad as the central religious authority for Muslims while at the same time establishing the primacy of the Scripture, the qur'ânic text.

Among the materials used by Ibn Ishâq was the *isrâ'îliyât*, a body of stories mostly derived from Jewish aggadic and midrashic treatises explicating Scripture. Ibn Ishâq's use of *isrâ'îliyât* linked the *Sîra* (Prophet's Biography) and the Qur'ân to previous Scriptures as a means of fostering the claim that Islam is the heir to Judaism and Christianity.

The Egyptian scholar Ibn Hishâm (834 C.E.), who produced a shortened version of Ibn Ishâq's *Sîra*, disposed of most of the *isrâ'îliyât*. His shortened version has been described as a categorical truncating of the original text, eliminating Ibn

Ishâq's worldview and catholic methodology. Significantly, Ibn Hishâm's abridged *Sîra* became the popular one.

Early Muslims looked to Jewish (and Christian) sources for traditions and legends related to the many biblical stories and themes in the Qur'ân. In most instances, the qur'ânic text is very succinct, whetting the reader's appetite to know more details of what happened. One way that the commentaries made the stories meatier was by adding details found in the sources of other traditions. The *isrâ'îliyât* consists of narratives brought into Islamic literature by Jewish converts or by Muslims who heard them from Jews. As this was a religious quest and not an academic endeavor, there are certain inconsistencies. Not all of the *isrâ'îliyât* can be found in Jewish sources, although they parallel biblical concepts and motifs. Furthermore, some of the materials considered by Muslims to be Israelite in origin are in fact authentically Islamic.

By the ninth century some Muslim scholars had come to distrust the *isrâ'îliyât* and ultimately rejected many of them as noncanonical or inappropriate to Islam, either because of their content (*matn*) or their lack of authentication (*isnâd*). Since Abraham was considered to have been a Muslim, certain legends about him had to be accepted as authentic. Legends about biblical figures mentioned in the Qur'ân served as the basis of important elements in Islamic practice, but a foreign origin for these legends, and thus for Islam itself, was unacceptable. Therefore, while most of the *isrâ'îliyât* were retained, others were banned because they appeared to run counter to Islamic dogma.

The issue of the *isrâ'îliyât* remains complex, with continuing, intricate repercussions affecting even present-day interreligious dialogue. One might think that the *isrâ'îliyât* would
constitute a bridge for interfaith understanding, because they
link Muslims and Jews, as well as Muslims and Christians.
However, those Muslims most given to dialogue, usually liberals and reformers, tend to be the most critical of the
isrâ'îliyât, while traditionalists and Islamists, who generally
have reservations with regard to dialogue, are less prone to
dispense with the *isrâ'îliyât*. The liberals and reformers are
mostly humanists or social scientists who are intellectually
comfortable with the idea of subjecting religious traditions to
scholarly analysis. The traditionalists and Islamists come
overwhelmingly from the natural sciences and are prone to
revere religious tradition as a fetish that is not to be dissected.

The belief in the Messiah, or the Mahdî in Islamic parlance,
is a case in point. The fourteenth-century Ibn Khaldûn, hailed
as the "father of sociology," believed that the concept of a
Messiah is a pre-Islamic notion that crept into Islam by way
of the *isrâ'îliyât*.[2] In the 1920s this view was elaborated by
Pakistan's Muhammad Iqbâl in his *Reconstruction*,[3] and following on Iqbâl's work, the Egyptian historian and Islamic
reformer Ahmad Amîn (d. 1954) devoted an entire treatise to
this question, entitled *On the Messiah and Messianism*.[4] All

---

[2] See Ibn Khaldûn, *The Muqaddimah: An Introduction to History*, translated from the
Arabic by Franz Rosenthal, edited and abridged by N. J. Dawood. Bollingen Series
(Princeton, N.J.: Princeton University Press, 1967), pp. 257 ff.

[3] See Mohammad Iqbal, *The Reconstruction of Religious Thought in Islam* (London and
Lahore: Sh. Mohammad Ashraf, 1930).

[4] See Ahmad Amîn, *Al-mahdî wa l-mahdawîya* (Cairo: dâru l-ma`ârif, 1951).

three, and many other scholars as well, reasoned that the belief in a Messiah was a remnant of pre-Islamic superstitions, and that Muslims should be glad that Islam emancipated them from such backward notions.

By contrast, traditionalists have a stronger faith in the Hadîth, the sayings of the Prophet; they accept as authentic what the reformers regard with skepticism. According to one Hadîth, the Prophet is reported to have said, "There is nothing wrong with the lore of the Children of Israel." Reformers doubt the authenticity of such statements, reasoning that Muslims do not benefit from the *isrâ'îliyât* because the myths and folklore they contain create barriers against historical truth. Medieval "fundamentalists," such as the famous scholars Ibn Taimîya and Ibn Kathîr, taught that the *isrâ'îliyât* could be helpful, provided they were not used as the basis (*i'timâd*) of an argument but only to corroborate (*istishhâd*) it.

In the year 2000 the *isrâ'îliyât* controversy became topical again because of a best-selling book on Adam. Influenced by new findings about the origins of man, the author explains Adam as the symbol of human consciousness. This explanation is by no means new; several Muslim philosophers and mystics referred to Adam as the first prophet rather than the first man, and the author, `Abdu-s-Sabûr Shâhîn, feels that the *isrâ'îliyât* block the way to this understanding. He wants people to place their trust in archaeology rather than mythology, and to recognize Kenya's Lucy, and not the biblical Adam, as the ancestor of mankind.

The Arabic language has a pun right at hand to express these two opposed concepts: *uhfûra* (excavation) as against *ustûra* (story). A traditionalist opponent quickly rose to the occasion, defending the *isrâ'îliyât* as a useful source of information about Adam and Eve and many things more. Yet he too condemns his opponent for being influenced by Jewish ideas. Shâhîn, he says, sees a contradiction between the scientific view of the age of the human species and the short biblical time span. Why, he asks, does Shâhîn allow himself to be impelled by such Jewish myths?[5] He ought not to rely upon *isrâ'îliyât*; they are to be used only to corroborate what is mentioned in Islamic sources.

In this way the *isrâ'îliyât* remain a topical issue, and, what is most convenient for Muslims, no one is to be blamed but the Jews, either way. Quite a few Muslims have an attitude toward the *isrâ'îliyât* that resembles the attitude of many Christians toward the apocryphal writings of their religious heritage. The apocryphal gospels and the *isrâ'îliyât* are apprehended by ordinary believers very differently from the way they are understood by scholars who specialize in these subjects.

---

[5] The controversy was highlighted by `Abdu-r-Rahmân Al-Mutawwa` in the newspaper *Ash-Sharq Al-Ausat*, February 8, 2000, p. 14.

8

Between *Convivencia* and Pogrom:
From the Eighth Century to the Seventeenth

THE SPANISH SYMBIOSIS

In 711 Muslims from North Africa invaded Spain to expand the caliphate. At that time Spain was ruled by the Visigoths, a Germanic tribe that was not popular with the masses of serfs, most of whom were indigenous Ibero-Celtic peoples. In secret many still adhered to Arian Christianity,[1] which had been in vogue before the seventh century, when the Visigoth court converted to Catholicism and forced its subjects to follow suit. The Muslims are likely to have known that the religiously and socially oppressed populace of Spain would not resist their invasion. Among all the forms of Christianity, Arianism is closest to Islam, a fact that explains the mass conversions to Islam in Andalusia and Bosnia, the two centers of the Arian heresy.[2]

---

[1] Named after Bishop Arius (also known as Areius) of Alexandria.
[2] Ulfilas, a disciple of Arius, translated the Bible into the Visigothic language, then dominant in Andalusia and Bosnia. The Arian Christians, like the Muslims after them, saw Jesus as a prophet rather than as a part of the godhead. For this reason the Bosnians have for centuries taken pride in the fact that they were Muslims "even before Muhammad."

The Jews of Spain, who were persecuted under the Catholic dispensation, welcomed the invaders,[3] and the Muslim conquest resulted in a significant improvement in their situation. Many Jews rose to high positions and wealth through land ownership, finance, and trade or achieved success and fame in the sciences, especially medicine. Some reached the highest ranks of the political hierarchy. For example, Hasday Ibn Shaprut, a famous physician, outstanding translator of Greek, and skilled diplomat, served as vizier (a kind of prime minister) in tenth-century Córdoba, under both `Abdu-r-Rahmân III and his son, Al-Hakam. Samuel Ha-Levi Ibn Nagrila Ha-Nagid, known as "the Prince," was both an artist and a scientist who served as a prime minister under the ruler of Granada. Upon his death in 1056, the post was passed on to his son, Joseph.

Granada became the apex of Andalusian culture under Muslim rule and continues to be celebrated in poems and songs. It was an island of cultural splendor throughout the fifteenth century. For Muslims, Granada is Paradise Lost, the romantic dream of their bygone glory. Few are aware that during the fabled Golden Age, roughly half of Granada's population was Jewish. With the shrinking of Muslim territo-

---

[3] Three elements, sometimes said to be legendary but of fairly well substantiated historicity, combined to facilitate this extraordinary military feat. (1) Ceuta (Septa), still a Spanish possession on the Moroccan coast, was under Spanish (Visigothic) rule in the eighth century. There was a feud between King Rodrigo in Toledo and Count Julian, its governor, who turned to the Muslims for help. (2) The Spanish Jews had suffered pogroms under the Visigoths; some of them approached the Muslims in Morocco to help them and became guides for the invading army. (3) The invaders were led by an outstanding commander, Târiq, after whom the major peak on the Spanish coast was named Mount Tariq, in Arabic *Jabal Târiq*, today known as Gibraltar.

ry in Spain as the Christians began reconquering the country, many Muslims and Jews flocked together in this last Muslim principality on Iberian soil. In a sense it was but natural for the vizier to be Jewish while the head of state was Muslim. In 1492, however, Granada fell to the Christians.

The Muslim presence in Spain led to close interaction between the three monotheistic faiths. Western civilization was deeply influenced by the converging ideas of Jewish, Christian, and Muslim theologians, philosophers, and mystics. Yet in our modern world, the Islamic element is frequently ignored, and reference is made only to Judeo-Christian civilization.

From the ninth to the twelfth century, the eastern part of Islamic civilization was symbolized by the glory of Baghdad, for some time the cultural capital of the world, famous for its arts, sciences, and intellectual life, not to mention its wealth and splendor. Córdoba had much the same role in the western part of the Islamic world. So great was Córdoba's attraction for the rest of Europe that Roswitha von Gandersheim, a nun in a German monastery, glorified its uniquely advanced civilization in an enthusiastic poem that became a literary masterpiece. There was, however, a major difference between East and West. In the East the chief educators of Muslims were Christians and Zoroastrians, whereas in Spain the main influence on Muslims came from Jews. The Jews, in turn, were deeply influenced by Muslim art, culture, and spiritual concepts.

While in basic religious matters Jews and Muslims remained apart, in philosophy they became almost indistinguishable. A characteristic feature of the Jewish-Muslim symbiosis was the Hellenization of Jewish thought, which was due largely to the impact of Muslim philosophers who were under the spell of the ancient Greeks. On the Jewish side, the symbiosis was personified in the figures of Saadya Gaon, Shlomo Ibn Gabirol, Bahya Ibn Paquda, Moshe ben Maimon (Maimonides), and Judah Ha-Levi. Their Muslim counterparts were Ibn Bâjja, Ibn Tufail (Aventofail), Ibn Rushd (Averroes), Ibn Sînâ (Avicenna), Al-Fârâbî, and Al-Ghazâlî (Algazel).

Islamic theology and philosophy make much of *ijtihâd* ("intellectual effort" or "independent reasoning") for better understanding, though most scholars of the law impose varying degrees of restrictions in order to avoid *bid`a* ("innovation"). Medieval Muslim thinkers hotly debated the issue of freedom of thought, but even for the most daring it was different from how it is understood in the modern West. Sarah Strousma holds that "Arab intellectuals were aware of the fact that even solitary meditation requires a certain degree of liberty. In this context the opposite of liberty is not slavery, constraint, or repression, but often the loyalty to one's traditions. Arab thinkers called this loyalty *taqlîd* (imitation)."[4] Religious education and the faith itself are obviously conditioned by customs or social habits. Many Western philosophers have dealt with this issue from their own social and historical perspectives. Like Aristotle, the medieval Arab thinkers used the notion of custom to explain the language of

---

[4] Sarah Strousma, "Habitués religieuses et liberté intellectuelle dans la pensée arabe médievale," in *Monothéismes et Tolérance, colloque du C.R.J.M.*, ed. Michel Abitbol and Robert Assarraf (Paris: Albin Michel, 1998), p. 58.

the legislator. For the philosophers, "To follow what one is accustomed to may not always be commendable, but it is inherent in human nature, in all societies. Therefore, the good legislator will not commit the error of neglecting it."[5]

Since different nations have different customs, they develop distinct legal systems, symbols, and religious expressions, and the result is conflict between disparate groups.[6] Prominent among those who have given serious thought to the role of custom in human thinking was Maimonides. In the *Guide for the Perplexed* he cites as one cause of discord "custom and education, because it is in the nature of man to like what he is familiar with and in which he has been brought up, and that he fears anything alien. The plurality of religions and their mutual intolerance result from the fact that people remain faithful to the education they received."[7]

The Muslim West included Spain and parts of North Africa, the Maghreb. The Golden Age of Jewish-Muslim history was based on a kind of partnership or commonwealth among a group of sister cities: Ceuta, Fez, and Tetuan in Morocco, and, respectively, Lucena, Córdoba, and Granada in Spain. In this intellectual climate, the Jewish intellectuals of the Maghreb were the masters of Andalusian Judaism. Even the grammarians and poets among the founders of the Spanish school came from the Maghreb.

In the ninth century, Yehudah of Tahert (now Algeria) became famous for his *Epistle to the Jews of Fez*, a comparative grammar of Semitic languages. He criticized those who

---

[5] Ibid., p. 61.
[6] Ibid., p. 62.
[7] Maimonides, *Guide for the Perplexed*. Quoted in ibid., p. 62.

neglected the study of Aramaic, the language of the Targumim, the traditional Aramaic translations of the Bible. Among the Maghrebi intellectuals who enriched Hebrew language and poetry were Jacob bar Dunash and Adonim bar Nissim Ha-Levi. Yehudah ben Samuel Ibn Abbâs Al-Maghrebi, a twelfth-century poet and scientist, was a friend of the poet Judah Halevi (Yehudah Ha-Levi, 1075–1141).[8] Halevi became famous for a composition inserted into the Sephardic liturgy for Rosh Hashanah and Yom Kippur. Around 1160, Maimonides himself spent some time in Fez, then and now the spiritual center of Morocco and much of Northwest Africa.

Despite the flourishing of Jews in the West, their cultural roots remained in the East, where the Talmud had been compiled and where the geonim (heads of the talmudic academies) had developed an elaborate religious culture in the Babylonian academies of Pumbedita and Sura. Some Jews became important figures at the caliphal court in Baghdad. Netira (d. 916) enjoyed high social status under Caliph Al-Mu`tadid. The financier Joseph Phineas (d. 928) had major dealings with the vizier of Caliph Al-Muqtadir; he and Aaron Amran became the official bankers of the caliph. Several Jewish families rose to prominence by providing various Muslim states with some of their best civil servants for many generations, until the mid-twelfth century.

---

[8] See Franz Rosenzweig, *Ninety-two Poems and Hymns of Yehuda Halevi*, translated by Thomas Kovach, Eva Jospe, and Gilya Gerda Schmidt, edited and with an introduction by Richard A. Cohen (New York: SUNY Series, 2000).

Rabbi Saadya Gaon (882–942), born in the Egyptian oasis of Fayoum, was one of the rare "outsiders" on whom the title of gaon ("excellency") was bestowed, a prestigious office reserved for the intellectual and socioeconomic aristocracy of Baghdadi Jewry. Figures like Saadya were the products of a society that might be called symbiotic; whatever changes occurred in intellectual and spiritual life, Jews and Muslims underwent them together. Platonism, for example, was adopted not only by Muslims but by Jews. In this context Saadya became a central figure of Jewish philosophy. After the great Muslim philosophers, he was the first to build a rationalist system of religion in which faith and reason merged. Saadya Gaon wrote the *Kitâbu l-imânât wa l-i`tiqâdât* ("Book of Beliefs and Convictions"), a classification of the precepts of the law (mitzvot). His dichotomy between "rational precepts" (`aqliyât*) and "traditional precepts" (*sam`iyât*) was probably inspired by the rational theology (*kalâm*) of the Mu`tazilite school (mainly Baghdad and Basra), taught by both Muslim and Jewish theologians. With his book *What Is Most Useful for Man to Do in This World?* he contributed to the study of ethics.

The grandeur of Jewish intellectual and religious thought was expressed in the Arabic language, making the symbiosis genuinely Judeo-Islamic. Centuries later, Prime Minister David Ben-Gurion would spend his lunchtimes learning Arabic in order to read the works of Maimonides in the original text.

THE IDEOLOGY OF "DHIMMITUDE"

The status of non-Muslim minorities in Islamic lands evolved unevenly. In several places Christian attitudes toward Jews and other minorities had hardened shortly before the advent of Islam. The new attitude included prohibitions on the feast of Purim and the building of synagogues. More restrictions followed under the Byzantine emperor Justinian I, such as forbidding the practice of Judaism altogether in the North African territories that Rome reconquered from the Vandals. There was active interference in Jewish doctrinal matters as well: stipulations as to which Targum was to be used, and prohibitions on the use of the Mishnah (the core of the Talmud) for matters regarding the Torah.

At first the Muslim conquest brought relief to many oppressed peoples in the Mediterranean and beyond. In later centuries, however, Muslim governments sometimes emulated the oppressive behavior of those they supplanted. Once their political power began to wane, some Muslim rulers turned tyrannical in their treatment of minorities.

At times this issue became a matter of hot dispute among Muslims themselves, and occasionally even the cause of civil war. In the Indian Moghul Empire, for instance, a sûfî-inclined crown prince, Dârâ Shîkoh, wanted to maintain the equality between Hindus and Muslims that had characterized Muslim rule for several generations. This stance cost him the throne, as a "fundamentalist" contender for power proved to be the better military commander. The discrimination against non-Muslim subjects introduced by the new ruler contributed to the "Great Divide" that still bedevils relations between Hindus and Muslims in the Subcontinent.

Our concern here is with Jews and Christians as minorities under Muslim rule. The qur'ânic term "People of the Book" (*ahlu-l-kitâb*) applies primarily to Jews and Christians, though later Muslims sometimes extended it to others, including the Zoroastrians and certain sects of Hindus on discovering that some of them were monotheists and possessed a revealed scripture in such works as the *Bhagavad Gita*. The Buddhists were less fortunate. The word *budd* (from Buddha) came to mean "idol," with numerous derivatives, such as *budd shiku-ni* ("iconoclasm").

Jews and Christians were considered spiritual cousins of the Muslims, and were often treated as religious relatives, in line with qur'ânic teachings:

> Among the Peoples of the Book are upright ones who are very devout in their worship of God. They believe in Him and the Last Day, standing for what is right and opposing what is wrong. Keen to do good they are among the righteous (Sûra 3:113).

The Qur'ân explicitly states:

> I am not going to worship whom you worship
> and you are not going to worship whom I worship.
> To you your religion, and to me mine
> (*lakum dînukum wa liya dîni*) (Sûra 109:4–6).

Accordingly, the "People of the Book" were protected minorities free to follow their respective faiths and run their own religious courts. This was the theory, and it was also true in practice for much of the time.

A member of such a protected minority was called a *dhim-mî*, initially a positive term, because it means that the person's protection is obligatory upon Muslims. In the course of time, however, it acquired a negative connotation and came to mean something akin to second-class citizen, if not worse. Dhimmîs were exempt from military service, partly because it was felt that they could not be expected to fight against their brethren in faith. They were also exempt from paying the *zakâ*, the tax that is one of the five basic pillars of Islam; instead, they paid a different one, called *jizya*, which entitled them to protection by the Muslim rulers. This gave rise to all kinds of misinterpretations, and sometimes it was argued that Muslim rulers were tolerant because they wanted their subjects to remain non-Muslims so as to extract the jizya from them. While there were instances in which this was the case, it was hardly the rule.

An instance from India illustrates what was most problematic about the jizya. Under the first Moghul emperors, all citizens paid the same taxes. When the fundamentalist Aurangzeb assumed power after defeating the legitimate heir to the throne, he introduced the jizya. A Hindu delegation petitioned him not to do so. The jizya was less than the taxes they had formerly paid, but separate taxation divided people of the same village. The Hindus preferred to pay more but remain citizens with the same legal status as their Muslim neighbors.

In general the Muslim state did try to protect its dhimmî subjects against mob violence. While most of the time the dhimmî populations were tolerated, there were periods when they were subjected to violence and faced prohibitions, primarily during wars with non-Muslim powers.

The millet system created under the Ottomans has often been praised as progressive in comparison with conditions prevailing in Europe from the tenth to the seventeenth century. In modern Persian and Turkish the Arabic word *milla* (*millet*) denotes "nation." Originally it meant "religious community," scarcely different from the term *umma*, which is used today for the world community of Islam. The Qur'ân speaks of Islam as being the *millat Ibrâhîm*, or "religion of Abraham," with the connotation of "community." The subjects of the Ottoman Empire were divided according to their millet, or religious affiliation. The Christian millet was subdivided into ethnic millets on the basis of their churches. There was, for instance, an *ermeni* (Armenian) millet and a *yunani* (Greek) millet. All millets enjoyed considerable cultural and legal autonomy, at least during the better days of the six-hundred-year-long Ottoman Empire. This freedom helps explain why these nations are still Christian despite centuries of Muslim rule.

Right from the beginning Jews and Christians were regarded not only as spiritual kin but as religious rivals, and Muslims were instructed to differentiate themselves from them in dress, customs, and manners. Some scholars hold that this idea goes back to instructions given by the Prophet himself, but apparently the Hadîth to this effect was regarded as not very authentic; and these rules were not always strictly enforced, and often not at all. At times, however, there was a backlash and great emphasis was placed on such distinctions, especially after the Ottoman advance into Asia Minor and southeastern Europe.

Originally such measures may have served to protect the Muslims, who in many places were a ruling minority. Jews and Christians were required to wear not only clothes of distinctive colors but a patch of a different color on their outer garments. Later, however, the sartorial distinctions sometimes had the purpose of humiliating non-Muslims and making them feel inferior, or of punishing them when they "forgot their place." Anyone familiar with the yellow star Jews were forced to wear by the Nazis and their sympathizers during the Holocaust will find it difficult to rationalize such practices.

Muslim women were expected to cover their faces, as will be discussed in another chapter, and one of the most offensive practices was the requirement that non-Muslim women do the opposite. The veiled face was associated with virtue, whereas the uncovered face signified the opposite, thus putting a person on the same level as a slave woman.

Looking specifically at Jewish life in Muslim history, we find that hostility toward Jews undeniably existed and occasionally flared up, even taking the shape of pogroms. Mistreatment of Jews occurred in various parts of the Muslim world in different historical periods. While it was rarely a permanent feature of any society, there was only a handful of places where it did not happen at one time or another. In the 1830s, under Muhammad `Alî, the founder of a new dynasty in Egypt, a previously deplorable situation was partly remedied. As one observer wrote:

> At present, they [the Jews] are less oppressed; but still they scarcely dare to utter a word of abuse when reviled or beaten unjustly by the meanest Arab or Turk; for many a Jew has been put to death upon false and malicious accusations of uttering disrespectful words against the Qur'ân or the Prophet.

Another example is Tunisia, where in 1857 a Jew allegedly insulted Islam while intoxicated. Tunisia was then following the Hanbalî school of jurisprudence, under which he would have received a light sentence. Instead, the case was referred to the court of the more rigorous Mâlikî school, thus ensuring a death sentence.

The history of Jewish-Muslim relations is so complex that one can list as many positive as negative examples of their interaction. The Islamic code regarding the protection of minorities failed to prevent the development of what has been called a whole ideological structure of "dhimmitude," based on the differentiation between Muslims and others ("infidels"), the segregation of the various communities, and the humiliation of the dhimmîs. Their inferiorization was projected as a theological principle. Theologians in the service of

the empire justified it by interpreting verses from the Qur'ân
as legitimating the practice. The fact that more conscientious
Muslims took such treatment of minorities to be alien to the
teachings of the Prophet proved of little help. Today, in cos-
mopolitan societies where Jews, Christians, and Muslims live
in relatively harmonious social, political, and religious envi-
ronments, Muslims cannot imagine the slave-like conditions
under which dhimmîs sometimes lived. Because they cannot
imagine such distortions, they refuse to acknowledge these
sad chapters in the Muslim historical record and continue to
glorify a mythic vision of a perfectly harmonious and tolerant
past.

Generally such deterioration was sporadic, interrupting
periods of tolerable relations between the communities, and
overall, problems were certainly less severe than in the
Christian world. This is not to argue that Islam is superior to
Christianity, but simply to reflect the historical record.
Christian hostility was linked to the notion of Jews as the
killers of Christ. Muslim prejudice toward Jews stemmed from
the historical enmity of the Jews in Medina toward the
Prophet. But early Muslim-Jewish squabbles were recalled far
less often in Muslim societies than was the image of Jews as
Christ-killers in Christian societies, and with much less fervor.

Islam's more tolerant attitude toward Jews derives in part
from the fact that in the Qur'ân Jews are mentioned both negatively and positively, with a noteworthy distinction: the negative references speak mostly of Yahûd ("Jews"), the positive
ones generally of Banî Isrâ'îl ("Children of Israel"). With reference to the conspiracy of the pagans in Mecca and the Jews

in Medina against the nascent Muslim community, we read in
the Qur'ân: "You will see that the Believers' worst enemies
are the Jews and the idolators" (Sûra 5:82).

That this does not represent a wholesale condemnation of
Jews (Yahûd) is evident from another passage:

> The Believers, the Jews, the Christians, and other
> monotheists, all who believe in God and the Last Day
> and do good will be rewarded by their Lord; they need
> not fear anything nor be despondent (Sûra 2:62).

Thus it is possible to see a Jew from a double perspective:
either as one of those who conspired against Muhammad in
Medina, or as an heir to the biblical prophets. As a result,
some Muslim peoples, such as the Pashtûn, proudly claim
descent from the Lost Tribes, and in Afghanistan and
Pakistan some give their children the name Isrâ'îl.

The double-image of the Jew in the Qur'ân may account
for the fluctuations in Muslim attitudes toward Jews, alter-
nating from *convivencia* (amicably living together) to hostility.
A study of the image of the Jew in the *Arabian Nights* yields
no negative references. In that world-famous collection of
folk tales and legends, the Jew appears mostly as a sage, very
much on the pattern of *Nathan the Wise*, a play by Lessing, a
German pillar of the Enlightenment. The Jew of the *Arabian
Nights* is often a medical doctor, a humanitarian who never
fails to help.

Strange as it may appear today, some researchers see the
roots of anti-Semitism in Christendom in the medieval

Christian perception of Jews as allies of the Muslims, a fifth column for Islam in Christian territory. Spaniards commonly refer to Jews as traitors (*el judío traicionero*) because they were said to have assisted in the Muslim conquest of the Iberian Peninsula. Other Christians of Western Europe, too, tended to view Jews and Muslims as twins. The bluntest expression of this notion was voiced by Peter the Venerable, who was of the opinion that "a Jew is not a Jew until he converts to Islam."[9]

After the fall of Granada in 1492, Muslims and Jews were both expelled from Spain. Many members of both groups avoided expulsion by converting to Catholicism, becoming Moriscos (converts from Islam) and Marranos (converts from Judaism). Later even these converts, or rather their offspring, were expelled. The last such expulsion occurred at the turn of the year 1608–1609. Significantly, Muslims and Jews mostly went into exile together, settling primarily in Morocco and the neighboring countries of North Africa. Others, mainly Jews, went as far as the Balkans, then part of the Ottoman caliphate.

---

[9] Allan H. and Helen E. Cutler, *The Jew as an Ally of the Muslim: Medieval Roots of Antisemitism* (Notre Dame, Ind.: University of Notre Dame Press, 1986), p. 335.

9

Together on the String:
The Eighteenth and Nineteenth Centuries

A Religion of Force and Violence?

Christians have, for the most part, considered force to be a major characteristic of the Islamic religion and have often viewed themselves as its victims; Muslims generally see it the other way round. Sometimes it is not clear, in metaphorical terms, who is the Christian and who the Muslim. Among the most despicable of Serb war crimes in the recent Balkan wars was the chopping off of two fingers from the hands of several hundred Bosnian children. The perpetrators of the crime wanted them to have only three fingers, symbolizing the cross of the Serbian Orthodox Church. One is surely not wrong in arguing that those Muslim children are the real Christians bearing the cross, and not those who mutilated them in the name of Christianity. The same applies to the "lucky" Bosnians who had crosses cut into their flesh and survived, bearing the symbol for the rest of their lives.

While Christians accuse Muslims of jihâd, Muslims blame Christians for the Crusades, and both have adjusted their religious teachings and histories accordingly. Muslims often forgot the Greater Jihâd (spiritual self-purification) and turned the Lesser Jihâd (defense of religion) into imperial conquest. The Spaniards developed a totally different type of Christianity parallel to the ordinary version. The place of Jesus, the peacemaker, was taken by Santiago Matamoros (St. James the "Muslim Killer"). Today Spain is threatened by increasing desertification. A sarcastic explanation offered for the scarcity of forests is that too many trees were needed to fuel the fires of the Inquisition when *los hijos de Dios quemaron a los hijos de Alá* ("the sons of God burned the sons of Allah").

The Crusades were conceived of as a holy war, aimed at recovering land the church believed belonged to Christendom. There is a parallel between this attitude and the caliphate's doctrine that opposes *dâr al-islâm*, the "Abode of Islam" (i.e., peace), to *dâr al-harb*, the "Abode of War." We call this doctrine Muslim rather than Islamic because it does not figure in the Qur'ân but is a product of political history, no matter the religious overlay and ramifications.

There are two opposing Western myths regarding Muslim tolerance: (1) Muslims are seen as fanatics offering a choice between the Qur'ân and the sword; (2) the Islamic East was a utopia in which Muslims, Christians, and Jews worked together in harmony as equals. Both views are simplistic. In medieval times not many Christians or Muslims regarded religious tolerance as a sacred principle, though some rulers, such as Fredrick II of Sicily, did so ardently.

European apologists sometimes argue that ruthless oppression of non-Christians began during the Renaissance, when Christian Europe saw itself threatened by the Turks. In reality, Catholic Hungarians and their Croat vassals carried out Crusades much earlier, against Muslims and also against Christian "heresies" in the Balkans, especially in Bosnia, which was forcibly converted from its Patarene Christianity to Catholicism before the Ottoman Turks arrived. Muslims were strongly represented in the Balkans several centuries before the Ottomans, and many Bosnians embraced Islam before the first Turk converted. Needless to say, the long history of the violent suppression of Judaism in Europe came hard upon the heels of Christianity's becoming the official religion of the Roman Empire, many hundreds of years before the dawn of the Renaissance.

Pogroms and the expulsion of Jews and Muslims from much of the empire accompanied the Hungarian Crusades. This change from the remarkable tolerance of the early Hungarian rule to Catholic exclusivism was not due solely to external threats. In Bosnia the Ottoman Turks were received as liberators from the Catholic yoke, just as the arrival of the Arabs in Spain was seen by the people of Andalusia.

The fourteenth-century advance of the Ottoman armies into Eastern Europe provoked anti-Muslim propaganda in neighboring states that felt threatened. The Reformation brought about some changes, to the extent that quite a few Hungarian Protestants migrated to the Ottoman Empire, where ultimately they embraced Islam. The Turks profited from the influx of such Europeans, who were often among the best and brightest. One Hungarian Protestant turned Muslim, Ibrâhîm Müteferrika, introduced the printing press to the Ottoman Empire.

During the European Enlightenment in the eighteenth century, the old hostility to Islam was partly reinforced, but essentially as a relatively marginal byproduct of an internal cultural critique. Opposed to the obscurantism of the Catholic Church, the new rationalists attacked religious intolerance. Often, however, they used an allusive as well as evasive literary device. Instead of directly attacking Christianity, they employed Islam as a foil. Attacking Islam was a safer strategy than attacking Catholicism and its clergy head-on.

The other trend, lavishing praise on the mythic Islamic utopia, started almost simultaneously. Thinkers like the German poet-philosopher Goethe emphasized kinship with Islam as a monotheistic religion and reasoned that "We all live and die in Islam, since it means submission to God" and is "a system in which nothing is lacking."

Others contrasted Catholic bigotry with Muslim tolerance. Enlightenment writers like Lessing compared the noble and tolerant Saladin, who had reconquered Jerusalem, with the cruel and ignorant Crusaders. With his famous play *Nathan the Wise*, Lessing became a precursor of interreligious dialogue and the idea of Jews, Christians, and Muslims as one family in need of reconciliation. In the nineteenth century, the era of European romanticism, with its almost cultish fascination with Spain, Victor Hugo and Washington Irving extended the romantic myth from Christian to Muslim Spain.

Jews did not lag behind in this reevaluation of Spain's Muslim past. European Jews, referred to by Christians as Semites and Middle Easterners, identified themselves with other Semites and Middle Easterners, particularly with the Arabs of Spain. The British politician Benjamin Disraeli and

the German poet Heinrich Heine found in the example of
Muslim Spain both personal solace and a reproach to their
intolerant fellow citizens by glorifying medieval Islamic tolerance. As Jewish-born converts to Christianity, they
deplored the fate of the *moriscos* (Spaniards of Muslim ancestry) as an indirect way of decrying Jewish suffering. This feeling was especially typical of those who, like Heine, had converted to Christianity only to discover that this step did not
bring the acceptance they had yearned for.

The actual historical record, situated somewhere between
the two extremes, is more ambiguous. Muslim rulers did on
occasion discriminate against followers of other religions, but
such behavior was the exception rather than the rule and, in
relative historical and cultural terms, Muslims can rightly be
considered tolerant. Although strongly egalitarian in some of
its teachings, Islam, both in doctrine and in practice, does recognize and enforce certain inequalities, notably between man
and woman, master and slave, believer and unbeliever.
Enshrined in the holy law, the sharî`a, these distinctions pre-
sent contemporary Muslim leaders with a difficult choice:
whether to remain isolated because of traditional dogma or to
rethink qur'ânic teachings to make them compatible with the
concepts of human rights that are gaining universal recognition, at least among enlightened elites.

THE DIVISIVE ROLE OF COLONIALISM

Only a generation ago there were large Jewish communities
throughout the Arab world, with a total population estimat-
ed at approximately eight hundred thousand. Many Jewish

communities had been present in these countries prior to the Muslim conquest in the seventh century, and thus preceded the Arabs. This once-vibrant presence has been reduced to a fraction—just about sixteen thousand—and it continues to decrease. The near-extinction of Arabic-speaking Jewry was due not to annihilation, as in Europe during the Holocaust, but to emigration.

The Jewish exodus from the Arab world was caused by several factors and passed through various stages. One of the important factors was the European penetration of the Arab world. Napoleon Bonaparte's expedition to Egypt in 1798 is reckoned as the official beginning of this process, but it was preceded by various colonialist adventures marked by bitter rivalries among the European powers, in particular between Britain and France. After World War I, London and Paris coordinated their geopolitical ambitions in the region. The effects of European dominance on society in the Middle East and North Africa were profound, with a lasting effect on both Muslim and non-Muslim inhabitants.

The majority of Middle Eastern and North African Jews were poor, like the majority of the population in general. As late as 1910, 60 percent of the Jews of Baghdad could be classified as poor, and another 5 percent as beneath the poverty line (beggars). They lived a life of social degradation and even physical isolation, increasingly confined to a crowded ghetto-like area sometimes called the Hârat al-Yahûd (Jewish Quarter), and in Morocco called the Mellâh.

Though a small number of Jews and Christians were wealthy and privileged, this by no means always protected them against the negative effects of dhimmihood. They prospered in crafts and professions regarded as lowly by Muslims, such as gold and silver smithing and moneylending. Some of them acted as intermediaries between local Muslim rulers and European commercial interests.

The ruling class, which often had scant interest in religion per se, tended to look down upon Jews and other minorities, on ethnic as well as religious grounds, but generally found them useful in administrative, social, or economic functions. Because of their educational attainments and mastery of foreign languages, members of the Jewish elite were able to perform important state missions, something they had already undertaken in medieval times. From Tangiers to Istanbul, the Sephardic upper class spoke Arabic and Spanish. The Livornese Jews of Algeria and Tunisia spoke Italian. Iraqi Jewish merchants who did business in India knew English. Jews and Christians were also in demand at European consulates. In Baghdad, the British consulate and commercial companies at one time employed twenty-eight Christians, fourteen Jews, and four Muslims. Throughout the Maghreb, native consular agents, vice-consuls, and honorary consuls were invariably Jews.

While in Egypt in 1798, Napoleon invited the Jews of Arabia and Africa to reestablish their kingdom in Jerusalem, under his banner, of course. In a parallel move, the German kaiser, on a visit to Morocco, offered Prussia's sword to protect Islam. The geopolitical rivalries of the European powers provided an opportunity for non-Muslims in the Middle East and North Africa to exploit the tensions in order to gain free-

dom from their dhimmî status. At the same time it forced
Muslims to reassess the compatibility of their culture and
social norms with those of the dominant powers of the modern world.

In the Ottoman Empire the first official step toward
improving the status of non-Muslims occurred in 1839. An
edict issued by the sultan/caliph listed reforms similar to
those in the French Declaration of the Rights of Man, extending civil equality to non-Muslims, at least in theory. This was
followed by another edict in 1856, elaborated with the assistance of Austria, Britain, and France, Turkey's allies in the
Crimean War. The purpose of this edict, with its far-reaching
human rights guarantees, was to elicit Western recognition of
Ottoman territorial integrity and to mark the empire's entry
into the European concert of powers. (For this reason it is all
the more bewildering that at the beginning of the third millennium Turkey is still striving to pass the human rights test
in order to become a full member of the European Union.)

The Jews who participated in the implementation of such
reforms were members of the elite families of Baghdad,
Aleppo, and Cairo. Having held leadership positions for generations, they were influential at home and abroad. Their
modern education and knowledge of European languages
assured them of Western connections, and some of them were
instrumental in modernizing the Jewish communities.

Most of the reforms pertaining to non-Muslims were part
of a wider process known as *tanzîmât*, a kind of Ottoman per-
estroika. In North Africa, French influence and the important
role of Jewish institutions, such as the Alliance Israélite

Universelle, began to have an impact on Muslim-Jewish relations. In Morocco it took the spirit of reform longer to have an effect, however, and it was here where the largest Jewish population of the Arab world lived. Lobbying by British subjects of Moroccan-Jewish origin led to the special mission of Sir Moses Montefiore to Morocco in 1863. And yet, Jews began to benefit from reforms only when France gained control of Morocco. As a result of the early and long-lasting French presence in Algeria (since 1830), its Jews were more affected by European influences than those in neighboring states.

Before the French Revolution, Europeans cared little about the welfare of Jews even within their own borders, and there was not one country that had fully emancipated its Jewish citizens. Gradually, though, the values of the Enlightenment began to bear fruit. By the turn of the nineteenth century, public opinion was beginning to have an impact on domestic and international affairs, and at times political motivations were accompanied by an authentic sense of morality. Understandably, this development was not smooth, and there were frequent setbacks, such as the Dreyfus Affair, symptomatic of earlier historical conditions. In the Middle East and North Africa, the European powers espoused the cause of minorities. Tolerance was preached to the natives not only for the sake of human rights, but also to emphasize the moral superiority of the imperialist powers, especially where religious tolerance was concerned.

During World War II, the sultan of Morocco, Sidi Mohamed V, and the bey of Tunis, Sidi Moncef Bey, came out in defense of their Jewish citizens, courageously withstanding

Nazi pressure with strong public declarations. While a few
North Africans were lured by Nazi propaganda, the majority
protected their Jewish neighbors in various ways.

The situation changed during the struggle for independence following World War II. In keeping with colonial policy everywhere, minority communities were used as buffers
between the rulers and the majority population. In East and
South Africa, the Indian communities were converted into a
buffer between the British and their African subjects. As a
result, the Indians later suffered, especially in Uganda and
Kenya. Unable to strike at their British oppressors directly,
the African population sometimes turned its wrath on the
Indians, whose fault was that they were neither African nor
British.

In North Africa, Jews were driven into a somewhat similar
position. They certainly could not be blamed for having taken
to French education and trying to improve their living standard. At the same time, doing so earned them some privileges
from their colonial masters, and in the eyes of the less-privi-
leged majority population, their status made them appear
like collaborators. The French certainly did not consider them
French, but to Muslims they looked like an appendage to the
colonial master.

Such situations often end in tragedy, as has repeatedly
been witnessed in Indonesia and Malaysia, with Muslim
mobs turning against the thriving Chinese minority. The
transformation of a minority into a buffer between rulers and
ruled has happened many times in many parts of the world,
and it has never been easy to find a way to maintain social

harmony once this occurs. It takes time to realize that both parties were but puppets pulled by their masters in the colonial setup, and even more time to overcome the resentment resulting from this situation.

The colonial buffer phenomenon was particularly acute in the Spanish-ruled territory of Northern Morocco. At a time when Spain was still forbidden territory for Jews, the colonial authorities attracted Jews to the Spanish protectorate in Morocco, where they served in the lower echelons of the administration. The result was Muslim hostility against the Jews as an intermediary class assisting the foreign power.

Surprisingly, this situation was not the main reason that so many Moroccan Jews left for Israel. While it must be conceded that in most other Arab countries hostility drove the Jews out, in Morocco it was also Jewish messianic expectations that prompted large numbers to migrate to Israel; the belief that the Messiah was about to appear grew steadily in the 1940s.

A healing of wounds began in the early eighties when Moroccan Jews now living abroad as emigrés began again to participate in the *hailûla* pilgrimage to the shrine of Rabbi Chaim Pinto, a Jewish saint, near Fez in Morocco. Traditionally there are more Muslims than Jews at the shrine, but now the *hailûla* has become a joint enterprise once again, and the country's leading filmmaker, Muhammad Lutfî (Mohamed Lotfi), has captured this Jewish-Muslim spiritual event in an award-winning documentary, entitled *La Hiloula*.

10

Fresh Wounds and Dim Hopes:
The Twentieth Century

AFTER THE HOLOCAUST: BOSNIA

In 1933 the Nazis came to power; in 1999 the genocidal campaign against the Muslim people of Kosova, an extension of the ethnic cleansing that began in Bosnia in 1992, came to an end.[1] From the beginning of the ethnic cleansing inflicted on the Bosnian people, Jews and Christians differed as to whether it constituted another Holocaust. Many Jews said it did; most Christians said it did not. Muslims do not insist on calling the destruction of Bosnia a Holocaust, but many were consoled by the stand that most Jewish organizations and many prominent Jewish individuals took in publicly denouncing those crimes against humanity as a Holocaust. Jews often did so in the face of opposition from those who disputed the enormity of the crime in Bosnia or sought to

---

[1] The principle of ethnic cleansing, as devised in Croatia in 1941, states that "one third of the enemy population should be killed, another third expelled, and the remaining third assimilated." In the ethnic cleansing carried out in Bosnia, forced conversions of Muslims to the Orthodox Church may have been fewer than 100, as against some 200,000 people killed and 750,000 expelled. In other words, what happened in Bosnia was closer to genocide than to ethnic cleansing.

minimize it, equating victim and aggressor and averring that "all are the same and equally to blame."

In addition to identifying with the suffering of the Muslim people of Bosnia and seeing it as reminiscent of the past suffering of their own people, many Jews were also in the forefront of humanitarian efforts in and on behalf of Bosnia. Jewish organizations and individuals sent large quantities of baby clothes, often packed by volunteers in American synagogues, while Islamists distributed scarves to little girls shivering in Austrian refugee camps, showing greater concern for the children's religious conformity than for their well-being. On April 6, 1995, the third anniversary of the aggression, a pro-Bosnia demonstration took place on Capitol Hill in Washington, D.C. Fifty of the participants were Jews, forty-eight were Muslims, and two were Christians.

Bosnia is not the only example of sympathetic action by Jews on behalf of Muslims suffering oppression. During the Soviet invasion of Afghanistan, it was striking to see that most of the young people from the West bringing humanitarian relief to the suffering Afghans in the war zones were Jews. Rather than associate with the Islamists dispatched from Iran and Pakistan, these young volunteers worked with the indigenous resistance in the interior, where they never received a share of the millions of dollars lavished by the United States on the Afghan resistance.

The young relief workers rarely made headlines. Anna Layla (Behrend) from Geneva, Switzerland, spent several months in the Afghan mountains, accompanying a group of students from Kabul University who were undergoing guerrilla training, the only group in the Afghan resistance that had women fighters in its ranks. At the end the group was wiped out—not by the communists, but by Islamists who could not tolerate independent nationalists. Anna Layla's life was saved and she is back in Geneva, spending the best years of her life as a severely handicapped person. Her father was a hero of the resistance against the Nazis in the Warsaw Ghetto.[2] Many Afghans are eagerly waiting for their chance to honor such supporters once the Tâlibân nightmare is over.

An attentive reading of the Qur'ân leaves no doubt that Muslims cannot remain indifferent to the crime of genocide under any circumstances. The Sacred Scripture explicitly condemns the persecution of all believers and the destruction of human life. The passage that justifies Muslim resistance to persecution mentions the destruction not just of mosques but also of monasteries, churches, and synagogues:

> Permission to fight is given to those against whom war is waged, because they are wronged. Surely God is able to help them. Those who have been unjustly thrown out of their homes. All they did was to say, "Our Lord is God." God took a group of good people to push back a group of bad ones, otherwise those would have pulled down monasteries, churches, synagogues, and mosques wherein God's name is much mentioned (Sûra 22:39).

Churches, monasteries, and synagogues are mentioned even before mosques. Thus the wording of this Sûra tells

---

[2] A journalist by profession, Anna Layla wrote a moving account of her experiences with the Afghan resistance. Unfortunately, it is available only in French. See Anna Layla, *Afghanistan Libre: Moments avec la Résistance Démocratique* (Geneva: Editions Poésie Vivante, 1991).

Muslims that they should make no distinction as to whether the persecuted are Jews, Christians, or Muslims.

In the face of this qur'ânic moral imperative, it is deplorable and shameful that the Holocaust has not evoked a stronger response among Muslims. The Arab-Israeli conflict over Palestine is no excuse for Muslims to adopt an attitude of indifference with regard to the enormity of the Holocaust: the teachings of the Qur'ân are explicit on this point. As mentioned earlier, there was a handful of notable exceptions, such as the late Sultan Mohamed V, who resisted pressure to enact the Nazi anti-Jewish laws in Morocco.

Professor Zuhdî Sharrâbî (Zehdi Charabé), a Sunni Muslim from Aleppo in Syria, managed to hide his Jewish wife and her mother in the heart of Berlin throughout the Nazi period. He refused to have his story told because he felt that he had done nothing other than his most basic Islamic duty. The thriving Charabé family that he left behind in Berlin bears testimony to his qur'ânic ethics. A Bosnian Muslim woman sheltered a Jewish family in her Sarajevo home during the Nazi occupation. Fifty years later she was invited to Israel and received special recognition for risking her life.

One would expect the film *Schindler's List* to be attacked by neo-Nazis in Western Europe, not by leaders in the Muslim world, but this did indeed happen. Such depraved insensitivity is particularly painful to contemplate when one recalls such things as the widely appreciated contribution to present-day Islamic thought made by Muhammad Asad (Leopold Weiss), a Jewish convert to Islam. He lost his relatives in the

Holocaust, and had he not happened to be in Arabia at the time, he himself would have suffered the same fate.[3] Today many Muslims consider Asad's rendering of the Qur'ân to be the best English translation.[4] Dr. Hamîd Marcus, another convert from Judaism, translated the Qur'ân into German, only to die in a concentration camp, totally unsung in the Muslim world.[5] The Nazis did not care what religion he professed; to them he was a Jew. More recently, in Bosnia and Serbia, non-Muslims have been killed because one of their parents happened to be a Muslim.[6]

In a speech on the Holocaust, Sanâullâh Kirmânî, an Islamic scholar from India residing in the United States, highlighted the morality of remembrance as a triumph over evil, giving as an example Eli Wiesel's reference to Bosnia in his address at the dedication of the Holocaust Museum:

> Some Jewish communal leaders were the first to recognize publicly the "ethnic cleansing" in Bosnia for what it is and to speak out against it. . . . As a Muslim I am grateful for that remembrance. The greatest triumph of the victims in Auschwitz, Treblinka, Babi Yar and other horrible places is to be a collective and ever-present

---

[3] See Muhammad Asad, *The Road to Makkah* (New Delhi: Islamic Book Service, 1994). This is an Indian pirated edition. The original bore the title *The Road to Mecca*.

[4] See Muhammad Asad, *The Message of the Qur'ân* (Gibraltar: Dar al-Andalus, 1980).

[5] Hamîd Marcus was a sûfî type of person who shunned fame. The translation was published in prewar Germany under the name of Maulana Sadruddîn, a Pakistani preacher who became a kind of guru to Marcus. Sadruddîn's knowledge of German never advanced beyond the elementary stage. The translation is so excellent that it has several times been reprinted in recent years.

[6] For a more detailed study of this topic, see Khalid Durán, "Bosnia: The Other Andalusia," *Journal of Muslim Minority Affairs* 13:2 (July 1992): 390–400.

remembrance to all the children of Abraham. May we, the children of Abraham, always remember and jointly raise our hands and voices to proclaim our remembrance against such evils happening to any people ever again.[7]

There are individuals and governments in the Muslim world that applaud the Holocaust revisionists in Britain, France, and elsewhere. Most eager to patronize Holocaust deniers is the regime in Tehran, which regularly sends Nazi old-timers to the United States to entertain its followers with anti-Semitic outbursts, especially on the anniversary of Khomeini's death. Evidently they are impervious to the lessons of history.[8]

Already we are witnessing the blossoming of revisionism with regard to the ethnic cleansing in Bosnia, even though there is incomparably more information and abundant, tangible evidence available about these crimes against humanity. While the ethnic cleansing was going on from 1992 to 1995, hundreds of journalists from all over the world interviewed thousands of torturers and their victims, filmed them, took their pictures, and recorded their statements. After World

---

[7] Sanâullâh Kirmânî, "The Holocaust: Reflections of a Muslim," *Journal of Ecumenical Studies* 34:2 (Spring 1997): 222. The lecture was presented at Temple Israel, Silver Spring, Maryland, on April 8, 1994, as part of an interfaith Yom Ha-Shoah service.

[8] One such "entertainer" is Dr. Ahmad Huber, a retired journalist from Switzerland. In a lecture at the Islamic Education Center (a Khomeinist institution) in Potomac, Maryland, he explained that the figure of 6 million Jewish victims of the Holocaust was invented to offset Hitler's unparalleled achievement of getting 6 million jobless off the streets by providing them with employment. Huber's lectures are available on videotape.

War II many prominent Nazi criminals went into hiding. By contrast, only a handful of the Serb chauvinists who committed these crimes felt compelled to do the same, and very few have been caught and tried. Indeed, thousands are living openly, enjoying undisturbed normal lives. While many deny having committed any crimes, just as many openly take pride in what they did.

The victims, too, are very much with us. More than ten thousand raped women, mostly refugees from Bosnia, are being cared for by international organizations. Those interested in helping them may contact the groups that provide the multiple forms of assistance the victims require (almost all of it is provided through private initiatives, with no UN, government, or church funding). The facts about the atrocities committed against the Bosnian people can be verified by picking up the phone or by even popping in unannounced.[9] Many of the victims were only eleven or twelve years old when they were raped by a dozen drunken soldiers, day after day, for weeks or months on end. Now they are like living corpses, damaged beyond repair both psychologically and physically. In Bosnia rape was not done for sexual gratification, but as a means of striking terror; it was part of a planned political campaign. The idea was not to make the victims disappear, but rather to create as many surviving warnings to the enemy as possible. Conservative estimates vary between fifty and sixty thousand rape victims, but even some UN

[9] For instance: Medica mondiale, Hülchrather Str. 4, 50670 Cologne, Germany. Tel. 011\49\221\931-8980. E-mail:medicamondiale@net.cologne.de.- www.medicamondiale.org.

agencies put the figure as low as ten to twenty thousand. The dispute over the figure of six million Jews killed in the Holocaust has made us become all too familiar with the malice behind such number games.

Despite the abundant evidence of atrocities, there is fierce denial in many quarters that any of this happened. In Greece, Russia, and some other countries, it is dangerous to even mention the issue, since doing so could provoke violent reprisals. France leads the pack in the production of revisionist writings with regard both to the Holocaust and to ethnic cleansing. Muslims who do not protest against this revisionism neither heed qur'ânic teachings nor see the moral imperative that is clear to most of the world's people regardless of their religious culture or ethnic background. Such Muslims would be well advised to reflect on the implications of Holocaust denial for their own future. In Germany a macabre racist joke asks: "What is the difference between a Jew and a Turk?" The answer: "The Jew already got his lesson, the Turk has yet to get it."[10]

Awareness of this linkage is growing, and even an Islamist journal pointed out the connection between the Holocaust and looming dangers for Muslims. The journal, a publication of the U.S. branch of the Islamist subsection called Salafîs, reports with considerable detail on the cooperation of large parts of the German population with the Nazi crimes against the Jews, in this way unambiguously taking the side of the victims. The journal quotes Elie Wiesel at some length and

---

[10] "Der Jude hat es bereits hinter sich, der Türke hat es noch vor sich!"

without any of the reservations commonly seen in Islamist publications.[11]

There have always been Arabs and Muslims who identified unreservedly with the victims of the Holocaust, but these individuals, who also spoke out courageously on other issues, usually paid with their lives for their principles. Their number includes the Algerian freedom fighter and humanitarian lawyer `Ali Mécili (assassinated in Paris in 1987), the Afghan resistance leader Professor `Abdu-l-Qayyûm Rahbar (assassinated in Peshawar in 1990), the Iranian human rights activist Kâzim Rajawî (assassinated in Geneva in 1990), and the Palestinian politician Dr. `Isâm As-Sartâwî (assassinated in Lisbon in 1984). Most were murdered because they opposed the policies of Iran's "Islamic Republic," but they were also targeted because of their unbiased attitude toward Jews as fellow human beings whose extraordinary suffering as a people should never be belittled.

THE ARAB-ISRAELI CONFLICT

There have been and still are many positive interactions between Jews and Muslims, and they need to be highlighted to prevent their being completely overwhelmed and utterly lost amid the many negative aspects of the relationship between the Children of Abraham. At present, however, the general picture is bleak. There is deep suspicion between many Muslims and Jews, reinforced by the Israeli-Palestinian

---

[11] See Bâsim Khafâjî, "Muslims in the West and Ethnic Cleansing," *As-Sirât Al-Mustaqîm*, no. 57 (July 1996), pp. 14–15.

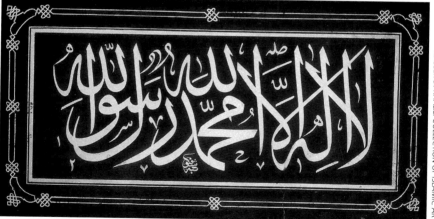

These two exquisite examples of Islamic calligraphy from 19th-century Ottoman Turkey are of the *shahada*, the classic Muslim profession of faith. The language of the profession is: "There is no god but God and Muhammad is the Messenger of God." The utterance of the *shahada* (Arabic for "to affirm") is the central act of Muslim piety; it is both the most important and the most simple declaration of Muslim faith. In the Hadith, the collected sayings and stories attributed to Muhammad, it is reported by Abu Sa'îd El' Khodri that the Prophet reassured a visitor concerned that he was not fulfilling his religious obligations of the *shahada's* significance: "... these few words are equal to one third of the Qur'ân."

A manuscript of the Qur'ân, from Iran, c.1820, in the Arabic naskhi script, with insertions in Persian nastaliq script. In Islamic belief, the Qur'ân is God's final message to humanity. God (Allah) revealed His word to the Prophet Muhammad through the Angel Gabriel, and Muhammad then recited the verses of the non-mediated revelation to a growing following who memorized them. ("Qur'ân" means recitation.) The Qur'ân conveys God's word directly in lyrical Arabic considered so incomparably beautiful no translation has remotely done it justice. The Qur'ân makes believers submit to Divine will and believe in God's justice and kindness. It prescribes the duties of Muslims and the guidelines for individual behavior and social norms. The Qur'ân was revealed first in Mecca (611-622), and then at Medina (622-632). The heart of Islam, in the centuries since, the Qur'ân has been learned by heart in Islamic schools, meditated upon and copied, sung and chanted in mosques, and widely translated.

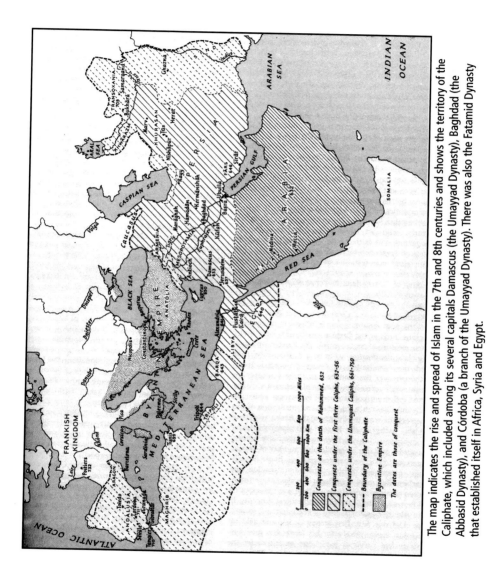

The map indicates the rise and spread of Islam in the 7th and 8th centuries and shows the territory of the Caliphate, which included among its several capitals Damascus (the Umayyad Dynasty), Baghdad (the Abbasid Dynasty), and Córdoba (a branch of the Umayyad Dynasty). There was also the Fatamid Dynasty that established itself in Africa, Syria and Egypt.

Begun in 786, the great mosque of Córdoba is one of the finest examples of Moorish architecture in the world. From the 8th till the 13th century, Córdoba was the Western counterpart to Baghdad. During its cultural zenith, it was arguably the most advanced and civilized city on earth. Its contribution to intellectual life was enormous, personified by three great philosophers who were its products: the Roman Seneca, the Muslim Ibn Rushd (Averroës), and the Jew Maimonides.

The famous Court of the Lions in the Alhambra Palace in Granada. The last great Moorish city to fall to the Christians during the Spanish *Reconquista*, Granada was captured in 1492 by the armies of King Ferdinand and Queen Isabella, whereupon all Muslims and Jews were expelled from Spain.

A map of the Ottoman Empire at its height in the mid-16th century during the reign of Sultan Sulayman I, "The Magnificent." In addition to the historic Turkish heartland of Anatolia, the Empire held much of North Africa, Asia Minor, the Crimea, Armenia, and Georgia; and its Asian borders pushed deep into Persia and Arabia. Its European conquests included the Byzantine Empire, Greece and Macedonia; much of the Balkan Peninsula: Bulgaria, and most of Hungary. Transylvania (Hungary and Romania), Walachia and Moldova (Romania) were reduced to tributary principalities.

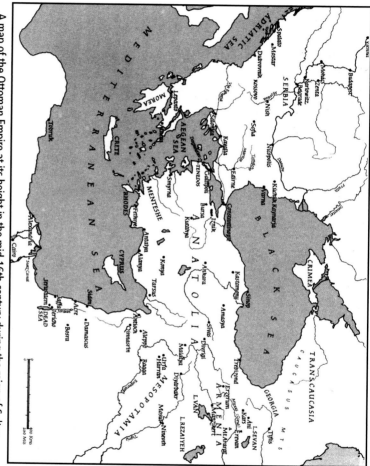

Noah and his family are safe in the Ark during the great flood. This illustration appears in a late 16th-century Islamic manuscript, *Qisas al-anbiyâ'* (Stories of the Prophets). Rendered in the Persian style with Persian calligraphy, it was painted by unidentified Ottoman artists. The lives and deeds of biblical figures considered as prophets by Muslims are briefly mentioned in the Qu'rân, and are often depicted in Persian and Ottoman art.

A muezzin chanting from the minaret of a mosque summons the faithful to prayer five times a day.

ROLI BOOKS

The faithful in prayer at Jama Masjid (Friday Mosque) in Delhi, India. The mosque was built in the 17th century during the reign of the Mogul emperor Shah Jahan, who also built the celebrated Taj Mahal.

Facing toward Mecca, as do Muslims the world over, these Indonesians are gathered in one of the capital's public squares for the observance of Idul Fitri, marking the end of the fasting month of Ramadân.

PHOTO RESEARCHERS, INC.

A sufi Muslim at prayer.

The mausoleum of Hazrat Massoumeh in Qum, Iran, is one of the holiest shrines of Shi i Muslims.

This is the beautiful central courtyard of the Isfahan Shah Mosque in Isfahan, Iran.

Pilgrims in Mecca performing the rite of circling the Ka`ba, the most sacred shrine in Islam, seven times. According to the Qur'ân, the Ka`ba is the oldest temple for the worship of the one God. After the angel had provided Abraham a ram to sacrifice in the place of his son Ishmael, Abraham and Ishmael praised God by rebuilding the temple that lay there in ruins. Among other stones, they used a black meteorite, which still forms part of the building; lucky pilgrims who manage to touch it feel that they have shaken hands with Abraham.

Standing on Mount Arafat is one of the most important rites practiced by pilgrims, or hâjis, during the pilgrimage, or hajj, to Mecca. It was here that the Prophet Muhammad spoke to his followers shortly before his death. At Mount Rahma (or Mount Mercy), pilgrims spend their day in meditation and recitation that culminates in prayer at sunset. The gathering is called a "Rehearsal for the Day of Judgment" when all humanity assembles before God to account for their deeds.

In the Marrakesh Square of Djemaa el Fna in Morocco, veiled Muslim women do their marketing as well as visit medicine men, watch magicians, and listen to traditional storytellers.

In Tehran, Iran, schoolgirls enjoy an outing in the Mellat (People's) Park, formerly Shahanshai Park. The *hijab* (Islamic veil) is part of the uniform.

A British street scene shows Westernized young men of Pakistani origin "hanging out" while an elderly bearded Pakistani immigrant in traditional dress walks past, surveying them. Tensions between the older, often religiously fervent generation of Muslim immigrants in Britain and the younger, more assimilated ones, often British-born, are rife, and are treated in such films as *East Is East*.

Members of the Muslim community assembled at an outing at Coney Island, New York. New York, like other major American cities, has a substantial and growing Muslim community, a product of large-scale non-European immigration since the mid-1960s; as a result, Islam is the fastest growing religion in the country. As is true throughout the United States, most come from Pakistan and Bangladesh, but there is also a sizable Arab community.

Students in Sarajevo, Bosnia-Herzegovina, in October 1995. During a lull in the fighting, a downtown public school opens for class. Though predominately Muslim, in keeping with the tolerant traditions of Bosnian Islam, the school welcomed students from all the ethnic groups of the former Yugoslavia.

Muslim fundamentalism (Islamism) is spreading in the tropics. Muslims in Malaysia have decided to set an example by Islamicizing their country with a fervor rarely seen elsewhere. This fragile, multiethnic nation is witnessing the rapid growth of Muslim militancy, and its sizable non-Muslim population feels threatened. The Malay government is finding it increasingly difficult to resist demands for an Islamic state. This political and religious phenomenon is also spreading among the Muslim minority of southern Thailand.

Impassioned Islamists (fundamentalists) chanting and brandishing weapons at a rally.

The late Ayatollah Khomeini of Iran, father of the Iranian Islamist revolution and an icon of Jihadists around the world, tucked into a machine gun belt. Among other human rights abuses, Khomeini's rule resulted in unspeakable crimes against women, including a "theology of rape" enacted upon thousands of female prisoners.

The caption on this drawing of Usâma Bin Lâdin, considered the mastermind of global Islamist terrorism, reads: "Made in USA. Warning: no method has yet been devised to dispose of this product." Few Americans know that many Muslims believe Islamism is an American creation, part of a Western conspiracy to keep Muslims backward. American support for the Afghan resistance is often cited as "evidence." The CIA, in fact, had little direct dealing with the Afghan resistance, and even less with such "Arab Afghans" as Bin Lâdin. Pakistan directed the resistance, seeing the war as an opportunity to control Afghanistan. But throughout the Muslim world many assert that the Americans have no one to blame but themselves. Many Islamists adore Bin Lâdin, and regard him as a revolutionary hero, a Muslim version of Ché Guevara.

Made in USA
Warning:
no method
has yet been
devised to
dispose of this
product

جريدة أي رب

أتحاد سوفياتي

أبدأ من النهاية فأقول:
إذا أراد عربي أو إسرائيلي أو أميركي أن يعرف لماذا يجب انتهاء
مفاوضات السلام في الشرق الأوسط بحل عادل وشامل.. وسريع،
فعليه أن يتجه بنظره نحو موسكو.

المراقب العربي مثلنا يعرف بالتجربة أن قوة الحدس عند اليهود مرتفعة، وأن الجالية اليهودية في أي بلد عادة ما تكون أول من يشعر برياح التغيير، فإذا كان الحدس اليهودي في روسيا هو ما نقدر، فإن الأيام حبلى بعظائم الأمور.

غالبية اليهود الروس التي كانت تتظاهر قبل أشهر قليلة تأييداً للرئيس بوريس يلتسن تلزم الصمت هذه الأيام، وهي بالتأكيد تلزم بيوتها ولا تتظاهر.

ومنظمة "بعاد" التي تعمل كمظلة للنشاط اليهودي الروسي كانت أيدت ميخائيل غورباتشوف علناً وبشجاعة في آب (أغسطس) ١٩٩١، خلال محاولة الانقلاب الشيوعية، إلا أن نائب رئيسها يفغيني سانانوفسكي يقول اليوم "بعاد الآن تتزن موقف الحياد السلم، ولم نرسل إلى الرئيس يلتسن برقية تأييد كما فعلنا خلال محاولة الانقلاب، فنحن الآن محايدون، وهو الموقف التقليدي لليهود".

في غضون ذلك، زادت طلبات الهجرة إلى الخارج التي يقدمها اليهود الروس، والرسالة واضحة، فمع أن اليهود الروس يؤيدون يلتسن، ومع أن كثيرين منهم من أنصار الليبراليين في البرلمان، فإنهم أكثر حذراً وحكمة، من أن يراهنوا على حصان خاسر، ويواجهوا غضب المنتصرين عندما يسقط.

وواضح أن روسيا تقف على حافة الهاوية اليوم، وربما نجد الولايات المتحدة وحلفاؤها في مساعدة يلتسن على الصمود، وربما سقط رغم كل المساعدات.

اليوم تحاول موسكو وتفشل في بسط سلطتها على جميع أنحاء البلاد المترامية، وإذا سقط النظام فقد تنهار روسيا، وتنقسم في دويلات ومقاطعات على أسس طائفية وعرقية ويقتل الجميع في ما لا نهاية أو ربما خلف يلتسن بعض المعتدلين الذين يواصلون سياسته، ولكن مع التمتع بقبول عام فقده الرئيس الحالي، وربما أطيح يلتسن وسياسته وتسلم الحكم وطنيون متطرفون أصحاب نزعات غير ديموقراطية، بمن فيهم الشيوعيون السابقون، يعيدون نظام الحزب الواحد تحت اسم ومفهوم آخرين لهذه المرة.

ويهمني من الاحتمالات السابقة آخرها وأقواها، وهنا أعود إلى ما بدأت به من ضرورة الوصول إلى تسوية شاملة وعادلة في الشرق الأوسط قبل فوات الأوان، فالأرجح إذا سقط يلتسن أن يخلفه القوميون المتعصبون، والأرجح عند ذلك أن يمارس هؤلاء السياسة الاستعمارية التي انتهجها السوفيات على مدى ٧٠ سنة، حتى مع اختلاف التسميات.

وأتصور أن هذا السيناريو إحدى الفرضات التي تمسك بها صدام حسين وهو يغرق، فهو في البداية لم يعرف أن الاتحاد السوفياتي انهار عملياً، وأن المواجهة بين الشرق والغرب انتهت، وعندما دفع الثمن أخذ يراهن على عودة الوضع القديم، وينتظر حتى نحن فرصة مرة ثانية.

إذا قام نظام قومي متعصب في موسكو فسيكون ظاهرة مناقضة للفكر السوفياتي الساقط، إلا أنه سيسعى من منطلق العداء للغرب والإسلامية والشوفينية، إلى تحقيق الأهداف نفسها، بما في ذلك التنافس على المصالح والنفوذ في الشرق الأوسط والخليج تحديداً. وسيسعى القوميون الروس في البحث عن حلفاء لهم، لا يهم أن يكون هؤلاء دولاً مثل العراق وليبيا، أو منظمات إرهابية متطرفة، وربما نجد بينها بعض المنظمات الجديدة التي تريد المصالح الغربية بحجة الدين أو غيره.

ولا نتصور أنه لن يوجد عاقل يمكن أن يستبعد أن يجد الروس دولة أو أكثر ومنظمات من كل لون تتحالف معهم في السر أو العلن، وتزيد المنطقة خراباً فوق خراب (العاقل كذلك يدرك أن الولايات المتحدة لم تكن مرتاحة كثيراً لسقوط الشيوعية، فهي كانت الشرير الذي أذكى روح المنافسة، وجعلها تجتهد لتتفوق، وإن تركها سقوطه من دون هدف، فأصبح هناك من يريد أن يجعل الإسلام هدفاً أو عدواً جديداً).

وهكذا فقد وصلنا إلى السباق بين السلام في الشرق الأوسط وعودة الاتحاد السوفياتي باسم آخر، والعربي والإسرائيلي والأميركي العاقل هو الذي يعمل لتحقيق سلام عادل وشامل قبل فوات الفرصة.

والدنيا كلها فرصة، إذا اقتنصها الإنسان في الوقت المناسب فاز، وإذا تردد خسر.

THE ARABIC NEWSMAGAZINE AL-WASAT

The cartoon from the Arabic-language press spoofs the shifting political alliances involving the Islamists. Before the war in Afghanistan, the Soviet Union was an important backer of many Muslim radical religious groups as a way of destabilizing Western-leaning regimes and putting pressure on Israel. Now Russia sees itself imperiled by Islamism, and the Islamists regard Russia as an enemy.

من وأنا لطفلة كنت أحب
أتذيّع على الناس.. ولما كبرت
اشتغلت داعية..

The cartoon from the Arabic-language press mocks the arrogance and intolerant religiosity of the Islamists. One of the freshly trained fundamentalist female preachers is asked what made her choose this unusual profession. She answers: "Since I was small I have always liked to give people a hard time, so when I grew up I decided to work as a preacher."

ROSE EL-YOUSSEF

conflict, which every now and then rages at fever pitch, and the wars between Israel and its Arab neighbors. The "common man" in the Muslim world is mostly fearful and suspicious of Jews. These attitudes stem largely from the news he hears about attempts against places sacred to Muslims in the geographical areas under dispute, especially the attempt to burn the Al-Aqsa Mosque, the shooting at the Dome of the Rock, and the 1994 massacre at Abraham's shrine in Hebron (the Tomb of the Patriarchs).

There is also a widespread belief that the Jews aim to create a Greater Israel stretching as far as Medina in Saudi Arabia. As mentioned earlier, in the Prophet's day Medina's population was partly Jewish, and thus some Muslims believe that it is an object of Jewish vengefulness and Israeli irredentism. Islamists use this notion as a propaganda weapon to further their own ends.[12] It is a bitter irony that scarcely any Jew is aware of the background to these fears, except for a few specialists on Islamic affairs.

One of the most powerful expressions of this mood was the political slogan chanted by tens of thousands of demon-

---

[12] Bassâm Al-`Ammûsh, an Islamist deputy in Jordan's parliament, delivered a lecture at the 1994 Jerusalem Day in Chicago, ruminating in a manner that one could describe as "pathological archaeology of religion":

"Our brothers in Saudi Arabia, those who live in Medina or close by, know the fortress of Ka`b Ibn Ashraf [a Jewish leader at the time of the Prophet]. It is still there, as it was, unchanged. According to what I have heard, and I suppose it is correct, this is because of the Zionist lobby in the world. They have made it a condition that Saudi Arabia must not effect any changes in those areas. Everything should remain as it is until they come to claim it because it belonged to their ancestors. In 1967, what did Golda Meir say? Or at least it has been attributed to her that she said 'I smell the fragrance of my ancestors, my ancestors in Khaibar.'"

Khaibar was a Jewish village in Arabia in the time of the Prophet. Islamists never tire of claiming that Israelis plan to conquer Arabia in order to get Khaibar back.

strators in Pakistan to voice their rejection of the power-hun-
gry Islamist leader Maudûdî: "Ek Maudûdî—sau Yahûdî!"
"One Maudûdî is worse than a hundred Jews." It is, on the
one hand, a sad indication of how the word *Yahûdî* has
become synonymous with enemy. On the other hand, it
shows that people cannot easily be duped, and that they
eventually discover the true identity of their real enemies:
Maudûdî rather than Yahûdî. The slogan has to be seen in the
context of Islamist polemics. Here the Pakistani masses tell
the Islamist minority: "You are blaming the Jews for everything, whereas in actual fact you are a hundred times worse
than they."

The Palestine issue has given enormous impetus to the
Islamists. Initially, Arabs and other Muslims took great pains
to point to the racial and religious bonds between Jews and
Muslims, stressing that the conflict was political, not religious. The line of argument ran that they were opposed to the
Zionist ideology and the State of Israel, not to Judaism as a
religion or the Jews as a people. In the course of time, however, the Arab-Israeli conflict has generated abysmal hatred
in many people on both sides. In the sixties some Islamists,
notably the Egyptian Sayyid Qutb, took this conflict out of the
realm of politics and made it over as a theological issue. This
trend has steadily intensified, and we are now witnessing the
production of a literature that is outright anti-Jewish, not just
anti-Israel. Some Islamists argue that the conflict is primordial and existential: the world has room for only one of the
two, and the Almighty prophesied the end of Jews; Palestine

will be their grave, this being the only reason they have gathered there. It is a "struggle for existence between Qur'ân and Talmud."[13]

Judaism and Islam, such Islamists aver, are incompatible and mutually exclusive. One of the top leaders of the worldwide Islamist movement, the Tunisian fugitive Râshid al-Ghannûshî, takes the ultimate step toward Nazism by declaring Jews to be the enemies not just of Islam but of all humanity, of all positive values.[14]

This trend is relatively new and therefore has not yet been rebutted by many Muslim thinkers. In fact, many are not even aware of the poison brewing in Islamist literature. Others know and are deeply shocked, and are seemingly paralyzed by what seems to them monstrously outrageous. They consider this kind of propaganda not only un-Islamic but also profoundly anti-Islamic, and they regard the evident borrowing from European anti-Semitic outpourings as shameful for Muslims and harmful to the cause of Islam.[15]

---

[13] This is the title of a book by 'Abdu-s-Sattâr Fathullâh Sa`îd: *Ma`rakatu l-wujûd baina l-qur'ân wa t-talmûd* ("The Struggle for Existence Between the Qur'ân and the Talmud") (Plainfield, Ind.: MAYA [Muslim Arab Youth Association], 1980).

[14] More recently he sounded the alarm because of "the Judaization and Americanization of the region." See Ash-Shaikh Râshid Al-Ghannûshî, "Hal li-mihnati l-walîma . . . ," *Ash-Sharq Al-Awsat*, June 26, 2000, p. 8.

[15] Among those alert to the new trend toward an anti-Jewish theology is Professor Rashîd Ahmad Jâlandharî, head of the Institute of Islamic Culture in Lahore, Pakistan, and a former director of the Pakistan government's Islamic Research Institute. He has condemned such misinterpretations of Islam in numerous lectures. The same holds true for Professor Smail Balic from Bosnia, retired chairman of the Muslim community of Austria and editor of the journal *Islam und der Westen*, published in Bosnian, German, and Turkish. The late Omar Juma, a Kenyan broadcaster, devoted many of his sermons to anti-Jewish distortions of Islam's ecumenical message.

Lately some Islamists have adopted the blood-stained medieval European ploy of condemning Jews as Christ-killers. (By the same illogic the Arabs could be collectively condemned as the people who opposed Muhammad and nearly killed him.) The Qur'ân does not hold Jews collectively responsible for the death of Jesus. Some Arabian Jews seem to have teased their Christian opponents by boasting that they had killed Jesus, but the Qur'ân refutes this idea by stating emphatically that "they killed him not" (Sûra 4:157). The Qur'ân does mention that Jews sometimes killed their prophets, as did other peoples, Arabs in particular.

In general, Islamist literature presents an undifferentiated image of the Jews by means of scriptural card-stacking: making use only of qur'ânic verses that speak of Jewish sinners. For someone unfamiliar with the text as a whole, such stigmatizing is convincing. But one could just as well infer the opposite by pointing only to the instances of divine grace showered upon the Jews while omitting the instances of sin and transgression. If one were to weigh both elements in the Qur'ân, negative images of Jews as transgressors are less frequent than positive references to Jews as examples of close communion between man and God. The Qur'ân presents many of the biblical prophets as recipients of divine grace and friends of God. With two or three exceptions they are all Jews, and are the heroes of the qur'ânic narrative. The Qur'ân goes further than Judaism by elevating David and Solomon to the rank of prophets:

To you [Muhammad] We have sent inspiration as We sent it to Noah and the Messengers after him. We sent inspiration to Abraham, Ishmael, Isaac, Jacob and the Tribes, to Jesus, Job, Jonah, Aaron and Solomon, and to David We gave the Psalms (Sûra 4:163).

For Jews, David and Solomon are national heroes, center-pieces of the Israelite pantheon, yet millions of Muslims are named David (Da'ûd) or Solomon (Sulaimân). And how many carry the name Jesus? His name (`Isâ) is more common among Muslims than among Christians. In the Hispanic world the name Jesús is not uncommon, but even that stands no comparison to the frequency of `Isâ in the Islamic commu-nity. The Qur'ân speaks of Jesus as a prophet to the Children of Israel, stressing his Jewishness rather than his universality:

In their footsteps We sent Jesus, the son of Mary, con-firming the Torah that had come before him. He was no more than a servant. We granted him our favor and made him an example to the Children of Israel (Sûra 5:46 and 43:59).

Most important, the Qur'ân explicitly speaks of the divine blessing upon Isaac, Jacob, and their offspring. The revelation also tells us how to understand passages that speak of Jews negatively:

We gave him the good news of Isaac, a prophet, one of the righteous. We blessed him and Jacob. Of their prog-eny are some that do right and some who obviously wrong themselves (Sûra 37:112–113).

The history of Jewish-Muslim relations, especially within the framework of Islamic rule, has been a history of contradictions, of paradoxes, and finally of tragedy in the twentieth century because of the Palestine question. But is it more tragic than what happened to Jews in Europe during World War II? Is the enmity between Arabs and Israelis, between Muslims and Jews, worse than what used to be the Franco-Prussian enmity? Is it worse than the Jewish-German enmity after the Holocaust? Following in the steps of David Ben-Gurion and Yitzhak Rabin, Ehud Barak visited the new Berlin in 1999 without forgetting the Jewish martyrs who perished in concentration camps. Do Muslims belong to so different an order of humanity that we cannot forgive and ask for forgiveness? Certainly, there are the issues of Jerusalem, of Palestine, of Arab solidarity and Islamic brotherhood.

Yet even while the Israeli-Palestinian conflict rages, in Israel "new historians" have already undertaken the courageous task of revisiting the recent history of the conflict and reassessing the ambitious dreams of classical Zionism. Schoolbooks are being reexamined in order to put an end to what may have been deemed necessary for psychological warfare when Israelis saw themselves as besieged in their garrison state by unremitting enemies. Schoolbooks that dehumanized the Palestinian people by annihilating their identity are being rewritten to tell a more balanced and complete story. After half a century, Palestine is to be a land of two peoples, whatever ultimate territorial solution comes out of the negotiations. There is still room for the worst and the best both in Israeli-Palestinian relations and, more generally, in Jewish-Muslim relations. Leaders with courage and vision are needed on both sides in order to secure a brighter future in terms of relations between the two peoples and the two faiths.

The ongoing efforts of people of goodwill are focused on the future, but it is also necessary to keep alive the positive aspects of the past. We ought to cleanse our collective memories of the wrongs committed by our ancestors and by recent generations in order to lay the foundation of a better future. Those who will be leaders in the twenty-first century are still contaminated by the intoxicating propaganda of the 1980s and 1990s.

Jewish thought and art, the Jewish scientific mind, and Jewish linguistic and diplomatic skills were and remain to this day major components of Islamic civilization. If Jewish scholars acknowledge Islam's influence and the use of Arabic by some of their greatest thinkers, why should Arabs and Muslims be reluctant to admit Jewish influence on their culture and society? Many Muslims immediately reject a cultural element or influence the moment it is identified as Jewish. If it is accepted as part of authentic Islam, then by definition it is not Jewish but divine in origin, and if there is something similar in Judaism, it is because the Jews also received divine revelations.

11

A New Page for Other Priorities:
The Twenty-first Century

Jerusalem is not only of prime importance to Jewish-Muslim relations, it is the whetstone; and simplistic, one-sided formulations will not help solve the problem. It cannot be solved by the Jewish argument that since Muslims have Mecca and Medina they have no claim on Jerusalem. Nor by Muslims claiming that Jerusalem has the same religious significance to Islam as Mecca and Medina. A solution would be easier if the Muslims in Palestine were descendants of the Romans who destroyed the Temple. In that case, it could be argued that they ought to give Jerusalem back to its rightful owners. But when Arab Muslims first came to Jerusalem under Caliph `Omar, there was barely a Jewish presence in the city, and the Temple Mount was desolate. The Dome of the Rock was built on that site in homage to the Temple, not as an act of Muslim triumphalism. That is one reason a solution is so difficult.

The situation was entirely different when the Ottoman Turks conquered Constantinople; they seized this capital city from its original Greek inhabitants and conducted themselves with strident triumphalism. Hagia Sophia, the great cathedral of Orthodox Christianity, was not really needed as a mosque, but the sultan, nonetheless, had it turned into one as a symbol of victory. Since the Greeks and their Orthodox Church are still present in Istanbul, Hagia Sophia ought to be given back to them. Atatürk found a way out by turning it into a museum, thus making it belong to everybody.

Many non-Muslim scholars argue that Muhammad changed the direction of prayer from Jerusalem to Mecca because of his disappointment when the Jews of Medina failed him, but the point is debatable. He made Muslims focus on Mecca, and succeeded at getting back into his city. According to Islamic eschatology, at the end of times the direction of prayer will again be toward Jerusalem, where most of the eschatological events will take place. This expectation may be of doubtful authenticity; it is not enshrined in the Qur'ân, but it exists as an element of popular faith with millions. In the meantime Muslims speak of Jerusalem lovingly as *al-qiblatu l-ûla* ("the first direction of prayer"). It sounds almost like *al-qublatu l-ûla* ("the first kiss"), and that is indeed what it is, in a spiritual sense.

The Temple Mount is holy to Muslims because of its biblical history, Islam's Jewish legacy. The Prophet felt himself taken to Jerusalem and then ascended into the seven heavens, meeting with Moses and Jesus and all the other prophets. The spiritual airport for this mystical night journey was the Temple Mount; Muhammad did not dream of St. Peter's in Rome. The Qur'ân refers to this event as a journey from the Holy House in Mecca to "the farthest mosque," an expression Muslims have always understood as referring to the spot on the Temple Mount where the Aqsa Mosque is situated. *Aqsa* means "farthest." Attempts to find a different geographic location or religious explanation for this term have failed.

It has to be borne in mind that *masjid*, the Arabic word for "mosque," means a place of prostration before God. In this sense, a place of worship other than a Muslim mosque can also be called a *masjid*. This applies all the more in the case of Jerusalem, because of the belief that originally it was all Abrahamic *islâm* before it became Judaism and Christianity. The Ka'ba, Muslims believe, was always *baitu-llâh* ("God's House"), despite the idols that were put there for a century or more. Al-Aqsa may have been a church for some centuries, built on the remnants of the Temple; but essentially it has always been a *masjid*.

The Muslim relationship to Jerusalem was superbly expressed by a tribal chief from Baluchistan upon his return from making a pilgrimage to Arabia. "Mecca," he exclaimed, "I respect her like my wife, but Medina, I love her like my daughter!" Asked about Jerusalem, he was astonished how someone could even ask. "But Jerusalem is my mother!" was his answer. In the Qur'ân, Mecca is called the "Mother of Cities" because it is said to be home to the oldest house of monotheistic worship, but in popular piety the expression resembles more closely the attachment one might feel for a remote grandmother. As for Jerusalem, the memory is vivid because of the qur'ânic stories, as if it had all happened only a generation ago.

Non-Muslims may think it contrived when Muslims today

speak of Jerusalem as "the third of the two holy shrines" (*thâlithu l-haramaini sh-sharîfain*); the expression is a clumsy, evasive-sounding formulation. There has always been a difference of categories, with Mecca and Medina belonging to one and Jerusalem to another. In the course of the centuries many cities became holy to Muslims, and among them Jerusalem is the queen. Jerusalem is surely hallowed, but it belongs to the second category.

Islam may be called lucky in that its grown-up children do not insist on sharing the parental home. The Baha'is disclaim any relationship. The founder of Sikhism, Baba Guru Nanak, was a sûfî who made the pilgrimage to Mecca. His followers, however, have a Ka`ba of their own, the Golden Temple in Amritsar, India. The Sikhs do not insist on having a share of Mecca; they have broken the bonds and no longer belong to the Abrahamic family. Jews, Christians, and Muslims are united by this special family relationship; if they cannot share Jerusalem, the Abraham family will break up and cease to exist.

An obvious solution would be for all to pray together on the Temple Mount, making the dream of an Abrahamic platform come true. For demographic reasons, however, at this point in time this would prove to be more like a nightmare than a dream.

Jerusalem poses a great challenge for Jews and Muslims. But a compromise solution is surely possible, and they must arrive at one. They owe it to themselves, to each other, and to the rest of humanity. A complex religious issue is made much more difficult by conflicting national claims to the same holy ground. There are Jews with an exclusivist attitude based not on religion but on the national identity that was born here three thousand years ago. And there are Palestinians for whom Jerusalem is simply an ancestral home, irrespective of their Christian or Islamic faith. They did not get to Jerusalem by throwing out Jews and occupying their houses. Therefore they do not live with any consciousness of being in the wrong place, one that rightfully belongs to others.

If Jerusalem were purely a religious question, it would be difficult enough, but it would probably be more easily solvable. So far the intransigent positions have been voiced more forcefully, and the violence and high level of tension make compromise appear all but impossible. Still, there is no dearth of opinion-makers among Arabs and Israelis, Muslims and Jews, who want the twenty-first century to witness the end of the Arab-Israeli struggle.[1]

PROSPECTS: INTIMATE BUT INCOMPATIBLE?

Although the early Jewish-Muslim experiment in Medina failed, in later centuries Jews and Muslims learned to turn the page and coexist in many parts of the world. Their relations were by no means always ideal, and yet when the initial experiment was given a second and a third try, it worked more often than not.

---

[1] See Sâlih Al-Qallâb, "The Arabs' Number-One Priority in the Twenty-first Century," *Ash-Sharq Al-Ausat*, January 14, 2000, p. 6

Jewish refugees from Spain introduced Moorish culture to Bosnia at the end of the fifteenth century. On two occasions, Turkish governors tried to instigate pogroms against the Jews in order to confiscate their property, but Bosnian Muslims resisted these attempts and protected their Jewish fellow citizens. In fact, at one time the sultan had to appoint a new governor in order to avoid an uprising by the Muslims of Bosnia, who were protecting their Jewish fellow citizens.

Bosnia's current ambassador to the United States, Sven Alkalaj, is Jewish, a descendant of Spanish Jews who found refuge in the Ottoman Empire; the name Alkalaj (Al-Qala`î) points to Alcalá de Henares in Spain. The ambassador is a friend of a former prime minister, Dr. Hâris Silajdzic. Theirs is a second-generation friendship, because their fathers (a rabbi and an imâm, respectively) suffered together while drafted in the Yugoslav army, where the Serbs forced them to eat pork. Hâfiz Kâmil Silajdzic (d. 1997) was imâm at Europe's most important mosque, the Husrefbeg Dzamija in Sarajevo, and he was one of the century's outstanding Muslim humanists, deeply opposed to all forms of discrimination and hatred.

What do these experiences demonstrate? Many Muslims and Jews understand that the conflicts that occurred during the Prophet's life in Medina were an isolated instance that should not be generalized into an everlasting struggle between Judaism and Islam. The successful *convivencia* in Andalusia, Bosnia, and elsewhere was possible because people realized that the clash in Medina was a unique one, restricted to a particular time and place. There always was, and still is, scope for a fresh start, always a new opportunity to become what we once dreamed we might be.

Muslims learned to judge the Jews in Spain, Morocco, and the Ottoman Empire on their merits, and often they felt very close to them. So much is similar in the religious observances of the two groups that to an outsider, such as a Confucian, they look like twins.

A Jewish professor at the American University in Cairo, `Abdullah Schleifer, converted to Islam on rediscovering the spirit of Jewish orthodoxy in a Moroccan Muslim environment strictly ruled by the sharî`a. He felt that the ritual differences were immaterial compared with the oneness in essence. His impression was that such oneness is not found between any other two religions; he encountered this spirit only with Jews and Muslims.

The sameness that impressed Schleifer as positive has impressed others as negative. Old European prejudices against Jews are today voiced against Muslims. Turks in Germany are subjected to the same insults once hurled at Jews.

Some two dozen of Morocco's leading families are of Spanish-Jewish descent, and so is Touitou, a leader of the Islamist insurgency in Algeria. Since Islam was the religion of the majority for many centuries and Muslims held political power, it was only natural that many Jews converted to Islam, as had happened earlier in the Middle East during the first expansion of Islam. These Moroccan aristocrats have been Muslims and pillars of the state for centuries; nevertheless, they do not deny their Jewish origins, despite the Arab-Israeli conflict that has poisoned the atmosphere. One of the many sûfî fraternities is that of the Cohen, a clear indication of the founders' origin in Judaism. Similarly, many Jews from North Africa (in Israel, France, and the United States) are proud of their roots in Moorish culture.

Many roadblocks obstruct Jewish-Muslim understanding, yet the significant areas of religious and cultural commonality can help overcome them and help Jews and Muslims find common ground. The important thing is for Muslims to spell out their fears, and for Jews to reflect upon them patiently. Muslim fears ought not to be dismissed as mere fantasies of political propaganda. Divisive issues need to be analyzed and addressed creatively, with positive assurances. Muslims need to listen to Jewish voices of reconciliation instead of collectively imputing to Jews motives of which the vast majority of Jews are not even aware. If these far-fetched alleged motives were known to Jews, they would be rejected out of hand, thus allaying Muslim anxieties.

In terms of religious controversy, Islam and Judaism have major complaints about one another, and many tragic confrontations might have been averted had these issues been spelled out clearly in the form of sincere dialogue. Throughout history many Jews have been offended by the supersessionist attitude of Muslims who would argue, indirectly and directly, that Judaism was past history, obsolete and moth-eaten. Muslims, in turn, are angered by the refusal of Jews to recognize Muhammad as a prophet.

What can be done about these complaints? A few Jewish scholars have pleaded for Jewish acceptance of Muhammad as a prophet in line with the non-Jewish prophets included in the Hebrew Bible, such as Job. They base their reasoning on a suggestion that Maimonides is reported to have put forward.

Muslims should have no difficulty in qualifying their supersessionism by greater emphasis on the principle of competition in pious deeds as enshrined in the Qur'ân:

> We have prescribed a law and an open way for each one of you. God could have made you a single people but He wants to test you and see what you do with what He has given you. Therefore compete with one another in all virtues, as if in a race. You all have the same goal: God. He will let you know about the matters you are in disagreement about (Sûra 5:48).

In the sources of both religions there is a divine threat that both peoples should heed: if they do not prove to be up to the mark, God will replace them by another people more deserving of His favors.

Part IV
Religious Life and Society

If the whole of mankind and all the spirits would cooperate to produce a Qur'ân like this, they would not be able to do it even if they worked closely together, everyone of them assisting the other (Sûra 17:88).

12

The Sources

THE QUR'ÂN

What Kind of Book Is It?

The Qur'ân (pronounced *Kurr aan*) is the Holy Book of Islam. Many Muslims believe that it is entirely the word of God, from cover to cover—not composed by the Prophet Muhammad but revealed to him by the Almighty. Muhammad's sayings, his opinions and directives, judgments and instructions, were collected separately; all these statements of the Prophet are called Hadîth ("novelties"). Muslims often compare the Hadîth to the New Testament. The Qur'ân, however, is to Muslims what Jesus is to Christians, that is, God's earthly manifestation, His revelation to man.

The Qur'ân is God's creative word (*kalima* in Arabic, *logos* in Greek) in history. Muslims see God incarnate in the Holy Text almost as Christians see God incarnate in Jesus. For many the text of the revelation is part of God; it is divine. They believe that the Archangel Gabriel showed it to Muhammad, and Muhammad read it to humanity. Therefore, the revelation is called a "reading" or "recitation" (Qur'ân). A dialogue between God and humanity, the Qur'ân is full of divine messages that warn, advise, and exhort. A faithful Muslim is expected to base his life on the Holy Scripture and be guided by its teachings.

The Qur'ân is divided into 114 sûras (chapters); the Arabic plural is *sûwar*. The first chapter is called *al-fâtiha* ("The Opening Chapter"); it is a short prayer, sometimes called the Lord's Prayer (Paternoster) of Islam. The other chapters are arranged roughly according to length, starting with the longest, chapter 2. With one exception, all the sûras begin with the invocation "In the name of God, the all-compassionate, the all-merciful." This is the *basmala*, the most frequently spoken or written sentence of the Qur'ân. In the Islamic world it is written on walls and especially above doorways, often in beautifully decorative calligraphy. Pious Muslims rarely begin any activity without first saying the *basmala*, which in Arabic reads: *bi-smillâhi-r-rahmâni-r-rahîm.*

At the time when the Prophet's Companions were compiling the book by assembling the various sûras, they were still under the spell of spiritual events. They had witnessed the Prophet in moments when revelations descended upon him. To them, the sequence of events did not matter; the experiences were too powerful to be subjected to an academic recording. What mattered to the Prophet's Companions was the comprehensiveness of the message—not its dissection for the purpose of historical analysis.

There is no division according to themes or topics in the Qur'ân; it is not a manual with a clear-cut order. Someone reading it like a textbook might be astonished by the repetitions. Anyone who reads the Qur'ân in order to mark the sentences that seem the most important to him is bound to miss its purpose and to overlook its full meaning. Every verse has individual value and can be understood separately; every phrase conveys a message. There are no superfluous or meaningless words.

As a result of this holistic view, we find the earliest sûras, those that ushered in the experience at Mecca, at the end of the Qur'ân, because they are the shortest revelations. (See below in this section the example of chapter 114, *sûratu-n-nâs.*) The long sûras at the beginning of the book, on the other hand, were revealed in Medina, at a much later date. Muhammad received revelations over a span of twenty-three years.

This is not to say that the time factor was immaterial. The second generation of Muslim theologians began to pay close attention to the context in which each revelation was received, and this became a special subject of research, eventuating in a separate discipline within Islamic theological studies: the study of *asbâbu n-nuzûl* ("the causes of revelation"). The fact that there could be no text without context was clearly recognized by the early scholars of Islam. The Prophet received the revelations of the Qur'ân one by one; each occasion was a special experience. The best way to understand the book is to seek to partake of these experiences, to absorb each revelation as it was lived by the Prophet, to grasp these occurrences in their context and unfolding. The reader will then discover that the Qur'ân speaks to him directly, answers his questions, and addresses itself to the particular situation in which the believer finds himself.

Muhammad received the first revelation in his hometown, Mecca, when he was still a persecuted preacher; he received the later ones in Medina, where he was the head of a city-state. These two phases were markedly different from one another. The revelations started with the enunciation of moral precepts. In the first sûras, from the time of Mecca, one finds, *inter alia*, the Ten Commandments inculcated in a novel and highly emotional way. The same is true of the commandment to love your neighbor as yourself; altruism is basic to Islam.

The early sûras are primarily impassioned pleas for social justice:

Just look at that one.
He is poking fun at religion.
He is maltreating orphans
and does not feed the poor.
Look at those pretenders.
They are not really praying,
they are only putting up a show,
and refuse to feed the hungry (Sûra 107:1–7).

In Medina the Prophet tried to implement the principles of justice and solidarity as far as was possible under unfavorable circumstances. To facilitate the arduous task, new guidelines were revealed to him that were practical and down-to-earth, among them a detailed law of inheritance.

Some Muslims regard the resultant Medinese polity as a model to be emulated, and for some this assumes a reactionary character. Others take it as an example of how to go about implementing the moral precepts under the given circumstances of each age and applying them in order to approximate the ideals of Mecca as fully as possible.

In Mecca, God Almighty told Muhammad: "You are not to dictate to them." In other words, you cannot force the obstinate among the people to become more human, you need not thrust Islam down their throats. God sent the Prophet "only as a warner" (Sûra 7:184, 188) and a "missionary" (Sûra 3:144), to reform those who were prepared to listen. In Medina, this essentially democratic attitude led to the emergence of *shûra*, a system of consultation embodied in a form of community council based on the crypto-democracy practiced by the tribes. (Sûra 42 is entitled *ash-shûra*, "The Consultation.")

Many Islamic scholars hold that the task of interpreting Islam does not mean sticking blindly to ancient patterns. Rejecting the theological version of strict constructionism, they believe that in every age the Islamic experiment needs to be renewed. Every generation faces the difficult challenge of deciding for itself what practical shape to give to the ethical principles enunciated in Mecca. It requires Muslims to exert (*ijtihâd*) themselves intellectually to the fullest in order to make God's word prevail and become meaningful amid ever-changing circumstances. This is the task assigned to the believer in the Qur'ân, which says that man was appointed as God's vicegerent (caliph) on earth: "Let man prove that he is really up to the task" (Sûra 2:30, 33:72).

What Muslims Do with the Qur'ân

Many Muslims who read the Qur'ân often—and a significant number have memorized the full text—begin to think in its terms and within its conceptual framework, conversing with themselves in the language of the Holy Book. Because of their familiarity with the Qur'ân, one or another sentence from it will occur to them at any given moment, providing solace or even a solution to a vexing problem.

Muslims admonishing one another to be patient usually do so by quoting one or two phrases from the Qur'ân, such as "Verily, God is with the patient ones" (Sûra 2:45) or "Patience is beautiful and help is to be sought from God" (Sûra 3:186). The same happens when someone is to be rebuked for arrogance: "God does not love those who show off" (Sûra 31:18). Someone who spies on others or spreads rumors is likewise reproved with verses from the Qur'ân condemning such behavior.

In a case of calumny, a judge will commence his verdict with a sentence from the Qur'ân vituperating calumny as a particularly heinous transgression (Sûra 9:79, 24:22). Idlers and squanderers of money are called "satanic" (Sûra 17:26, 25:67), and these verses serve Muslims who wish to reproach those in their community who are given to profligate spending. In recent history, these verses have been directed at individuals who waste the wealth acquired from the oil boom.

Through the moral power of such admonitions and exhortations, the Qur'ân is a living force in the life of most Muslims. It also plays a decisive role whenever the necessity arises to defend one's country and freedom. The Afghans conducted a seemingly hopeless struggle for independence against the overwhelming might of the Soviets. The Bosnians resisted the genocide perpetrated against them by Serb chauvinists. People fighting for survival derive strength from relevant qur'ânic verses, such as:

If there are twenty among you, patient and persevering, they will vanquish two hundred (Sûra 8:65).

How many times has God allowed a little troop to beat back a huge army! God is with the steadfast who persevere. . . . David killed Goliath. God gave him power and wisdom and taught him whatever He wished. Had God not made some people keep others in check, the world would be one big trouble (Sûra 2:249–251).

Moral edification is also conveyed by means of stories about bygone events, whether actual history or legends familiar to seventh-century Arabs. Many of these tales read like an Arabic version of biblical parables and exempla. The longest chapter, for instance, Sûra 2, entitled "The Cow," relates the Exodus from Egypt. Chapter 12, *Sûrat Yûsuf,* is the Joseph story, and is almost identical to the biblical text.

The Qur'ân is the highest and most authoritative source of normative Islam. A categorical qur'ânic statement on any subject is regarded by the overwhelming majority of Muslims as decisive and beyond question. The Qur'ân, however, is not primarily a book of laws and regulations that deals directly with every conceivable issue or problem. Rather, it is a book of divine wisdom meant to guide human beings so that they can realize their potential as creatures made "in the best of molds" (Sûra 95:4) and can become God's vicegerents on earth.

Many Muslims are fond of opening the Qur'ân at random and reading whatever portion they happen upon. As this practice illustrates, Muslims generally do not engage in systematic study of the revelation, but it is certainly considered meritorious to read the entire book from beginning to end on a continual basis. This is done especially during Ramadân, a month of fasting, repentance, and introspection. To facilitate this practice, the Qur'ân is divided into thirty sections, one for each day of the holy month.

Those who know the entire book by heart recite it to others, especially during Ramadân. Those who are illiterate listen to the recitations. One who has memorized the entire Scripture is called a *hâfiz*, a title of honor. It is especially the blind who continue the tradition of memorizing the Holy Book by means of frequent recitation, although the Qur'an is, of course, available in raised-print editions.

Melodious recitation of the Qur'ân is an art with its own conventions, and there are many variants. During the 1960s and 1970s, the Egyptian `Abdu-l-Bâsit became famous as a *qârî* (someone specializing in the recitation of the Qur'ân). Westerners would probably find recitations from East Africa more appealing because of their melodiousness. The most musical recitations can be heard in Indonesia. It has become customary to hold international competitions in reciting the

Qur'ân. All age groups of both sexes participate in the competitions, and many a *qârî* achieves childhood fame.

The first competitions of this kind took place during the lifetime of the Prophet. More than a dozen of his Companions memorized the entire revelation and meticulously compared each recitation to stabilize a precise narrative; thus the authenticity of the book is not in doubt. After Muhammad's death it was easy to collect all the revelations and edit them in one book, the Qur'ân, without distortions and dispute. By then so many Muslims knew the entire revelation by heart that there could be little error in editing it. Fifteen centuries later we know for a certainty that the Qur'ân we possess is the same as the revelation received by the Prophet in seventh-century Arabia. If Muslims do not feel comfortable with a particular passage, they cannot claim that it deviates from the original text. What we have is the original, and so there is only one choice: to accept it or not.

In Islam no distinction is made between purity of the heart and cleanliness of the body or of dress; for Muslims these are two sides of the same coin. That is why they normally do not touch the Qur'ân without first washing themselves. In the Arabic original the following sentence is usually printed on one of the front pages: "Only the clean shall touch it!"

LANGUAGE OF THE ANGELS

Although it is not a work of poetry, parts of the Qur'ân are composed in rhymed prose, or at least appear rhythmical,

such as chapter 114 (the last chapter), *Sûratu n-nâs*, the con-
cluding prayer in the Qur'ân:

> *a`ûdhu bi-rabbi n-nâs*
> *maliki n-nâs*
> *ilâhi n-nâs*
> *min sharri l-waswâsi l-khannâs*
> *aladhi yuwaswisu fî sudûri n-nâs*
> *mina l-jinnati wa n-nâs*

> I seek refuge with the Lord of men,
> the King of men,
> the God of men,
> from the evil of the stealthy seducer,
> who infiltrates into the hearts of men,
> refuge before the spirits and men.

For many Arabs, and other Muslims too, the strongest
proof of the Qur'ân's divine origin is the magnificence of its
language. Awed by its beauty of style and power of expression, they conclude that it cannot be of human origin. Non-
Arabs, and particularly non-Muslims, mostly do not quite
know what to make of such reasoning, and without a glimpse
at the historical background, this exotic argument in favor of
the Qur'ân's supernatural origin is difficult to grasp.

Arabia is a land of very ancient civilizations that vanished
when fertile lands turned into deserts. The peninsula may in
fact be the cradle of human civilization, but few traces of its
early cultures were left in sixth-century central Arabia. Music

and the pictorial arts were rudimentary, at best. Architecture was impressive in Yemen, but not in the Hijaz, where Mecca is situated.

There was one cultural arena in which Arabs excelled, however, and that was their mastery of language. Their artistic genius and creativity went into verbal eloquence, expressed in rhetoric and in poetry. Like the ancient Greeks at Corinth, Arabs held annual competitions in these arts, at Mecca and elsewhere. Obviously this tradition of poetic oratory had to peak at some point; someone had to be the best of the best, just as among thoroughbred Arabian horses one had to be the swiftest. Caruso, Pavarotti, and the many other famous singers of Italy are the result of a tradition that in their country is stronger than any other.

By origin and upbringing Muhammad was in every respect preconditioned to become the poet of poets, but he experienced an epiphany that changed everything. When he reached the rhetorical apex he could not accept that this art, this remarkable power of expression, had its source within himself, that it was the result merely of his constant refinement of speech, his mastery over a tradition of eloquence that valued noble oratory above all else. The way Muhammad was seized by thoughts and articulated them in a state of trance made him feel that this speech came from outside of himself, and that he was merely a medium to convey the message, like the Aeolian harp of the Greeks. During the initial phase, while he was still in Mecca, the revelations were accompanied by seizures, and he experienced them as interventions from on high.

Muhammad wanted to be a moral reformer, whereas the poets of his time were given to immorality, seeking to excel one another in licentiousness. This was one reason he did not want to be reckoned a poet. His religious message had to rise above the rivalries of the obscene poets. Yet all the same, he drew on the poetic traditions of his culture, and many qur'ânic verses have a strongly poetical character that exerts a powerful hold on the Arab listener; they still enchant as they did in the beginning. `Omar, the future caliph, for instance, was furious on learning that his sister had become a follower of Muhammad. But she only had to recite one of the early revelations and `Omar was a changed man:

> We did not send you the Qur'ân
> to make you feel unhappy,
> but as a reminder to the God-fearing.
> It is a revelation from Him
> who created the earth
> and the heavens on high.
> The most Merciful
> is firm on His throne.
> To Him belongs what is
> in the heavens and on earth
> and all that is between them,
> as well as what is beneath the soil.
> You may speak the word aloud—
> He knows the secrets,
> even the most hidden ones.
> God; there is but He.
> His are the most beautiful names (Sûra 20:1–8).

In the Arabic original this is set in rhymed verse, and the words are skillfully chosen from among numerous synonyms, a specialty of the immensely rich Arabic language.

And yet, there have always been those who did not share this view of `ijâzu l-qur'ân*: the Qur'ân as a linguistic miracle. They reason that its divinity is evident from the meaning of the words, not from their poetry. The Qur'ân itself states that God's message to man is written down on a well-preserved tablet, so whatever revelations humanity possesses are mere copies, some more exact, some less. The Arabic language of the revelation, rationalist theologians insist, is but a temporal human device to express the eternal divine message. It is not the words that come from God, but the meaning; it is not the language that is divine, but the message.

This ancient dispute will probably continue forever. Already in the ninth century some literati went so far as to argue that there could be a more beautiful Arabic than that of the Qur'ân. Linguistic beauty is, after all, a matter of taste, and standards change with the passage of time. To others this opinion is outright blasphemy. Contemporary orthodox Muslims are outraged by the suggestion, made at a conference in Kuwait, that the revelation should be translated into modern Arabic.

Through Islam, the Arabic spoken in seventh-century Mecca and Medina became the standard language of the Arab world. In the sixteenth century there was an analogous development when Martin Luther translated the Bible into German, the German of his region. This led to the emergence of a standard language for all Germans, putting an end to the diversity of tribal languages and regional dialects. However, in the twenty-first century that language, called *Luther-Deutsch*, is no longer spoken, and many Germans have difficulty reading and understanding it. The same holds true of qur'ânic Arabic, despite the tradition of learning the book by heart and keeping the classical language alive as much as possible. Languages cannot be made to stand still; they keep changing from generation to generation and from place to place.

Because of the belief in the divinity of the Qur'ân, there has always been much resistance to having it translated, and yet Islam's Holy Book has been rendered into many languages throughout the centuries. This activity has been the source of another ongoing dispute. For instance, in the twelfth century the Qur'ân was translated into a Moroccan Berber language, and the translation was widely used. Today only fragments of this translation survive, because the ideal of using the original Arabic language reasserted itself. In the twentieth century Muslims in different parts of the world, citing the Berber example as a model, wanted the Qur'ân and the entire ritual to be available in their own languages—Turkish, Indonesian, Urdu, Kiswahili, and so on. The controversy goes on and on.

Before the age of the printing press, the pious would copy the entire Holy Book in their most beautiful handwriting. This was considered to be a meritorious work, especially among the upper class. Many rulers and their ministers bequeathed to posterity a copy of the revelation in their own handwriting. Following this tradition, prominent figures of the twentieth century tried their hand at translating the Qur'ân into English. Among more than a hundred translations there is one by a former foreign minister of Pakistan who was also head of the International Court of Justice in The Hague, another by a former adviser to the president of Pakistan (written during his prison term), and there are many other examples. But because of the idea—a dogma with some—that there can be no real translation of a divine text, many of these translations bear the title "The Meaning of the Glorious Qur'ân."[1]

Large parts of Islam's Holy Book are composed in rhymed prose, which a few translators have tried to reproduce. The most successful of them was Arthur Arberry, one of the twentieth century's great scholars of Islam.

The belief in the divinity of the Qur'ân led many to think that the Arabic language itself was divine, and that the Quraish tribe of seventh-century Mecca spoke the original language of mankind, as taught by God and the angels. Few believers appear to recognize that many people in other cultures hold the same view of their own language. But there are also many Muslims who deride this claim about Arabic, such as a satirical Urdu poet who wrote:

What shall we do when we get to paradise?
It is said people over there speak Arabic,
whereas here we have learned such a chaste English.

[1] See `Abdullâh Yûsuf `Alî, *The Meaning of the Holy Qur'ân,* new edition with revised translation and commentary (Brentwood, Md.: Amana Corp., 1992). Also, *The Holy Qur'ân: English Translation of the Meanings and Commentary,* revised and edited by the Presidency of Islamic Researches, IFTA (Madinah: Call and Guidance, 1993).

How then shall we converse with the celestial maidens?
What shall we do when we get to paradise?[2]

The poet's irony stands in sharp contrast to the mindset of
the Yugoslav deputy who declared in parliament that Serbian
is the only language in which one can communicate with
extraterrestrials. Had anyone dared to contradict him or
merely to smile at this absurdity, he would have drawn his
pistol. Unfortunately, in some places, such as Southern
Sudan, there are Muslims who show a similar attitude and try
to enforce Arabic on Africans as if this were the only path to
salvation. But it is important to note that the majority of
Muslims are opposed to a supremacist linguistic policy.

THE SUNNA

Sunna means custom, habit, the proper way of doing things.
By inference it means rule (rules of conduct), even law, like
the laws of nature or the laws God has prescribed for the universe (*sunanu-llâhi fî-l-kaun*). In Islam, Sunna came to denote
the Prophet's *praxis*, his way of life, his acts—distantly comparable to the Acts of the Apostles in the New Testament. In
theology, *sunnatu-n-nabî* (the Prophet's mode of doing things)
has become a technical term on which many tomes have been
written.

On a popular level, various Muslim peoples have taken one
element or another of the Prophet's Sunna and elevated it

---

[2] *Bihisht-e barin le kar ham kya karenge?/ Suna hae wahan zaban hogi ahl-e `arab ki,/ yahan
to ham ne sikhi hae inglish ghazab ki./ Hurun ki bat kaise samjha karenge?*

above the rest, and when they talk about Sunna, they sometimes have very different things in mind. A graphic example is
the way ordinary people in Turkey understand the word *sünnet* in Turkish. To them it means circumcision. In the sultan's
palace in Istanbul, now a museum, tourists may visit the ornate
sünnet odasi ("Sunna Room"). It is the special chamber where
the princes used to be circumcised with great ceremony.

The importance the Ottomans attached to this ritual surprises many Muslims from countries where circumcision is
performed in a perfunctory manner, usually by a barber, with
little more fanfare than one associates with having one's hair
cut. These other Muslims call circumcision by its proper
name, *khatna*. It would never occur to them to call it Sunna,
because circumcision is but a minor part of the Prophet's
practice. Thus, popular conceptions of the Sunna vary from
country to country.

The word also denotes a part of the ritual prayer. Certain
parts of the ritual are *fard* ("obligatory, absolutely essential"),
and others are *sunny* ("additional," "desirable," or "recommended"), so called because the Prophet performed over and
above what is considered mandatory. *Sunna* comes from the
part of the sharî`a, Muslim canon law, that pertains to rituals,
and this particular use of the word *sunna* is known to all
Muslims. But this common usage among Muslims differs
from the way the Prophet employed the term.

In English we are able to write one with a capital *S* (Sunna,
the collectivity of the Prophet's acts, his *praxis*), and the other
with a small *s* (*sunna*, the additional part of the prayer). There
are no capital letters in Arabic, but Muslims know from the

context what is being talked about: either the Prophet's Sunna on the whole, or just part of it, the special prayer called *sunna*.

The following comparison will shed light on this distinction: when we talk about the Catholic Church, we mean the worldwide hierarchical establishment, with its headquarters in the Vatican in Rome. By contrast, when people say "On Sunday I am going to church," they are referring to a specific Christian house of worship. If the church is a Catholic one, it forms part of the universal establishment called Catholic Church. Similarly, the special prayer called *sunna* is part of the larger body of customs called the Prophet's Sunna.

Sunna has also acquired a communal or political meaning, denoting the 90 percent majority confession of Muslims who call themselves Sunnis or Sunnites in contrast to the minority confession calling itself Shi`is (Shi`ites). Sunnis call themselves *ahlu s-sunna wa l-jamâ`a*, "people of [the Prophet's] Sunna and the community [of Muslims]."

Sunnis use the term polemically to imply that they follow the Prophet's example most faithfully, whereas the Shi`is do not. In reality Shi`is, too, follow the Sunna. They, too, regard the Prophet as the "good exemplar." In matters of detail, though, there are minor variations in their interpretations of the Prophet's Sunna. These differences exist not only between Sunnis and Shi`is, but also among the "law schools" (comparable to the different rites of the various Christian denominations) belonging to both the Sunnis and Shi`is.

Again, we might compare this to the use of the word *catholic*, which is synonymous with "universal." The Church calls itself Catholic because it lays claim to universality. Most

Protestant denominations, however, do the same. Thus in the literal sense of the word, Lutherans or Methodists are just as catholic as the Catholics. Muslims, too, assert their universality or catholicity, whether Sunni or Shi`i. Because of the doctrines, liturgy, structure, and history of the Catholic Church, the word *Catholic* has acquired a particularist or communalist meaning; it is apprehended as a specific socioreligious phenomenon in history. The same applies to the term *Sunni Muslim*. We understand it as a sociopolitical term referring to a specific form of historical development, arising out of the primary concept of Sunna, that is, the Prophet's conduct and way of living his life.

We distinguish therefore between:

1. Sunna = the Prophet's *praxis*, as the original and overall concept.

2. Sunna = the majority confession of Muslims (Sunnis or Sunnites), a historical derivative serving as a denominational label.

3. sunna = the name of a special part of the ritual prayer.

4. sunna (*sünnet*) = circumcision. Here the name of the whole is employed to denote but one aspect of it. This is a regionalism, one of many peculiarities illustrating the conversion of religion into folklore.

Reformers discussing the concept of Sunna are less concerned with individual aspects, labels, and particularities. For them the primary question is what place to accord to the Prophet's *praxis*, how far and in what way to emulate his life. Are we simply to imitate him by dressing the way he dressed, eating dates instead of chocolates, using a *miswâk* (traditional wooden implement for cleaning the teeth) in place of a toothbrush? Or are we to deduce the larger meaning of what he did and wanted to be done? Are we not meant to concentrate on the intent and spirit of his acts and conduct, to imbibe the purport of his exemplary life and translate that into our own?

For example: Among the very few possessions the Prophet left behind was a mule. Translated into our lives in the industrial and postindustrial societies of the twenty-first century this would be the equivalent of a cheap used car. Many of the Prophet's contemporaries, including some of his Companions, owned beautiful horses and fast camels, the Eclipses and Jeeps of seventh-century Arabia.

Many Muslim thinkers regard the Sunna as much less essential than the revelation (Qur'ân). But most believe that without the Prophet's example we cannot fully grasp the meaning of many passages in the Holy Book, the Sunna being the primary guide on how to live by it, how to put the heavenly revelation into concrete reality, how to practice Islam.

How do we know the Sunna? Where do we acquire information about the Prophet and his deeds? As the primary sources of Islam we know the Qur'ân and the Hadîth (the sayings of the Prophet). What is the source of our knowledge about the Sunna?

The Hadîth tell us a great deal, but we must guard against the mistake of considering Hadîth and Sunna as one and the same. Many Hadîth, perhaps the larger part of them, do not provide us with details of the Sunna. But there are books by early Muslim historians about the Prophet's life that provide much additional information. These biographical sources are collectively referred to as Sîra, from *sîratu-n-nabî*—the Prophet's life story or procedure. The meaning of the word *Sîra* is close to that of Sunna; both can be translated as "behavior." (Matrimonial advertisements in the Urdu language ask for girls who are *khûb-sûrat* ["good-looking"] and *khûb-sîrat* ["well-behaved"]). As a technical term, however, Sîra now stands for "biography." As such, Sîra is a source of Sunna.

The established practice of the community is another, though more disputed source. Many theologians took it for granted that the earliest Muslim community was so heavily influenced by the Prophet's living example that their *praxis* had become more or less identical to his. The Sunna of the Companions was, therefore, a source for knowing the Sunna of the Prophet. This source is also known by the name of *ijmâ`*, which means "consensus," the practice of Islam on which there is agreement. These are matters not disputed by any of the Companions or early scholars, because all agreed that this was what they had learned directly from the Prophet, what they had seen him do, or what was reliably reported by his Companions that this is what he used to do. Thus, the sources of the Sunna are the Hadîth, Sîra, and *ijmâ`*.

13

The Practice

"Islam is built upon five," said the Prophet, and these five basic elements came to be called the Pillars of Islam.

They are:

1. The confession of faith: "I bear witness that there is no god but the One God, and I bear witness that Muhammad is His servant and messenger."

2. Prayer, more specifically the kind of prayer that is performed according to a prescribed ritual, five times a day.

3. Charity, also called the alms tax because it was institutionalized as a property tax. As a principle, however, it means self-purification, because by being charitable you do something not only for others, but also for yourself.

4. Fasting, especially in the month of Ramadân.

5. Pilgrimage to Mecca at least once in a lifetime.

Islam comprises an elaborate framework of rituals, some of which are very distinctive. The best known is the five-times-daily prayer, with its prescribed texts and body movements (prostration), its preparation in the form of the call to prayer (*adhân*) traditionally chanted from the minaret (instead of church bells), and the ablution. The ritual prayer determines the daily cycle of a Muslim's religious life. Called *salâ*, it is the second of the Five Pillars of Islam.

The weekly communal service takes place at Friday noon. In Arabic and in most other languages spoken by predominantly Muslim nations, Friday is called *jum`a*, from *yawmu-l-jumu`a*, "the day of gathering," or "assembly day." Central mosques (the principal cathedrals or main synagogues of Islam), meant to bring large numbers of believers together for the Friday service, are called *jâmi`* (assembly halls). Participation in the Friday service is obligatory. According to religious law, no funeral service may be held for someone who missed three consecutive Friday services, but this tenet is rarely acted upon.

Before Friday prayer a sermon is given that is supposed to deal not only with spiritual edification but also with concrete social issues and communal affairs. In pristine Islam, the Friday gathering used to have the character of a community council. In the twentieth century it has become a common feature of reformist writings to demand the restoration of the original unity between the spiritual and the temporal.

Friday is not necessarily a day of rest like the Jewish Shabbat or the Christian Sunday. During the morning hours, however, there is little commercial or other professional activity as people prepare for the noon service, taking their obligatory shower (ablution) and putting on fresh clothes before proceeding to the mosque. After the service, life follows its normal course, just as on every other day. The Qur'ân admonishes people to resume their normal activities and continue their work.

The question of Friday's status as a public holiday is controversial in a number of countries. During the colonial period Sunday was the customary day of rest. After independence, this was officially changed to Friday, but in practice the custom of refraining from work on Sunday continued to be observed in some countries. The argument in favor of Sunday is economic: businessmen want to stay in touch with the rest of the world, especially in banking. However, this means three holidays every week. Whether an official day of rest or not, on Fridays economic activity is reduced because of the disruption caused by the service at noon. With Sunday as the official holiday, little economic activity takes place between Friday and Sunday. The result is that there are practically three days of rest, something developing economies can ill afford. Some believe that an Islamic solution would be to stop work on Thursday noon and resume Saturday morning. Recently it was suggested to have Friday/Saturday in place of the Western Saturday/Sunday, but some were quick to object that this would too closely resemble Jewish practice.

In the seventies a Muslim scholar wrote her Ph. D. dissertation on the Friday controversy in just one country, Lebanon. That the issue is as intractable as ever became evident in 1998 when a Pakistani government changed back from Friday to Sunday, after it had taken decades of heated debate to change from Sunday to Friday. The government that took over in 1999 again made Friday the weekly day of rest.

Some of those who always argued that decolonization would not be complete unless Friday replaced Sunday are now having second thoughts. Where Friday is the public holiday, many people go to the beach rather than to the mosque. The effect on religious observance is negative and is getting worse. For this reason some of the traditionalists now believe it is wiser to keep Assembly Day and public holiday apart: Friday for prayer, and Sunday for the games.

The two major Muslim holidays (according to the fundamentalists the only two) are linked to Pillars 4 and 5, fasting and pilgrimage. Muslims conclude the month-long fast of Ramadân by celebrating the `îdu-l-fitr* (Feast of Breaking the Fast), also called *al-`îdu s-saghîr* (The Little Feast), because it is the lesser of the two holidays. Turks call it Sheker Bayram (Sugar Feast) because of the many sweets eaten on that occasion.

Two months after the Little Feast comes the Big Feast, called `îdu-l-adha* or Kurbân Bayram (Feast of Sacrifice), when animals (mostly sheep or goats) are slaughtered to commemorate Abraham's sacrificing a ram instead of his son.

A third holiday is *al-mawlidu n-nabawî sh-sharîf* (the Prophet's Birthday). Most Muslims celebrate it, some as fervently as the other two feasts. Fundamentalists, however, loathe this holiday as an innovation, and in Wahhâbî-dominated Saudi Arabia it is prohibited. They base their rejection on a remark supposedly made by the Prophet according to which "every innovation is from the devil." Others counter that only bad innovations are evil. Celebrating the Prophet's Birthday, they reason, is a *bid`a hasana* (good innovation). The holiday had its origin in the Moroccan coastal town of Ceuta (Septa) in the twelfth century, when a *qâdî* (judge) became angry on seeing Muslims join Christians in the celebration of Christmas, and this made him begin celebrating the Prophet's Birthday. Today only a few historians know about its origin, and worldwide Muslims celebrate the *mawlid* as if it had been an Islamic holiday from the start.

Fundamentalists tend to regard every celebration other than `îdu-l-fitr* and `îdu-l-adha* as sinister attempts to supplant Islam or undermine its centrality in the believer's life. They even object to celebrating Mother's Day on these grounds. Other Muslims counter that celebrating the Prophet's Birthday fosters Islamic consciousness. The celebrations are marked by nightlong recitations of poetry in praise of Muhammad and the chanting of religious songs.

The Shi`is celebrate the two major feasts of Islam, but their most important holiday is `Ashûrâ', the Tenth of Muharram, when they commemorate the martyrdom of Imam Husain, the Prophet Muhammad's grandson, who was killed at Karbalâ in Iraq. In popular religion, Karbalâ is to Shi`is what Golgotha, the site of the crucifixion, is to Christians.

As was mentioned earlier, in the 1980s Sunni fanatics in Pakistan began to celebrate an annual *Yawm `Omar* (Omar's Day) to commemorate the second caliph. This was introduced in response to Shi`i militants who stigmatize Caliph `Omar as the chief villain in early Muslim history and curse him in their prayers.

Islamic calendars generally show the Muslim New Year as a holiday, although there are scarcely any celebrations. Anniversaries of local saints are usually more important, but they are rarely mentioned on calendars because they belong to popular rather than official religion. Such festivities are somewhat similar to those of the annual *ferias* in Spain and some Latin American countries. In North Africa they are called *mûsim* (*moussem* in the French spelling, from *mawsim* in Arabic), in Bangladesh, India, and Pakistan `*urs* ("wedding" of the sacred and the profane), and in Turkey *mevlid* ("birthday," from Arabic *mawlid*).

RAMADÂN

Fasting in the month of Ramadân means daytime abstinence not only from drink, food, and sex, but also the cessation of fighting or quarreling, abusing others, and any kind of aggressiveness. These prohibitions are accompanied by the required recitation of extra prayers and intensified reading and reciting of the Qur'ân. Fasting is part of the annual cycle of the Muslim's religious life. Called *sawm*, it is the fourth of the Five Pillars of Islam.

Fasting is a recommended act, but during the month of Ramadân it becomes a religious duty. Fasting from sunrise until sunset not only means abstention from food, drink, and sexual pleasure, but also from evil thoughts and deeds. If Muslims curse or indulge in vile talk or obscenities, their fasting becomes invalid and they have to repeat the fast for an additional day. It may happen that people fast all day long, and then, half an hour before sunset, forget themselves, lose their temper, and say something offensive. In that case they must fast one more day after Ramadân is over, though not everyone, of course, strictly observes the law. Ramadân is a rigorous means of self-purification, provided it is practiced according to the religious precepts. Every night during Ramadân a special prayer is offered in the mosques during which the prayer leader (imâm) recites a thirtieth part of the Holy Book, the recitation taking about an hour. During the whole month of fasting, prayer is more intense than during the rest of the year. Many more people than usual are apt to pray five times a day, and there are additional prayers. The Qur'ân is read or recited, one part each day, so that the whole book is finished by the end of Ramadân.

In some countries, during the last three days, pious Muslims retire to mosques where they spend each night in religious seclusion. In other places, the nights of Ramadân almost resemble Carnival in parts of the Christian world, but the more religiously zealous regard this as a perversion. For them Ramadân is a month meant to approximate the spirit of monastic life.

Ramadân, the ninth month of the Islamic calendar, was chosen for fasting because it was in this month that "the Qur'ân was sent down as a guidance for mankind." Tradition has it that the first revelation to Muhammad occurred on the twenty-seventh of Ramadân, *lailatu-l-qadr*. "In this Night of Might the angels and the Holy Spirit descend to earth, and it is peaceful until the rise of morn" (Sûra 97:4–5). Muslims believe that on this occasion the heavens are more open to individual and communal prayer, so that both individual and community can purify themselves with the aid of divine grace, renewing the spiritual energy of society as a whole. The importance attached to this date differs from country to country. In popular mysticism (sûfism) it generally plays an enormous role. For some, *lailatu-l-qadr*, which might also be translated as the "Night of Grace," is the most important date on the Islamic calendar and is regarded as a night of miracles. It is "worth more than a thousand months," says the Qur'ân. For the mystics it is a period of maximum closeness to the divine, a night of visions. *Lailatu-l-qadr* is thus similar in spirit to much of the liturgy of Yom Kippur, the Jewish Day of Atonement, the Sabbath of Sabbaths, in which the Gates of Heaven are described as particularly open to human supplication.

Fasting has its spiritual significance because the believer is consciously obeying a divine command. It is the means by which we rein in our desires and passions. The experience of fasting makes us more appreciative of the gifts that God has bestowed upon us and that we usually take for granted.

Ramadân is a period for giving charity, sharing with those who have fewer material blessings than we do. One of the underlying purposes of fasting is to promote a feeling of oneness or solidarity with the poor. The principle is that people should know what it is to go hungry so that their charity comes from a sense of compassion and mercy founded on true empathy.

Those strong enough to fast for the whole month experience a sense of spiritual accomplishment. As a compassionate and flexible person, the Prophet allowed certain exceptions. For instance, pregnant and nursing women are exempt from fasting, as are the sick and travelers. Those for whom exemptions have been made are expected to fast later during the year, whenever circumstances permit. Children are not supposed to fast before the age of puberty, though they may share this experience for a few days in order to prepare themselves. The festive atmosphere during Ramadân induces many children to imitate the adults and fast for a week or two, and they experience a sense of pride and achievement.

The act of joining together in fasting and prayer for a whole month has a powerful socializing effect, helping to build a strong sense of community that is enhanced by the sharing of food at the end of the day. The evening ceremony of breaking the fast is usually celebrated among a large circle of relatives, friends, and even strangers. The emphasis on community is one of the key functions of Ramadân and, for that matter, of all Islamic rituals. Many do not fast for a variety of reasons, but they do not like to miss the festive atmosphere of breaking the fast on an evening of Ramadân.

It is hard for a Muslim to be alone during this month, and those living abroad in non-Muslim countries feel more homesick than usual. Many migrant workers take their leave at this time of the year in order to spend Ramadân at home. The annual migration to celebrate the holiday causes human stampedes and a logistical nightmare when half a million North Africans working in Europe travel home. Coming from Scandinavia, Holland, Germany, France, Belgium, they converge upon Spain in order to cross over into Morocco and Algeria. This poses a gigantic challenge for the united forces of the Spanish Red Cross and the Moroccan Red Crescent.

On the other hand there is no dearth of escapees who travel abroad in order to avoid the rigors of Ramadân; they flee both the scorching heat and the watchful eye of traditional society. Later it is easy to claim that the lost days have been made up for. In some of the Gulf countries, "running away from Ramadân" has grown to such proportions that the authorities have issued appeals to stop the practice.

Trade and industry are largely at a standstill during Ramadân, especially when it falls in the hot season when the days are extra long. The people are therefore all the more inclined to make up for the deprivations of the day during the night. As sleeping is not forbidden during the fast, the less pious often sleep during the day, which provides the energy for extensive partying and celebration during the night. In some areas the nights of Ramadân are the time for public entertainment, card playing, and other forms of amusement.

Some steer a middle course between asceticism and hedonism. Thus, in Turkey the nights of Ramadân are meant to be joyful but not frivolous. Many people take their children to the merry-go-rounds set up for the occasion. Folk dances from different regions are performed, as well as acrobatics and traditional show business routines. It has become difficult to find a soothsayer or one of the storytellers who used to be the main attraction in former times. But one may still come across the famous shadow plays known by the names of their popular heroes, Karagöz and Hajivat.

In many places it is traditional for a man to go from door to door in the morning to wake people up so that they may quickly eat something before the first call to prayer, signaling the beginning of another day of fasting. In some cities a shot is fired from a picturesque old cannon, one in the morning and one in the evening, indicating the beginning and end of the fasting time.

The Islamic calendar, like Judaism's, is a lunar one, so Ramadân falls at a different date on the solar calendar every year. Generally there is an eleven-day difference between the calendars. In this way Ramadân passes through all the seasons over a thirty-year period.

There is a hilarious aspect to Ramadân too, in that there is no precise way to determine when to end it. According to tradition, the new moon has to be sighted with the bare eye, which is not always possible, especially for the many Muslims who now live in the cloudy countries of the North. This problem has led to the creation of moon-sighting committees (a more accurate translation would be crescent-sighting committees), but the result is only a minor improvement. In America, the end of Ramadân is sometimes celebrated on four different days. One group says "today the moon was sighted," another group insists "the calendar tells us it was yesterday." A third group decides to celebrate "tomorrow, like in Morocco, the closest country of the Muslim world." A fourth group takes its cue from Saudi Arabia as the cradle of Islam. Nowadays the various groups hold joint deliberations, and when they reach a consensus on a single day, they report the sensational breakthrough. But the next year the problem again arises and the consensus rarely holds. In some countries, such as Pakistan, traditional scholars, representing the various sects and schools, board a special plane and are flown around for a few hours, but even they can't agree: one claims to have spotted the new moon while another angrily disputes this.

Many in the Muslim community, including statesmen like the late President Bourguiba of Tunisia, feel that the way Ramadân is practiced in modern times impedes social progress. It disrupts normal economic activity, leads to a reduction in learning in the schools, increases the number of accidents, and has a negative effect on discipline in the workplace. Advocates of the traditional way of fasting say that it is healthy, which is true for some, but there are many exceptions. For people with kidney problems or stomach ulcers, fasting is the worst thing they could possibly do. Among the 10 million Muslim laborers in Western Europe, the ratio of stomach ulcers, for example, is extraordinarily high, possibly as high as 50 percent, for a variety of reasons. Algerians in France, Turks in Germany, Moroccans in Spain are the groups with the highest percentage of stomach ulcers, and they are usually not considered sick enough to be exempt from fasting. Doctors advise them to take small bites every now and then instead of fasting followed by a sumptuous meal. Many, however, elevate tradition above reason—a universal phenomenon observable in many religions—and in this case the results can be truly pernicious.

THE FEAST OF SACRIFICE (`ÎDU-L-ADHA)

Two months and ten days after the end of Ramadân comes the most important of all Islamic celebrations. On that day, the pilgrimage to Mecca, which normally lasts two to three weeks, reaches its culmination. Those who do not perform the pilgrimage but stay home celebrate the Sacrificial Feast for about two or three days. The feast commemorates our spiritual ancestor, Abraham, who was prepared to sacrifice what was dearest to him, his son, for the love of God. In recognition of his *islâm* ("submission to the will of God") the Almighty granted him a dispensation from this supreme sacrifice and made him slaughter a ram instead. The Qur'ân tells us that this happened near the Ka`ba in Mecca. For this reason, slaughtering a sacrificial animal became part of the pilgrimage rites.

Those not on pilgrimage go to the mosque at home to perform the communal prayer on the first day of the feast. This takes place forty-five minutes after sunrise. After that there is a ceremony resembling the presentation of gifts on Christmas, although customs differ from country to country.

On the way back from mosque there is much embracing and the exchange of brotherly kisses, which continues throughout the day. Especially in the afternoon and sometimes until late at night, there is an unending exchange of visits. Either the entire family goes out together to pay a visit to relatives, or the father goes with his sons to visit friends just as the mother goes out with her daughters and the little ones to see their playmates.

After the morning ceremony when the children receive their gifts, the next item on the agenda is the ritual slaughter of the sacrificial sheep (or goat, cow, or camel). Whether on pilgrimage in Mecca or at home, a number of rules must be observed: the animal has to be drained of its blood. In some

Western countries it is quite difficult to slaughter according to Islamic precepts, because only government-appointed butchers are allowed to slaughter, not private persons in their homes. In some parts of Europe, Jewish butchers are exempt from the restriction, but Muslims have so far lobbied in vain to have this privilege extended to them.

Religious authorities in Turkey have declared that slaughtering by electric shock, a method widely used in Western Europe, does not run counter to Islamic precepts. However, a special sanctity attaches to the slaughtering on the day of the Sacrificial Feast. It is a ritual many believers wish to perform in the circle of their dear ones. Most important is that the name of God be invoked. Muslims have no problem employing Jewish butchers for this purpose because the formula and method are the same in both religions.

The sacrificial animal is a center of attraction for the children. For them the feast begins when they accompany their parents to purchase the animal and then are allowed to lead it home. Quite often this happens a week or two before the feast, and during this period the kids have ample opportunity to play with the sheep, decorating it with colored laces and painting its wool with bright colors. For many Muslim children the sacrificial sheep functions in a manner comparable to that of the Easter bunny or the Easter egg in some Christian cultures.

In the countryside this practice causes scarcely any disruption, and in suburban areas the only troublesome feature is the bleating of so many sheep on the porches and in the gardens. In the heart of urban centers, however, the concentration of so many sacrificial animals can assume chaotic proportions. Animals are kept in garages, on terraces, pavements, balconies, and, if there is no other place, in the bathroom, though generally just one day before the feast. Children, and even some adults, love the chaos around the sacrificial sheep. Not only is the animal adorned, but the place where it is sacrificed is also decorated. People then proceed to that spot, often in little processions. The sheep, the hero of the day, is accompanied as if in triumph. Then there is a final check to determine whether the animal is healthy and without any defect, because for this holy sacrifice only the best will do.

Many children are sad after the sheep is slaughtered, but they find consolation in the knowledge that next year there will be another one. Modern lifestyles, especially in Western societies, deprive many children of the fun of playing with the sacrificial sheep. Many will never get to enjoy the experience, and the feast loses some of its special flavor as a result.

The wealthy are expected to sacrifice two or even more sheep, a cow, or a camel. The meat is divided into either three or seven parts. One part (either a seventh or a third, depending on the custom followed) is kept for oneself; the remaining portions are distributed to relatives and friends who are less prosperous, and especially to the poor, strangers included. The main purpose of the feast is to demonstrate one's preparedness to sacrifice and to show brotherly feelings by letting less fortunate people share. The recipients need not be Muslims, they may be people of any faith who are not as well off as the donor. Given the poverty in much of the Muslim world, migrant workers in the West send money home so that their families may sacrifice on their behalf and make sure that the portions that are distributed go to people who are really in need. It is traditional for the children to be assigned the task of taking the donated portions to the recipients, and often they receive some sweets in return.

People sacrificing an animal in their own name may do so on one of the three holidays and keep a seventh part, as mentioned. However, someone sacrificing in the name of a deceased, to invoke special blessings upon that person, must do so on the first holiday and distribute the entire sacrifice rather than keep a portion.

The hides and skins of the many animals slaughtered are an important aspect of this event. They constitute a considerable wealth that is used primarily to support welfare institutions connected with mosques. In the Western world some Muslims donate the hides to the Red Cross, just as they would give them to the Red Crescent at home.

THE PILGRIMAGE TO MECCA

During the Sacrificial Feast people talk about friends who are on pilgrimage to Mecca. The pilgrims are given a rousing reception on their return, which constitutes another social event of great importance. This is the occasion to make plans for one's own journey to Arabia. Once the children are grown up and there is enough income to live debt-free, mothers tend to remind fathers that it is time to perform the pilgrimage.

This is an event of central importance in life, rivaling that of one's wedding day. It is a magnificent experience of communion with God and universal harmony with humankind. People from all parts of the world, identically clothed in the same type of white garments, spend a few days together, performing the common rites that make them feel part of a perfect union, as if they had been restored to the prelapsarian earthly paradise. Here the sacrifice is celebrated in a valley near Mecca. The festivities in the rest of the world express communion with the pilgrims who assemble at the gates of the "Mother of Cities" to worship God by sacrificing the ram of Abraham.

The `îdu-l-adha` is intimately connected with the Ka`ba in Mecca, which the Qur'ân says is the oldest temple in which to worship the one and only God; it symbolizes the beginning of faith in Allah. After Abraham was about to sacrifice his son Ishmael (not Isaac, as in the Jewish tradition) but was given a ram to sacrifice, father and son began to praise God by rebuilding the Ka`ba, which had been lying in ruins. Among other stones they used a black meteorite that happened to be lying there. It still forms part of the building. The lucky ones in the crowd of pilgrims who manage to touch it feel as if they have shaken hands with Abraham.

The pilgrimage belongs to the life cycle of a Muslim's religious practice, but it is also part of the annual cycle, because it takes place every year, which means that every year people see some pilgrims off and later celebrate their return from the hallowed places. Called *hajj*, the pilgrimage is the fifth of the Five Pillars.

On the day of the Feast millions of animals are slaughtered throughout the Muslim world. This massive slaughter has a devastating effect on the economies of many countries. It takes a significant amount of time to replenish the nation's livestock after such a slaughter on a single day every year. So far, governments have failed to stop the practice or even moderate it. Ayyûb Khân, while president of Pakistan, tried unsuccessfully to introduce reforms. The late Hassan II, king of drought-stricken Morocco, appealed to his countrymen to stop it, but many preachers opposed him and urged their parishioners to go on with the slaughter. The monarch, who was also the religious head of his country, tried to convince his people that it would be enough if he performed a sacrifice on behalf of the entire nation on television. In Morocco the dry season almost always results in the death of some animals. In times of drought tens of thousands of cattle and sheep die, and in the last two decades droughts have been frequent.

Abraham's sacrificing a ram instead of his son symbolized a much larger phenomenon in human history. As far as is known, all humanity practiced human sacrifice at an earlier stage, which was then generally replaced by animal sacrifice. A few Muslim mystics have reasoned that the animal sacrifice should now yield to a more symbolic act of surrender to the will of God.

THE "SIMPLICITY" OF ISLAM

Anti-Islam polemics, especially those emanating from Christian sources, have often condemned Islam as simplistic in a double sense. It is said to be morally undemanding and conceptually crude.

As for its alleged moral laxity, quite a few Muslims wish it were indeed so. We live in an age of massive migration from the Muslim East to the Christian West. For the great majority the motivation is economic, but there also are tens of thousands who emigrate in order to escape the rigors of traditional Islamic society. It is not so much a matter of leaving behind the prohibition against drinking alcohol and dating, both of which are unacceptable in many parts of the Muslim world. For many it is a wish to leave a world characterized by so powerful an emphasis on prayer and fasting.

It is difficult to imagine the severity of life in one of those strict communities where there is no fun during Ramadân, only abstinence; it is like spending one month every year in a monastery. One has to have lived through it in order to appreciate the hardship, especially when Ramadân falls in summer and the days are long and hot.

It is not only the rigors of Ramadân that engender this reaction but the routine of daily life. Rising for daily prayer at dawn is hard on most people, especially where it means going to the mosque first thing every day. During part of the year this means getting up at half past three in the morning.

After sexual intercourse a full shower is required before prayer. In the snow-covered mountain villages of Afghanistan and Turkey, this means getting up in the middle of the night to make a fire, heat the water, and get ready for the ablution necessary to perform the morning prayer.

These examples are just a fraction of the Muslim traditions that make religious practice a tough proposition despite Islam's traditional rationality, which teaches the proviso "If

this is not possible, then do it in such-and-such a way."
Anyone who thinks of Islam as morally undemanding has no
awareness or appreciation of the rigors of life in an orthodox
Muslim community and would almost undoubtedly find
them unendurable.

When Christians accuse Muslims of moral laxity they usually have sexual conduct in mind. Like Judaism, Islam does
not approve of celibacy. It is considered an unhealthy state of
affairs, not only for clerics and ordinary individuals, but also
for the whole of society. In traditional Muslim societies,
appointing an unmarried person as a teacher used to be
unthinkable, and in many places this attitude continues. Most
Muslims would argue even today that an unmarried man
should not be a judge.

Catholics who criticize Islam for the absence of celibacy
tend to overlook that the majority of Christians (Orthodox
and Protestants combined) do not practice celibacy either.
Polygamy is controversial among Muslims themselves. There
appears to be a consensus that it is permissible only under
special circumstances, but many polygamous Muslims interpret this in their favor. In some predominantly Muslim countries, polygamy is fairly common, while in others it is virtually unknown, and in several countries it is outlawed.

The controversy takes an ugly turn when missionaries
allege that the secret of Islam's success in gaining African
converts rests on its acceptance of polygamy. This has been
argued a thousand times, but the point is plainly absurd
because polygamy also continues to be practiced in a number
of Christianized societies. An example from Sierra Leone

places the issue in fine focus: A paramount chief belonging to one of the Protestant churches had twenty-two wives. On his conversion to Islam, he reduced the number to four, as demanded by the local Muslim preacher. After a while, finding this reduction too difficult, he returned to his former church and wives, celebrating the occasion by taking a twenty-third.

As for the conceptual simplicity of Islam, the great majority of Muslims see this as a virtue, not a shortcoming. This simplicity has historically been a major factor attracting people to Islam, just as there have always been others who find Islam too simplistic for their taste. The basic issue here is what people expect from religion, or what type of religion they are looking for.

If we look at the history of religion, we find a pattern that parallels the development of languages. Classical languages like Latin and Sanskrit have much more complex grammars than their linguistic offspring (Italian, Romanian, and Spanish or Bengali, Hindi, and Sinhali). Kiganda has a more complex grammar than a lingua franca like Kiswahili, and so on. Similarly, very ancient religions generally have a more complex salvation theory than relatively young ones, such as Zoroastrianism, Judaism, and Islam. If Christian theology is more complex, it is mainly because it absorbed so many pre-Judaic notions. The further back we go in religious history, the more labyrinthine salvation theories become. Modern teaching methods make ancient theologies more accessible to scholars, but whether they can be made spiritually meaningful and compelling to contemporary believers seems doubtful.

Islam relieves its adherents of the complexities that Christianity had acquired by the sixth century. In Islam the relationship of humankind with God is direct. Although on a popular level Muslims have created all sorts of intercessionary structures, the essential one-to-one relationship between God and human beings is not disputed. Christian complexity did leave some traces in the Qur'ân, such as the idea of the virgin birth, but it appears out of context from the Christian point of view. The references to Mary and Jesus are among but a handful of supernatural elements in the Qur'ân, and these appear more like a courtesy to Christians than anything else. Perceptive Christians are right when they complain that these elements are devoid of the meaning Christians assign to them.

The crucifixion is referred to only in passing: "They did not kill him, and they did not kill him on the cross either, it only looked to them as if" (Sûra 4:157). This succinct statement led most Muslims to believe that somebody else was crucified instead of Jesus, while some Islamic scholars reached the conclusion that Jesus survived crucifixion and left for another country. The essential point is that this story, no matter how the narrative is understood, is immaterial to Muslims, who believe that salvation is predicated on their belief in God and their own pious deeds.

THE GOLDEN MEAN

Muslim society is marked by many of the same divisions that characterize other religious communities, and these often have their roots in ethnic and/or regional factors. A few of the divisions in Muslim society may be unique to Islam, but most are of a universal nature. Anthropologists have difficulty applying the term *transnational* to Islam because they perceive a variety of Muslim cultures, and there has been some dispute as to whether there is such a thing as a *homo islamicus*, a "Muslim Man," as a cultural species. But there is more than a measure of justification in speaking of Muslims as representing a *sui generis* culture, provided this notion is sufficiently qualified by the many ways in which it is delimited. For a more detailed analysis one would have to speak of a plurality of Muslim societies. On the other hand, there are certain key notions and terms that legitimate the concept of one Muslim civilization, since the various Muslim societies share many characteristics that distinguish all of them from non-Islamic ones. It may not always be the phenomenon per se that is distinctly Muslim, but rather the way in which it is conceived and expressed, known and lived.

One of these commonalities is the division into legists (or legalists) and mystics, two worldviews that are often seen as mutually exclusive, although at times they converge and occasionally almost merge. In Muslim history, this has caused much conflict, but it may also be seen as a creative tension. The existence of these opposing worldviews has contributed to the enormous richness of Muslim culture.

As was mentioned earlier, seventh-century Arabia was a favorite refuge for hermits of various denominations. Many of the hermits were spiritualists who found the Christian societies of Syria, Byzantium, Egypt, and Ethiopia repugnant. One might call them the dropouts of imperial Christianity with its endless doctrinal feuds and theological squabbles. Muhammad met and spoke with several of them and was favorably impressed by their piety, but he felt that they had fallen into another extreme. He thus had two disparate images of Christianity. One was the imperial one, the aggressive Christianity of the Roman Empire that insisted upon everybody's subscribing to the doctrines of the church. The other was that of Christian dissidents, who were kind to the Arab in search of truth and encouraged him when he had his call to prophethood. When persecution of the early community in Mecca became unbearable, the Prophet sent a number of his followers to Christian Ethiopia, whose ruler received them warmly, as spiritual kin.

Muhammad envisioned his community as one treading the *via media*, the Aristotelian middle path, which he expressed in Arabic as *khairu l-umûri awsatuhâ*, "the best course is the middle course." The essence of Islam rests on the qur'ânic principle of equilibrium and compassion (`adl wa ihsân); this term is also translated as "justice and solidarity." Called the "good exemplar" in the Qur'ân, the Prophet personified the virtues of piety and purity, courage and generosity. Balanced in his lifestyle and in his dealing with others, he taught Islam as a religion of balance. The Qur'ân speaks of Muslims as a community in the middle, situated between the extremes of Judaism and Christianity as perceived by Muslims in the days of the Prophet. Islam was meant to be neither too worldly nor too otherworldly: "We made of you a community justly balanced, now you can be witnesses over the nations" (Sûra 2:143).[1]

Muslims tend to absolutize these images as if they were eternal and everlasting. Few Muslims show any awareness of the fact that a similar split into worldliness and otherworldliness occurred within the Muslim community itself, and the tension persists to this very day. The pendulum swings back and forth. What were once considered Jewish or Christian characteristics have long since become characteristics of Muslims too.

SÛFISM: THE COUNTERCULTURE

After the rapid expansion of Muslim rule over a large part of the world, the caliphate became exceedingly powerful. Soon a movement of social protest arose against the boisterous materialism that characterized the Omayyad caliphate. The conquest of so many lands made many Muslims immensely rich, and this wealth was reflected in their opulent lifestyle in Damascus, the new capital. Appalled by what they considered to be un-Islamic conduct, pious dissenters began to practice asceticism, shunning the caliphal court and retreating to provincial towns in order to flee the materialism and sinfulness of Damascus, Baghdad, and Córdoba as well as other imperial cities.

---

[1] A more literal translation is: "Thus We appointed you a midmost nation that you might be witnesses to the people." *The Koran Interpreted*, trans. Arthur J. Arberry. World's Classics (New York: Oxford University Press, 1982 ed.), p. 18.

The Prophet had ordered that silk and gold were to be reserved for women, and that men were to dress more simply in order to avoid class distinctions. But in the capital cities high society broke these rules. In protest against such indulgence, the pious began to wear garments of coarse wool (*sûf*), and this was the beginning of sûfism, often described as Islamic mysticism.

Later, many sûfîs provoked the authorities by concentrating their veneration on Jesus, until one of them, Mansûr Al-Hallâj, claimed to be the incarnation of divine truth and was crucified in Baghdad in 922. Others began venerating Muhammad in a way indistinguishable from the Christian worship of Jesus except for the formulation of doctrine. Muhammad was not made part of the Godhead, but some sûfîs endowed him with various divine qualities.

From the standpoint of the scholars of Islamic law, this type of veneration amounted to a reversion to paganism, and they became apprehensive of sûfism as a reassertion of pre-Islamic practices. The fourteenth-century Ibn Taimîya saw subversion at work and condemned mysticism as un-Islamic. (The Buddhist and Christian influences on sûfism are indeed unmistakable, but other religions had just as much reason to complain about Islamic influences on their believers, especially in the Balkans and in India.) The antisûfî Ibn Taimîya became the darling of the fundamentalists. Today's Islamists consider him to have been one of their forefathers.

In the discussion that follows we shall attempt to explain the nature of sûfism with the help of some categorizations, fully conscious of the fact that they are simplifications, but hopefully useful ones.

Islamic religious life can be seen as personified in two antipodes manifesting themselves as two separate types of persons or personalities. There are two distinct characters, two disparate mentalities, two different attitudes toward life, and two divergent forms of religious consciousness and practice.

One is the official or legist (legalist) type. Its protagonist is the scholar of the religious law (sharî`a). He is called, according to region and sect, either an `âlim (pl. `ulamâ' or ulema), a faqîh (pl. fuqahâ'), or a maulawî (with derivatives such as moulvi, maulana, mulla, mullah), or a mujtahid.

The other is the unofficial or mystic type. Its protagonist is the illuminated preacher, the freewheeling teacher of the tarîqa (the way to God). He is called either a sûfî (pl. sûfiyâ'), a walî (pl. auliyâ'), a faqîr (pl. fuqarâ'), or a darwîsh (also spelled dervish). The title shaikh (also spelled sheik) is used for both of them. It means "old man," or sage, or chief (of the tribe).

These distinctions are not always neat or watertight. Many individuals occupy a middle ground or wander back and forth from one pole to another, never making a final choice; others are indifferent to both. And still others succeed at combining elements from both sides within themselves, sometimes quite harmoniously. However, more often than not we encounter two parties that are opposed to one another, if not mutually exclusive.

This bifurcation has given birth to numerous conceptual pairs, such as sharî`a and tarîqa, both meaning "way" or "path," with the connotation of "way to salvation" or what Hispanic Catholics would call camino de gloria.

The 'âlim/faqîh follows the sharî'a, which has become synonymous with Islamic law. The sûfî/walî follows the tarîqa, which has become synonymous with the sûfî order or fraternity of mystics (brotherhood).

The 'âlim/faqîh treads a beaten path (the sharî'a). The sûfî/walî bounces along a shortcut (the tarîqa).

Usually the 'âlim/faqîh has no desire to go beyond the literal meaning of Scripture; he is content with what is apparent and clearly visible (*zâhir*). He is exoteric, that is, he believes in what is manifest on the outside. For the sûfî/walî, the externalities are not enough; he explores the inner meaning (*bâtin*) of the holy texts. He is esoteric, believing in what is hidden inside.

The 'âlim/faqîh believes in a transcendent God. His God is totally other than himself; his God is beyond him and without him. The sûfî/walî believes in an immanent God. His God is part of himself, just as he is part of God. God is within, permeating and pervading man.

The 'âlim/faqîh values sobriety, frowns upon music, and abhors dance and all other rituals except those prescribed by the sharî'a.

The sûfî/walî longs for ecstasy, adoring the Creator with music and dance.

The 'âlim/faqîh disdains the sûfî/walî as superstitious. The sûfî/walî pities the 'âlim/faqîh for being spiritually dead.

The 'âlim/faqîh accuses the sûfî/walî of being a heretic. The sûfî/walî denounces the 'âlim/faqîh as a hypocrite.

The 'âlim/faqîh insists on separate identities: A Muslim is

not a Jew, a Jew is not a Muslim. The sûfî/walî seeks to merge identities: A Muslim is a Jew too; and a Jew can also be a Muslim.

The `âlim/faqîh tends to be a communalist, a separatist. He is fond of erecting barriers between groups, such as followers of different religions, people of different generations, men and women—so that everything is in its right place and proper order. The sûfî/walî loves to break down barriers and bring all creatures together: animal and human, old and young, men and women, Moses and Muhammad, making them exchange seats.

The members of each group consider the other to be pretentious because the `âlim/faqîh endeavors to read at least one book a day, while the sûfî/walî seeks to forget at least a book per day.

There are arguably as many definitions of sûfism as there are individuals professing it. The sea is a favorite sûfî symbol because it is all-encompassing. One might say that there are as many different types of sûfîs as there are different fish in the sea.

If a set of common denominators can be found that distinguish sûfîs from nonsûfîs, it is their emphasis on emotion (*wijdân*, ecstasy), the priority of heart over mind, of intuition over reason, of cognitive knowledge (*ma`rifa*) over rational knowledge (`*ilm*). Someone placing the voice of the intellect over the voice of the heart could hardly pass as a sûfî. A sûfî may be a leading intellectual, applying analytical powers and cold reasoning to a variety of subjects, yet his value system will subordinate intellectual pursuits to illumination (faith).

Another chief characteristic that serves as a common denominator (although not as universally shared as the first) is ecumenism, commitment to a rapprochement between the followers of different religions, their fraternization and ultimately their unity, their oneness. Historically, this is a basic aspiration of Islam; as we have seen, Muhammad's primordial impulse was to unite Jews, Christians, and other monotheists on a common platform. Sûfîs have always emphasized this tenet more than other Muslims. While this teaching is the common legacy of all Muslims, the `âlim/faqîh tends to minimize it, the sûfî/walî to maximize it.

Another common denominator is the popular image of the sûfî as simple and unassuming, a meek human being whose ethical ideal is to be humble and kind even if he occupies a high position. He does good deeds without making a show of it and without seeking reward or recognition.

People tend to call any person who is neglectful of his outward appearance a sûfî. The traditional image is of a soft-spoken and helpful (or helpless) person, unkempt and untrimmed, wearing worn-out clothes, perhaps eccentric and distraught, but always kind and friendly. Taken to an extreme, we find some sûfîs resembling the Hindu sadhu more than any type of Muslim. Some live like the begging monks of Buddhism, wanting to demonstrate their "trust in God who will provide." Such persons do not necessarily share the philosophical views of the great sûfî masters; indeed they may know nothing of sûfî thought. They are identified as sûfî because they are so exceptionally gentle or lovable, often too naïve and guileless to manage in this world:

saintly fools, so to speak. In this sense, the term *sûfî* designates a certain character type, not a theological or philosophical position, but of course, often an intellectual position and
personal affect go hand in hand.

On the negative side, this "otherworldly" attitude sometimes degenerates into simple vagrancy. This is the *darwîsh*
(dervish) type of sûfî. Real vagabonds, in turn, love to pass
themselves off as sûfîs, and many are a bit of both. The line
between them is hard to draw.

Finally, there is the exotic incarnation of the sûfî who is
often an acrobat, juggler, or magician. Originally, individuals
of this type were renowned for eating fire and sleeping on
nails to demonstrate the choice of poverty (*faqr*) and self-
abnegation before God above earthly riches. Ultimately, they
may turn into performers, the opposite. This type is the *faqîr*
(ascete), whom Westerners know as a snake charmer (fakir).

It is because of the *faqîr* that many Muslims take sûfism to
be a perversion, if not a fraud. Fundamentalists and Islamists,
who are generally solemn and humorless, refuse to see in the
sûfî anything more than a charlatan, if not a heretic.

Sûfism is not just an individualistic way to God. It is equally an organized enterprise, in the shape of fraternities sometimes resembling monastic orders under a charismatic *shaikh*
(leader). The founding father of organized sûfism was Shaikh
`Abdu-l-Qâdir Gîlânî, who lived in ninth-century Baghdad.
His fraternity, the Qâdirîya, is still the most widespread
tarîqa (order), and all other sûfî orders are offshoots of the
Qâdirîya, or offshoots of the offshoots. Among the best-
known are the Chishtîya, found mainly in India and Pakistan,

and the Tîjânîya, mainly in Africa. Some are close to orthodoxy, such as the worldwide Naqshbandîya, while others,
such as the Qalandarîya (Afghanistan and Pakistan), believe,
like the Beatles, that "all you need is love, love is all you
need!"

Sûfism is often associated with fatalism, the belief in an
unchangeable fate. Western writings have sometimes stigmatized the entire Middle East as fatalistic. In reality this attitude is more a function of the prevailing *Zeitgeist* than of a
permanent mindset. Like other regions of the world, the
Middle East has known epochs of fatalism and epochs of
activism (voluntarism) when people upheld the freedom of
the human will and rejected the idea of predestination, insisting that man held his destiny in his own hands, that his fate
was not preordained. The Qur'ân is quite explicit in condemning fatalistic passivity: "God does not make things better if people do not do anything about it themselves" (Sûra
13:11).

Some sûfîs did indeed have difficulties with the unmistakable activism of the Qur'ân's message. They turned excessively fatalistic, and at times their actions—or inaction—gave
sûfism a bad name. The majority of sûfîs, however, are better
classified as pietists. Roughly speaking, this means that they
are inclined to otherworldliness. Their relationship with God
is so much more important than worldly concerns that some
shun public affairs altogether. Taking little interest in politics,
they can be very unwise when so many issues are ultimately
political and one is forced to make political decisions. Their
traditional apolitical stance has generally caused them more

trouble than not. Besides, it is part of normative Islam that people should be equally attentive to God and to the world around them, to their fellow beings. This requires a delicate balancing act. The Prophet is reported to have said: "Work for this world as if you had to live in it forever, and work for the world to come as if you had to die tomorrow."

BOOK RELIGION AND PEN CULTURE

The Middle East is home to a culture of writing. The alphabet was invented here, turning the people of the region into a "people of the book." Starting with the *Epic of Gilgamesh* and the Bible, literature became the major field of cultural creativity rather than music and painting, in stark contrast with America's pre-Columbian cultures. Little wonder, then, that here the strongest manifestation of God occurred in the form of a book, the Qur'ân, rather than in any other form of human creativity.

If we look for outstanding figures who exemplify Muslim cultural creativity, whether in the past or in the present, our attention is drawn, first and foremost, to great authors. Scholars of comparative religion like Ibn Hazm, philosophical novelists like Ibn Tufail, sociologists like Ibn Khaldûn, anthropologists like Al-Jâhiz were all among the greatest writers of past centuries. In recent years, Muslim authors have taken over the literature of their former colonial masters. Arguably, the leading figures in English and French literature are no longer British or French, but writers from the former colonies in Africa, Asia, and the Americas, often

Muslims. The Moroccan Tâhir Bin Jillûn (Tahar Ben Jelloun), who received the Prix Goncourt in France, V. S. Naipul, and the Indo-Pakistani Salmân Rushdî with his Booker Prize are some of the best-known examples among many. In Germany several Turkish-born women, such as Saliha Scheinhardt, have become leading authors and have received distinguished literary awards like the Bachmann Preis.

Poetry is the most important genre in Muslim literature. Poetry stimulated sûfism, and sûfism promoted poetry. The great cultural contribution of sûfism is its poetry and its devotional music, the latter emanating from the former. First there was the poet, then his verses were chanted. Famous sûfî poets of history are legion. One of the earliest sûfîs in recorded history was Râbi`a, a famous woman poet in Basra (Iraq).

Critics often fault sûfism for its overindulgence in poetry, which is often likened to an overdose of romanticism, using the term in the popular sense. This passion for poetry, it is argued, frequently engenders eccentric personalities and an outlook devoid of a sense of social responsibility and incompatible with the requirements of day-to-day life, especially in an industrialized society. It is no exaggeration to speak of an addiction to poetry (whether in Arabic, Kiswahili, Persian, or Urdu), more often than not linked to sûfism.

The twelfth-century mystic Ibn`Arabî of Murcia in Spain is acclaimed by sûfîs all over the world as *ash-shaikhu l-akbar* (the "Greatest Master"). Rûmî, the thirteenth-century Afghan/Persian mystic of Turkey, reverently called Mevlana ("Our Lord"), rivals Ibn`Arabî in name and fame. His pantheistic philosophy is expounded in the famous *Mathnawî*, a book in rhymed verse. It is mainly because of philosophical mystics that sûfism experienced a fascinating upsurge in the second half of the twentieth century, not only captivating large numbers of intellectuals from the Muslim world, but attracting tens of thousands of Westerners, among them a fair number of Jews. Interfaith associations like CRISLAM (standing for the togetherness of Christianity and Islam) in Madrid, take as their "constitution" a verse by Ibn`Arabî`:

> Before today I used to reject my fellow beings
> if they did not profess the same religion as I.
> Now my heart has become receptive to every image.
> It is a meadow for the grazing deer,
> a monastery for the monk,
> a temple for idols,
> a Ka`ba for the pilgrim,
> Torah scrolls and a copy of the Qur'ân.
> I profess the religion of love,
> wherever its caravan may turn to.
> Love is my law and my faith.

SOUNDS OF SIN OR SAINTLINESS?

Religious expression in the vast realm of Islam tends to be musical.

For 80 percent of Muslims, devotional songs, usually accompanied by a great variety of instruments, are part of their religious practice. Much of Middle Eastern music, including modern pop, has its origin in sûfî rites. For years, the most popular song in Pakistan was "La`l Shahbâz Qalandar." A love-stricken maiden, about to give in to the entreaties of her Romeo, goes to the shrine of the local saint, a famous member of a dervish order, and beseeches him to grant her the strength to say no: "Saint Shahbâz Qalandar, help me preserve my honor!" This song has continued to evolve with popular culture. It is available in some twenty versions, in all of the country's dozen languages. It can be heard in the most rustic form and in polished, sophisticated renditions, as jazz and also in disco versions. The Gypsy Reshma sings it as a haunting incantation.

The song is devoted to La`l Shahbâz Qalandar, who became the patron saint of artists, especially singers and actors. His birthday is celebrated at his shrine by the nation's celebrities with song and verse before crowds of thousands of pilgrims. Islamists, however, would like to put an end to this veneration, which they believe is heretical. They even tried to blow up the shrine of Egypt's patron saint, Sayyid Badawî, at Tanta.

What underlies the onslaught against music? In part it is the product of the fundamentalist strand in the new ideology of Islamism, which views many popular rites as holdovers from the *jâhilîya* (the pre-Islamic era). The Wahhâbî movement in eighteenth-century central Arabia wanted to banish all festivities, especially music and dance, whether secular or devotional. The state it created, Saudi Arabia, prohibited the import of records and cassettes and sees music of any kind as a gateway for corrupting influences. The Islamists may also recognize that music can be an effective means of forging bonds between people of different religions, something they cannot contemplate except on their own terms.

Singing and instrumental music have also been the subject of animated discussions among the sûfîs. Rûmî, the thirteenth-century poet-philosopher and sûfî master, whose disciples became famous as the whirling dervishes, called music the "creaking of the gates of heaven." When someone objected to the sound of creaking doors, Rûmî retorted, "You only hear it when the doors are being shut. What I hear is the opening of the doors."

In support of their jihâd against music, Islamists cite some of the Prophet's pronouncements. The Qur'ân does not deal directly with the issue, but several Hadîth seem to condemn singing and playing music. One of the fiercest current opponents of music is Ahmad Al-Qattân, a preacher in Kuwait who is a frequent guest speaker at Islamist rallies in the United States, and whose speeches are available on video and audiocassettes. In one of them, "Islam's Rule on Singing," he relates how one of the Prophet's Companions, on encountering a shepherd playing his flute, put his fingers into his ears and led his camel away from the sound of the flute, saying, "This is what I saw the Prophet do."

"And what do we do nowadays?" asks Shaikh Qattân. "Anyplace we stop, any shop we enter, any association we go to, any phone we pick up, we get to hear music. Do we put our fingers in our ears?"

Qattân issues dire warnings to his parishioners about the links between music and sin:

The Prophet's statement threatens all those who travel to Bangkok for sex, who go to foreign countries in search of musical instruments and singing girls, until they are seized and turned into apes and swine. The Prophet is reported to have said that "singing makes hypocrisy grow in the heart just as water makes plants grow." He also said that "singing leads to fornication." Yes, just listen to the words of the songs, listen to the texts of the tapes, and you will know what the Prophet was talking about.

It is more than moral outrage at promiscuity that impels the Islamist preacher to condemn all artistic creativity; he is critical of individual self-expression itself, and scornful of those attracted by Western music:

I ask many people, "When you listen to Michael Jackson, or Beethoven, or Mozart, what do you feel?" They tell me, "Oh, I feel my heart torn from the inside." I say, "Does it go that far?" They tell me, "Yes, by God, to that extent. I feel that all of a sudden I am flying. One moment I am crying, the next moment I am laughing, then dancing, then I am committing suicide."

Our Lord, we seek refuge with you from singing and its evils, and from the instruments of music, all those instruments in schools, restaurants, clubs, and everywhere. What about the Prophet's prohibitions, those Hadîth we have mentioned. All the instruments in use at the time of the Prophet were banned by him. A great affliction has befallen us!

The fundamentalist Shaikh Ahmad Al-Qattân and the mystic saint La`l Shahbâz Qalandar are worlds apart; it is as if they belong to different and irreconcilable religions. Islamists regard musicians as apostates, and apostates deserve death. The zealots believe that this should be the fate of some of today's musicians, as it was for those in the Andalusian civilization of eleventh-century Córdoba. The most advanced city in Europe at the time, it was razed to the ground by fundamentalists because of the population's fondness for music.

The Egyptian Sayyid Qutb, a leader of the Muslim Brotherhood Party, initially aspired to become a playwright but then chose to become a preacher of violence and is now celebrated as the ideologue of jihadism. His writings are reprinted by the millions and disseminated everywhere. Qutb was the brain behind an elaborate plan to murder the famous singer Umm Kulthûm, who was known as the Maria Callas of the Arabs, along with other artists. Ironically, the late Muhammad `Abdu-l-Wahhâb, one of the foremost composers and musicians in the Arab world, whom Qutb intended to assassinate, is generally referred to as the Immortal. This shows how deeply divided Muslim society is on the question of music.[2]

In the 1990s, Algeria's most popular singers, Matoub Lounès and Shâbb Hasanî, Sudan's Khojali `Othmân

---

[2] The controversy is reflected in a booklet in English by a fundamentalist author from Saudi Arabia that is offered for sale at Islamist functions in the United States. See Abu Bilal Mustafa Al-Kanadi, *The Islamic Ruling on Music and Singing— In Light of the Quraan, the Sunnah, and the Consensus of the Pious Predecessors* (Jeddah: Bilal Mustafa Al-Kanadi, 1985).

(Osman), and numerous other artists were assassinated. While fear has silenced some, others have become all the more forceful in their resistance. Marziye, sometimes called the Edith Piaf of Iran, was the most popular singer until Khomeini's rise to power, when she had to take refuge in a remote village at the edge of the desert. For fifteen years she sang alone in the wilderness, day after day. In 1994, seventy-year-old Marziye fled the Islamic Republic, and ever since she has been giving public concerts—in London, Los Angeles, Paris, Washington. Another example is Safî Wahhâb from Afghanistan, exiled in Germany. In addition to lyrics and patriotic songs, this Muslim composer sings about Rûmî, his sûfî master. His most popular song is one about Rûmî with his little lamp in pitch-darkness, symbolizing the beleaguered situation of the pious at the beginning of the twenty-first century, especially in devastated and oppressed Afghanistan.

Part V
Women: The Most Vexing Question

Men and women who surrender to God,
men and women who believe,
men and women who are truthful,
men and women who are steadfast,
men and women who humble themselves,
men and women who give in charity,
men and women who are abstinent,
men and women who stay clean,
men and women who are busy praising God,
they will be forgiven.
God has prepared a rich reward for them (Sûra 33:35).

14

What Does Islam Teach?

Religious tenets are almost invariably matters for dispute, but some are more controversial than others, and within Islam, those concerning women are clearly among the most fraught. There are some who allege that Islam is one of the most repressive religions as far as women are concerned; others argue that this perception is mistaken, and results from ignorance, misunderstanding, or prejudice. Irreconcilable views regarding women are found among Muslims themselves. Some project their religion as the epitome of women's rights and gender equality; others become apostates to protest what they regard as Islam's negation of women's rights. Many women leave Islam because they find it intolerable, and at least as many convert to Islam because they believe it is the ideal religion for women.

The issue is even more perplexing because women who join Islam often do so for diametrically opposed reasons. Some believe that Islam, rightly understood, elevates women more than any other religion. Others convert because they prefer confinement in the home and a position of childlike dependence; they wish to opt out of the rat race of modern life, even if doing so means acceptance of polygamy and the veil. Many of these are well educated, professional women; their catchword is "shelter" and their arguments constitute a counterrevolution to feminism. It is difficult to imagine viewpoints more divergent than the two extremes found among female converts to Islam.[1] Each camp, of course, claims to have the right understanding.

Interestingly, two prominent figures on opposing sides of this divide are Muslim women converts from Judaism. Margret Marcus from New York did not find Orthodox Judaism sufficiently patriarchal; therefore, she married Yûsuf Khân, a married Pakistani Islamist, to demonstrate her support for polygamy. In Lahore, now known as Maryam Jamîla (Jameelah), she collaborated with the Islamists' chief ideologue, Mawdûdî, in producing jihadist books that make even Khomeini and Usâma Bin Lâdin seem moderate in contrast. Her books are illustrated with the photo of a fully veiled woman, under which is written "The Author." Mainstream Muslims dismiss her as deranged, but her many books are still being sold at the Islamic Center of Southern California in Los Angeles and at Islamist establishments all around the world.[2]

On the other end of the continuum is Jemima Goldsmith, a close friend of the late Diana, princess of Wales. Jemima mar-

---

[1] There are now so many Western converts to Islam, especially women, that they can no longer be considered marginal. The number of German women converted to Islam, whether through marriage or not, is no less than the number of Muslim immigrants—2 million. A majority of these women, however, reside in the countries of their respective husbands. Several convert women have assumed important roles in the community, such as Emine Erbakan, the German sister-in-law of Necmettin Erbakan, the former Turkish prime minister who heads the (now banned) Islamist Welfare Party. Emine organizes the women of party members in Germany and acts as a spokesperson to the media.

[2] See Maryam Jameelah, *Islam versus the West*, 6th ed. (Lahore: M. Yusuf Khan, 1984).

ried Pakistani cricket star `Imrân Khân. She too lives in Lahore as a devout Muslim, but of the mainstream type. Islamists vilify her as a Jewish infiltrator, but most people adore her. Despite his popularity as a cricket superstar, `Imrân Khân failed to win a National Assembly seat. Jemima Khân would almost certainly win a seat if she were a candidate. Mainstream Muslim women love her because she is modern, goes unveiled, and yet knows how to stress Muslim identity.[3]

Jamila and Jemima stand at opposite ends of the spectrum. Here are two Jewish women who joined Islam, each one married to a Khân in Lahore (with little difference in social class between their husbands), yet they appear to belong to two different religions, so great is the difference between their respective positions.

All across Africa, from Ghana to Kenya, thousands of women with Muslim names like Saadatu and Salima angrily reject the religion into which they were born, complaining that "it is because of Islam that dad left my mom." Their fathers had several wives and frequently married and frequently divorced. Since there is no provision for alimony and child support, the divorced women and their children suffer considerable privation.

An examination of church registers in the United States reveals that every year at least a hundred women from families of Muslim immigrants convert to Christianity. Many do

[3] The religion page in the Saudi-financed daily newspaper *Ash-Sharq Al-Awsat* is generally more Islamist than Islamic in outlook, and yet it carried a feature on Jemima Goldsmith-Khan that extolled her as an exemplary Muslim woman, whereas her husband did not get such high marks. See Imâm M. Imâm, "Jemima Tackles the Cultural and Social Differences Between her Life Before and After Islam," *As-Sharq Al-Awsat*, December 21, 1999, p. 14.

so because they feel that in their community there is no religious life for them comparable to what Muslim men experience in the mosques.

Attending the mosque is obligatory for men, but not for women. The idea is not to exclude women from worship but to offer them a dispensation because of their demanding family obligations: minding the children, preparing food, maintaining the home, and so on. The results of this dispensation have varied, and the behavior of Muslim women diverges from place to place. In some countries as many women attend mosque as men, though the women sit separately, usually in the back rows. In other countries women are virtually excluded from the mosque, and meet separately for prayer sessions in private homes.

In most sûfî circles men and women pray together, and many times women predominate in number. In some countries, such as Egypt, there are female preachers, but they preach only to women and children. In the year 2000, a program was launched in Cairo to increase the number of female preachers, and there is no scarcity of women wishing to take up this task. Whether the program will work and what its consequences will be have yet to be seen. Just as ultraorthodox or fervently religious Jews refuse to believe that women should be ordained as rabbis, Muslim fundamentalists see the very idea of female preachers as absurd.

Enlightened Muslims often say that the practices reform-minded women rail against are un-Islamic, however widespread they may be. "Real Islam is different," the argument goes. Others accuse the protesting women of being rebellious, spoiled by the temptations of corrupt societies or lured into error by Christian missionaries.

Given the enormous divergence of views, many believers feel dejected and some have given up. Is it impossible to obtain a clear picture from the Islamic sources? What, then, is the true teaching and the wrong practice, or the right practice and the wrong teaching?

BETWEEN NORMATIVE ISLAM AND MUSLIM INTERPRETATIONS

Sociology uses the term *normative* to designate tenets that find the largest degree of acceptance, or, to put it the other way around, that encounter the least disagreement. What constitutes normative Islam? The essential principles include believing in the One God, His angels and prophets, revelation (the Qur'ân), the Day of Judgment, the hereafter, and the basic ethical principles (justice, love for peace, truthfulness, solidarity, altruism, charity, kindness, etc.). None of these elements can be deemed superfluous, no matter how dexterous the interpretation.[4]

There is , of course, much more in Islam's Holy Scripture, and no less than 85 percent of it is open to interpretation. Because so much is in dispute, Islam has spawned seventy-three different sects. Scarcely 15 percent of the revelation can

---

[4] There are widely different concepts of God among Muslims (from the totally transcendent to the purely immanent) as well as a thousand and one images of the angels. The crucial point is that one cannot ignore the issue of God and the angels and still be a Muslim in the religious sense. The believer has to come up with something, some notion of God and the angels, however individualistic; otherwise he or she could just as well be a Buddhist.

pass as normative Islam,[5] including two points concerning women: (1) their spiritual equality with men, and (2) the demand that they wear the type of dress traditionally called decent, modest, or "covering," that is, not sexually provocative. The dress code is stated unambiguously; there is no room left for dissent. In fact, the text states explicitly that except for the face, hands, and feet, the entire body is to be covered; there is no question of miniskirts or even short sleeves (Sûra 4:128).

A number of women's issues are open to dispute in the Qur'ân, such as the question of inheritance and of a woman's legal status (sometimes half the value of a man, sometimes only a quarter). Although the discussion of these details fills legal tomes, it can be reduced to one question: Does Islam place woman under the tutelage of man? The answer in the sharî`a is yes. It establishes a principle called qawwâma and also wisâya, which defines men as the guardians of women. A woman remains a dependent all her life and never becomes a full person. She is unable to get a passport in her own name but only as "daughter of," "wife of," or "widow of." If she has been widowed, she falls under the tutelage of her son or another male relative.

While many, including some Muslims, find this rule degrading, there are women who embrace it. They do not translate the term wisâya as "tutelage" but rather as "protection," and they appreciate the safety it implies. (Etymologically this interpretation is far-fetched. There are

---

[5] Some use the term normative in a different sense, but that discussion is not pertinent here.

many other words expressing "protection," whereas *wisâya* clearly means tutelage, guardianship, and mandate.)

Women are by no means treated as nonentities in Islam, but the Qur'ân entrusts leadership to men because men are "a degree above them" (Sûra 2:228). Compared to other patriarchal systems, Islam's is relatively benevolent because it emphasizes that with regard to most of life's circumstances men and women are equal and should treat each other with respect.

Muslims who feel uneasy about the treatment of women usually employ one of two different rationales in approaching the issue. One seeks to moderate certain rigors by dint of evasive, watered-down interpretations. For instance, the passage that allows husbands to beat their wives in case of disobedience (Sûra 4:34) is sometimes explained as implying only a spanking. Others go as far as to maintain that the word *daraba*, which in Arabic means, plain and simple, "to beat," can also mean something very different, such as minting a coin. Feminists will hardly be happy about this metaphorical interpretation. The idea of men "shaping their character" would be repugnant to them.

The other approach is to accept the facts and acknowledge that "to beat" means just that rather than "to caress." Since permission for the husband to discipline his wife is part of the *wisâya* principle (man's tutelage over woman), the only way out of the dilemma is to come to grips with the teaching itself. Once the principle of *wisâya* is reinterpreted so that it can be dispensed with on the practical plane, everything else will fall into place.

A common attitude among educated women with a liber-al bent of mind is simply to stipulate that Islam teaches this or that favored idea or practice. They assert, usually with gen-uine conviction, that certain things are Islamic teachings, but their interpretations are often little more than wishful think-ing. Loyal to their inherited faith, they long for an affirmative view of their identity within it, and so much is positive in Islam that it is tempting to discard the rest as an inauthentic excrescence.

Certainly it is arguable that much in the practice of Muslim peoples can safely be called un-Islamic even though it is pre-sented as Islamic. This applies to the position of women more than to any other aspect of Islam. A number of practices that have come to be seen as typically Islamic may actually be in blatant contradiction to Islamic teachings. The early and ide-alized Muslim community was a protest movement against a society that was enormously disadvantageous to women, characterized by frequent divorce or, rather, the peremptory repudiation of wives. This situation made the Prophet pro-claim that "among all the permitted things, divorce is the most hateful in the eyes of God." Many Arab societies have returned to "the good old days" before Islam (the stigmatized era of *jâhilîya,* or "barbarism"), at least as far as divorce (repu-diation) is concerned, with men having the power to impose their wishes, unfettered by law or custom.

Aside from the relatively thin basis of normative Islam, an ethos with regard to women is deducible from the Prophet's life and his views as expressed in conversations with his Companions. He emerges from the Scripture as a kind family man and a typical "daughter father," his sons having died in infancy. Much in what he did and said makes emancipated women feel comfortable with him. The positive image is so strong that it is hard to accept the apparently negative points as authentic, because they appear incompatible with the rest.

In some biographies of the Prophet from the sixteenth and seventeenth centuries, the founder of Islam looks like a paramount chief with some two dozen wives and concubines.[6] Some European attacks on the Prophet as profligate may have been prompted by such biographies. These documents reflect the values and attitudes of the period in which they were written, as well as the worldview of the authors, rather than those of nascent Islam. A good analogy would be the portrayal of Charlemagne as a womanizer by some medieval biographers, not because he was one, but because they wanted him to resemble King David. Some Muslim biographers departed from earlier images of Muhammad by describing him as an amorous chieftain because in their time that was a positive value. Biographies of the Prophet written in the twentieth century present him primarily as a social reformer. While this image, too, is an idealization, it is more in tune with the original sources.

The selective approach adopted by liberal Muslim women might carry greater religious authority if it were based on a better knowledge of the historical development of Islamic thought. Few of the Muslim women who interpret their religion as enlightened and humane distinguish between the

---

[6] See M. Sâdiq Fahmî Al-Mâlih's edition of Yûsuf Ibn Hasan Ibn `Abdi-l-Hâdî Al-Hanbalî, *The Book of the Prophet's Ancestors* (Damascus, 1904). The seventeenth-century original version was based on an older work by an unnamed author. The text, so far available only as a piece of art (calligraphy), has recently been translated and is expected to be published in 2001.

Islam they encounter when opening the Qur'ân, the primary source, and the Islam enshrined in the sharî`a, which is more than just traditional law. For radical traditionalists, and especially Puritan extremists such as Afghanistan's Tâlibân (and similar groups), the Qur'ân serves as little more than a text for recitation, a source of magical incantations. The radical traditionalists are not taught to interpret Scripture independently. They do not believe in exercising independent judgment; they are trained, instead, to see Islam through the lens of the sharî`a.

From the viewpoint of Muslims who read the Qur'ân with an independent spirit, a Muslim woman can be just like any other modern woman with conservative values and a conservative affect. Their image is of a woman who is a little old-fashioned in her style of dress and behavior, with a family life similar to that of a practicing Orthodox Jew or traditionalist Catholic. At the other end of the spectrum are the Tâlibân-type traditionalists who learn through the sharî`a; in their eyes women are simply inferior to men. They start segregating boys and girls in the nursery and believe it is harmful for females to learn more than prayers.

Some women scholars make a distinction between Islam per se and Islamic tradition; they hold the latter responsible for distorting the former. However, the term *Islamic tradition* is amorphous. There is much in Islamic tradition that is not part of the sharî`a, and the sharî`a is much too concrete a phenomenon to be subsumed under so general a concept as tradition. The sharî`a is only one of about a dozen strands in Islamic tradition, though certainly a major one. One of the few female theologians of Islam, Pakistani-born feminist

Rif`at Hasan, professor of religion at the University of Louisville in Kentucky, argues that "it is inappropriate to speak of 'the Islamic tradition' as if it were unitary or monolithic. Its various components need to be identified and examined separately before one can attempt to make any sort of generalization on behalf of Islamic tradition as a whole."[7]

A Straight Message from Conflicting Signals

In the course of countering Western criticism, Islamists are fond of insisting that their family relations are more affectionate and stable than is generally the case in Western societies. Many of their publications emphasize this aspect through illustrations, including cartoons. The Islamist family is presented as a unit bound together by love and devotion. Shaikh `Omar `Abdu-r-Rahmân, the leader of the Gamâ`a Islâmîya terrorist organization in Egypt, is a case in point. He is portrayed as an affectionate husband and father, and his wife is anything but a nonentity; one might even call her his coworker.

However, many other Islamist husbands are excessively authoritarian, and their severe family life is devoid of any perceptible affection; in many instances the husbands even eat separately from their wives and children. They explain this behavior as dictated by religion. Thus we are presented with the puzzling phenomenon of a culture with a kaleidoscope of attitudes, each presented as truly Islamic. What we

---

[7] Rif`at Hasan (Riffat Hassan), "Women Between Re-Islamization and Islamism," *TransState Islam* 5 (Spring 1997): 9.

have is the usual range of attitudes found in any society, reflecting human nature in its recurrent variations. What is distinct here is the religious frame of reference to which almost everybody resorts, and that frame of reference is anything but uniform. The diversity of interpretation seems to make Islam almost indefinable, at least as far as its position regarding women is concerned.

Some of the justifications Islamists offer for their attitudes toward women and the family look flimsy to scholars with an in-depth knowledge of Islamic history. There is unanimity among the Prophet's biographers that he was so indulgent with his children that they literally climbed all over him while he was performing his ritual prayers. He had nothing of the forbidding austerity that characterizes the many traditional households where there is no interaction between husband and wife except for sexual relations, and no emotional bond between father and children, hardly even any communication. In some of these settings the emotional bonds may actually be strong, but they cannot be openly expressed; tradition demands their suppression.[8]

People of different temperaments and inclinations stress different aspects of a religion's teachings; as a result, views emerge that are almost mutually exclusive and crudely reductive. For some, women are only half a man or less; they are to be firmly under the control of men, and through a good

---

[8] The syndrome of traditional relationships between spouses and between parents and children is the topic of an extraordinarily humorous and yet tender novel (largely autobiographical) by a Moroccan candidate for the Nobel Prize in literature: Driss Chraibi, *Mother Comes of Age* (Washington, D.C.: Three Continents Press, 1984). The original title is *La civilisation, mère!* which could be rendered as "Look, Mother, this is civilization!"

beating, if necessary. In their view, the prime purpose of woman is to serve man's "comfort" (sexual needs), which may require him to have four wives at a time, divorce them, and marry another four, as well as keep an unlimited number of concubines (sexual slaves).

For others, there is only one woman to one man; their relationship is one of equality and harmony, with partnership in God-fearing righteousness being more important than sexual gratification, as stipulated by the Holy Writ (Sûra 4:24 f.). Whatever part of the revelation appears to conflict with this idea of what constitutes the right bond between wife and husband they regard, and reject, as highly exceptional, restricted to some particular historical situation, time-bound and not eternally valid, unlike the basic ethical principles. For example, the spanking is symbolic, not corporeal. Again, because there is no authority or mechanism (i.e., no papacy) to decide in favor of one or the other approach, the controversy rages on.

Many take issue with the Islamic vision of paradise because men are promised virgins to be their sexual playmates. "Wrong," say some Islamic scholars; the reference is to their spouses, who shall be young again. "Nonsense," say others; the virgins of paradise are rewards; the greater the merit, the larger the number.[9]

Is the Qur'ân contradictory? It speaks of the equality of the sexes in one passage, but makes woman subordinate to male

---

[9] See `Abdullâh `Azzâm, `Ushshâqu l-hûr (Peshawar: Al-lajnatu n-nisâ'îyatu l-`arabîya, 1990). This book, written in Arabic, is about the Arab volunteers who died while fighting the Soviets in Afghanistan. The title means "Lovers of the Virgins of Paradise," meaning that those who were martyred fighting the enemies of God are now richly rewarded with numerous virgins in heaven.

authority in another. It extols the affectionate partnership of the sexes in marriage in one place, and seems to envision woman as man's sexual commodity in another (Sûra 2:223, "Your wives are your arable land, which you may plow when and how you please"). Yet the Qur'ân is emphatic in stressing that there is no moral difference between man and woman:

> People who do something good, man or woman, and have faith, We [God] will give them a new life, a good life, pure. We will reward them according to the good they have done (Sûra 16:97).

But the Qur'ân also declares that legally a woman is only half the worth of a man (Sûra 4:11 f.).

Some scholars see these seeming contradictions as a reflection of the differences in the societies that responded to the revelation, differences between the Arabian towns of Mecca (where the Prophet grew up) and Medina (where he later settled) in the seventh century. Some of the *muhâjirîn* (Muslim refugees from Mecca) worried that their womenfolk would be "spoiled" by the manners of the women in Medina, who were less submissive. Mecca was more urban, while the populace of the oasis town of Medina was more rural. Even contextual studies do not provide all the answers, however. The uninitiated reader of the revelation is still confronted with opposing statements that are not easily reconcilable.

Is it impossible, then, to give an authoritative answer to the question about Islam and women? The differences both in Muslim attitudes toward women and in the understanding of Islam's teachings can be mind-boggling. What can one say when somebody demands: "Tell me in a few sentences what is the position of woman in Islam," or "What does Islam teach concerning women?" Without making at least two dozen significant qualifications, any attempt at answering this question would be foolhardy.

We are confronted with a paradox because the Qur'ân is more explicit on the position of women than the Hebrew Bible and the New Testament, or the scriptures of several other religions. Confucius, for instance, found the subject so vexing that he gave up the attempt to issue guidelines. The Islamic revelation says much about women. Sûra 4, one of the longest chapters in the Qur'ân, is entitled "The Women," evidence of the centrality of the topic. But, in a nutshell, what does the Scripture really tell us?

One possible answer was given by the reformist theologian Mahmûd M. Tâhâ (d. 1985), who put all the "positive" statements into one drawer (Mecca) and the "negative" ones into another (Medina), declaring that the Medinese part was only for a bygone age.

Another possibility is to accept the apparent contradictions as such, take direction from the positive portions, and leave the rest to allegorical interpretation, as has been done by many believers throughout the ages. The positive statements are an inspiring reality, enunciating equality of the sexes and a position for women in tune with present-day notions of human rights.

Even among the most progressive Muslim scholars, few would say that at its inception Islam did not bring about an improvement for women or that its views are reactionary in toto. In the 1990s it was reported that in some rural areas of

China peasants were killing their baby daughters, usually by burying them alive. No fewer than five thousand such cases became known, and how many were unreported? In other words, in some societies daughters are still considered a disposable burden, as in ancient times. Exactly the same was done, in the same manner and for the same reasons, in Arabia in Muhammad's time. The Prophet succeeded in stopping this *jâhilîya* custom completely—no mean achievement. Some of the most moving passages in the Qur'ân are devoted to the subject:

> When one of them is told that it is a baby girl he looks unhappy and feels bad. He is so embarrassed by the bad news that he tries to hide, thinking whether to keep the child and suffer the contempt or bury it in the ground. What a terrible decision! (Sûra 16:58–59)
>
> [On the Day of Judgment] The question will be about the baby girl who was buried alive: For what crime was she killed? (Sûra 81:8–9).

In later history, however, the introduction of Islam among non-Muslim peoples did sometimes result in disadvantages for women. For critical Muslim scholars, the task is to reemphasize the initial impulse in favor of women's rights so as to bring Muslim societies in tune with their original ethos. The next step would be to admit that the advent of Islam did not bring about an all-comprehensive revolution in favor of women as some apologists would have us believe, although it did represent a historic step forward.

15

Gender or Sex?

The Arabic terms *hijáb* or *khimár*, the Persian *chádor*, and the Persian/Urdu *parda* literally mean "curtain" and are usually translated as "veil," though they may actually denote a scarf. But these terms have a broader meaning: they stand for gender segregation with all its ramifications. For instance, how many miles is a woman allowed to travel without a male guard? *Mahjubah* ("The Veiled Woman"), an English-language women's magazine produced by the "mullacracy" in Tehran, instructs its readers "How to Lower Our Gaze."[1]

Since the end of the nineteenth century, gender segregation has generally been on the wane, but some traditionalists are seeking to revive it and are enforcing stricter forms. In Afghanistan, for instance, the Tâlibân has not only prohibited white socks as sexually provocative but has also introduced separate footpaths for men and women, even though women are allowed to leave the house only in emergencies. In Algeria FIS stands for *Front Islamique du Salut* (Islamic Salvation Front), but people have come to read it as *Femmes Interdites de*

---

[1] See Sabeel Ahmad, "How to Lower Our Gaze," *Mahjubah: The Islamic Family Magazine* 19, no. 5, May 2000, p. 23.

Sortir ("women are not allowed to leave the house"). In Saudi Arabia the highest religious authority ruled that baby girls should not play with dolls representing males.

The Islamic vision of a happy people living in a harmonious society is built on the conviction that such happiness is conditional upon sexual orderliness. "Marriage is half the religion," the Prophet is reported to have said. Contrary to Hinduism, Islam is emphatic that widows and divorcees should remarry, and the quicker the better. Following this reasoning, people should be prevented from breaking the rules. There should be no sexual enticement, no temptation.

There is no unanimity of opinion as to whether men or women are the principal seducers. Volumes have been written on the negative image of woman as temptress in Islamic culture, but just as much on woman as the rock of stability, resisting the male's uncontrollable libidinous appetites. Muslim reformers point to the many disadvantages of gender segregation and argue that people should be educated in such a way as to make them behave responsibly in a gender-integrated society. There is a great deal of idealistic literature on this topic.[2] It has become customary for members of the new generation to complain in private conversation about "gender apartheid." The male translator of a famous woman writer in Pakistan may discuss some questions with her in the privacy of her home—in the presence of her husband, of course. But if he comes across her in the shopping center he is not supposed to greet her but to look the other way.

---

[2] See Mohamed Talbi, "Possibilities and Conditions for a Better Understanding between Islam and the West," in *Muslims in Dialogue: The Evolution of a Dialogue*, ed. Leonard Swidler (Lewiston, N.Y.: Edwin Mellen Press, 1992), pp. 155–168.

In the transition from a gender-segregated society to a mixed one many people lose self-control, and the result is sexual harassment on a scale unimaginable to Americans. In some present-day Muslim societies, it appear as if innumerable demons have been let lose after centuries of confinement. The ones who suffer most are working women, a relatively new, currently small, but growing sector of the population. One might reason that this situation should pose a special challenge to religious groups eager to make social reality conform to Islamic ideals. Some sûfî groups do indeed work hard to bring about a change of attitudes, though as yet with limited success.

Islamists, predictably enough, allege that it is all the fault of the evil West; and they are not altogether wrong. But the much-maligned TV-imperialism is not the only factor to blame, and perhaps not the primary one. A major cause is the rich nations' sex tourism. What Buddhist Thailand is to male sex tourists, Muslim Morocco has been to female sex tourists for decades. Of late, Morocco has come to share this honor with Tunisia, Gambia, Kenya's Muslim coast, and several other places. The effect on the local men's attitudes toward women is devastating. Since many make a living from "accosting" the tens of thousands of single women who descend every year on their bazaars and beaches, "sexual harassment" has become not just an ingrained attitude, but the art of the trade.

The problem with the Islamist solution is that unveiled women become targets of harassment even more because, according to the logic of the veil, it is all the fault of the victim and none of the aggressor's. The fact that the decrease in the number of unveiled women means that greater harassment is directed against veiled women does not go unnoticed, but it is not taken as a serious challenge to the Islamist principle.

Taking the veil does not provide the wearer with full protection against sexual harassment, but it reduces the problem considerably in some places, at least for a time. It is also argued, in its defense, that the veil relieves women of the costly competition in fashion that used to be a curse for middle-class women in Iran before the revolution, and continues to be so elsewhere. This obsession with fashion reached grotesque proportions at universities like `Ain Shams in Cairo, where female students would wear European high boots on the hottest summer days. Islamist garb is simple, egalitarian, and cheap because it is produced in Islamist factories and distributed almost free of charge, as a form of proselytism. The Islamists exploit to the fullest the general malaise and profound cultural anxiety created by the emerging gender integration. Western analysts adduce all kinds of reasons for the rise of Islamism, but rarely examine the gender issue, despite the fact that Islamist literature is more than 50 percent about sexual order.

As in Orthodox Judaism, the restrictive regulations in Islam concerning relations between men and women are predicated less on the assumed inferiority of women than on the perceived necessity of order. Both regard abstinence as an aberration. "Sex, yes, but rules and regulations are to be strictly observed: nothing premarital, nothing extramarital!" This is not to say that the patriarchal family structure does not aim at control. However, Westerners often think in terms of hierarchical power, whereas on the Muslim side the issue is viewed from a purely sexual perspective. This distinction underlies many misunderstandings between Western feminists and Muslim women, so much so that many dialogue attempts founder because the partners talk at cross-purposes.

For instance, the establishment of "women only" universities in several countries was welcomed by some Western feminists, but for reasons different from those of the Arab women concerned. In the Muslim world the creation of universities for women is not so much motivated by the idea of helping women achieve self-realization as by the necessity of a sober, desexualized atmosphere conducive to serious academic pursuits. Support for same-sex institutions does not arise from the fear that young women will run faster than young men or outperform them academically; the fear is that mixing could lead to unhappiness and suffering in this world and damnation in the next.

Others desire separate hospitals. Strangely enough, in much of the Muslim world there are relatively fewer women's clinics than in the West, but this is primarily a byproduct of a less-developed medical system due to the poverty of those areas, and is not a reflection of religious ideology. In some countries, such as Pakistan, hordes of young men throng the hospitals because they are among the few places where they can get close to women. While this is annoying enough for doctors and patients, for nurses it can become torturous.[3]

---

[3] In her UNESCO project on "The Empowerment of Women in South Asian Muslim Societies," Professor Rif`at Hasan (University of Louisville, Ky.), has the fate of nurses on her priority list.

The difference in perspective between radical feminists in the West and radical segregationists among the Islamists was illustrated at a meeting of an Islamist organization addressed by a member of the Jordanian parliament, Bassám Al-`Ammúsh. Veiled and seated in the back rows, a third of the participants were women. When some of them wished to pose questions, `Ammúsh requested a vote to determine whether they should be allowed to come to the microphone, like the men, or submit their questions in writing because *sawtu l-mar'a `awra* ("the female voice causes sexual excitement"). The vote was in favor of written questions only, but it would be a mistake to assume that this was about degrading or silencing the women. The women present were mostly university graduates, had their own printed program and speakers, and were treated with respect. They were not suspected of being evil temptresses. It was the men who were seen as the weaker sex; it was the men who needed protection against their own evil inclinations. Remarkably, this incident did not occur in the heart of Arabia, but in the American heartland, in 1994, at a regional convention of the Muslim Arab Youth Association (MAYA) in Detroit.

Throughout the 1980s and 1990s the "scarf controversy" made headlines, especially because of the ban on its use in French schools and the violent demonstrations in Turkey, where the government adamantly maintains the prohibition against the veil that accompanied the proclamation of the Turkish Republic in 1923. Much has been written on the subject, but unfortunately the most incisive discussion, by Yolande Geadah, is currently only available in French.

After two years in her native Egypt, the Canadian author returned to Montreal and was shocked to be confronted by the same veil controversy as in Cairo. This prompted her to write a book in which she analyzed the reasons for the spread of the veil or scarf (both are subsumed under the Arabic term *hijâb*) with all its ramifications. The present triumph of the scarf is dumbfounding to many observers, Muslim and non-Muslims alike, and her book was met with a sigh of relief by Muslim women and men around the world for its thoughtful treatment of the subject. Many Muslims feel steamrollered by media that focus on bigotry and the upsurge of anti-Western fanaticism but rarely mention the resistance to this new type of totalitarianism. Yolande Geadah entitled her book *Veiled Women: Unmasked Fundamentalisms*.[4] The author's insider analysis of the multiple pressures that force women under the *hijâb* gives the book a lead over many other writings on the subject.

Geadah observes that Islamist propaganda has caused many people to consider only veiled women virtuous, while unveiled ones represent the West's evil influence and are thus immoral. Behind all of this is the spiritual arrogance of the Islamists, who are the self-appointed judges of what is moral and immoral. They are not arbiters but controllers. The kind of veil and the behavioral norms that they decide are Islamic do not emanate from any strand of tradition, nor are they a matter of free choice from the rich historical legacy. Rather, they are prescribed by Islamists who believe they have the authority to regulate social behavior.

---

[4] Yolande Geadah, *Femmes Voilées: intégrismes démasqués* (Montreal: vlb éditeur, 1996).

The dictates result in an ageless form of human folly: an increase in hypocrisy. People's conduct does not become any more virtuous, since there are numberless ways of making a mockery of the veil, which is also worn by prostitutes. While the enforcement of veiling does not reduce promiscuity, it invariably diminishes truthfulness and helps propagate a culture of cheating and dissimulation, as well as one of intolerance. The women who most vociferously claim that the veil was their *free* choice also tend to be the ones who exert the most pressure on others to follow their example.

Among those refusing to take the veil there is usually less libertinism than among many of the veiled ones. Unveiled women feel obliged to prove the veiled ones wrong, and to do this they adopt more and more conservative attitudes and are exceptionally vigilant regarding their public conduct.

A common way of achieving Islamist supremacy is by making women believe that the veil will save them from eternal damnation. Wearing the veil is not just a means to an end (banning immoral conduct) but a virtue in and of itself, while going unveiled is sinful per se, no matter the circumstances. This teaching is highly persuasive to a large number of women, but it engenders confusion and cynicism with others.

In addition to promoting the veil through propaganda and religious casuistry, traditionalists often impose it by brute force. Incidents of zealots spraying acid on unveiled women—and the authorities not taking stern measures against such terrorism—have caused thousands of women to veil themselves to prevent physical injury. Public abuse, even of elderly women, meets with little resistance from a public afraid of reprisals. At a bus stop in the middle of Cairo, in broad daylight, a young girl accompanied by her mother was raped by two individuals while their accomplices kept the crowd at bay. When the culprits went to trial, their defense team of prominent lawyers was paid handsomely by an Islamist political party. The case received wide publicity, and the fact that the rapists went free gave a tremendous boost to the cause of the zealots. This is but one of many instances where the Egyptian state failed to provide justice to victims of such "holy terror."

Geadah generously concedes that in terms of personal safety she still feels safer in Cairo than in certain neighborhoods of New York or Montreal. The same could not be said about many cities in the Arab world—and certainly not about Pakistani cities like Karachi and Lahore. There are streets where no woman can venture out at all, whether unveiled or veiled, unless she is heavily guarded.

Geadah was shocked to observe that Egyptian society, otherwise known for its tolerant cosmopolitanism, is undergoing a transformation toward narrow-mindedness and fanaticism. Al-Banna, the founding father of the Muslim Brotherhood Party in Egypt, a precursor to Islamist organizations across the globe, used to condemn the superstitious practices of popular religion. A new generation, hailing from more rural origins, is steeped in this backward culture of superstition. To make matters worse, the Islamist Muslim Brethren has entered into alliances with radical traditionalist groups. The result is an upsurge of belief in demons (jinn) that seems bizarrely incompatible with the existence of a substantial secularist intelligentsia in Egypt, including a broad class of advanced scientists.

The jinn, who are repeatedly mentioned in the Qur'ân, can be good or bad spirits. The good ones were made famous by the fairy tale *Aladdin's Lamp.* In popular imagery, however, the jinn are more often than not evil spirits. Generally speaking, the belief in jinn has diminished, especially among the educated class, just as the belief in angels has lost much of the fascination it used to possess before human beings learned to fly. However, Shaikh Gáddu-l-Haqq (d. 1998), a rector of the traditional Al-Azhar seminary, ruled that doubting the existence of jinn is tantamount to apostasy, a ruling that had disastrous consequences for Egypt's intellectual life. As for women, it meant further buttressing of the veiling campaign, because women who refuse the veil are considered by the fundamentalists to be possessed by jinn. Where people have a strong faith in jinn, exorcism becomes an urgent necessity. Thus the veil becomes a form of exorcism. If women proffer a rationale for their refusal, they become apostates.

Anti-Islamists, both Muslim and non-Muslim, are tempted to ban the veil or scarf because of its political symbolism. Not taking any measures against it means allowing the zealots to continue their campaign of indoctrination and intimidation. But banning poses a tricky dilemma. It is an infringement upon human rights, an antidemocratic measure that turns the aggressors into victims. It also drives some conservatives into the arms of the Islamists.

Quite a few Muslim women don the veil or scarf as a matter of genuine free choice, among them college students whose mothers do not wear it and who advise them not to put it on. The young women use the veil as a means of keeping men at bay, a signal that they are not available for easy sex. Like Orthodox Jewish young women and conservative Christians, they intend to stay virgins till marriage, and the scarf symbolizes this conviction. A ban on the scarf forces these girls into the Islamist camp even though they may loathe it. Such girls may be strongly opposed to the Islamists. It is no exaggeration to say that the Islamists are not unhappy when the *hijâb* is banned, because on a tactical level it serves their purposes; the ban has become the zealots' best weapon because it allows them to pose as democratic defenders of human rights.

The French case is particularly illustrative, not only because the scarf controversy rocked the country for months, but also because of the way it started. Two Moroccan girls came to school one day wearing scarves and were ordered to remove them by the principal. Outside France it was wrongly assumed that this incident was the bigoted action of a French racist, but the reality was quite different. The principal is from a French-speaking island in the Caribbean, a black man with a strong commitment to multiculturism. There are thousands of Moroccan women in France who wear traditional dress, and had the girls come to school dressed in Moroccan style, it would never have occurred to the principal to prevent them from doing so. The two sisters, however, put

244 _Women: The Most Vexing Question_

on what has become a kind of Islamist uniform, something that distinguishes Islamists even in large crowds of traditionally dressed Muslims, whether in Morocco, Egypt, Turkey, or elsewhere (in South Asia the dividing line is less clear). The Islamist dress is not one of the traditional or regional costumes. A comparison might help to explain the point: In Germany and Italy, as in every country, there have always been people wearing brown or black shirts, but these were different from the party shirts worn by the Nazis and the Fascists.

An outsider may not notice the symbolic differences in the tying of the scarf, whereas many Muslims can tell from the scarf whether the wearer is an Arab (Sunni) and a pro-Iranian Islamist. Nowadays parks in Germany tend to be crowded with picnicking Turks, usually sitting in a circle. One circle may be made up of mainstream Muslims, steeped in their rural traditions, another may consist of the common run of Turkish Islamists, a third may belong to Khomeinist-inspired Islamists—and all can be deduced from the type of scarves the women wear and the way they tie them.

The principal of the French school knew that the girls' father had recently joined the Islamists and was now imposing the party line on his daughters. That is what the principal objected to, and it is the same objection most teachers elsewhere have as well, not only in France and Germany, but also in Tunisia and Turkey, Kazakhstan and Kirghizstan. Hassan II of Morocco prevailed upon the Islamist father to moderate his shrill tone, for which the king was cursed in the Islamist press. In the meantime there are many more such cases in

France and a dozen European countries, and little hope that the dispute will ever end.

TRENDS OF CHANGE

An overview of the current situation of women in the Islamic world reveals very disparate trends. Within such a vast realm, developments are naturally uneven, making it difficult to discern general currents. The situation differs from country to country, and in many countries there are striking variations from region to region, aside from the usual differences among ethnic groups and social classes, as well as between urban and rural populations. Urban women are by no means always freer than rural ones; in fact, it is often the other way around. In some places nomad women enjoy greater freedom than peasant women, and sometimes the reverse is true. There are also the political vicissitudes that impel or impede the emergence of female emancipation. In some countries where women had made significant headway, such as Iran and Sudan, they have suffered dramatic reverses; while in some very traditional societies, such as Morocco and Oman, there has been marked improvement.

Thus, it is as easy to paint a bleak picture of the state of Muslim womanhood as it is to render a euphoric account of breathtaking progress, and equally compelling evidence can be marshaled to buttress either view. Transitional periods know excesses in all directions. In a situation replete with contradictions, anyone attempting to present a general trend is sure to be accused of providing useless generalizations.

Both currents, the emancipationist and the antiemancipationist, constitute a mutually reinforcing dialectic, causing an escalation of controversy that makes it difficult to predict the outcome. Wherever female emancipation makes great strides, a backlash is almost certain. And wherever the backlash becomes overwhelming, with the antiemancipation movement coming to power and enforcing its norms (as in Pakistan in 1977, Iran in 1979, Sudan in 1989, and Afghanistan in 1996), opposition to it grows fiercer and the emancipationist movement gains more strength than it might otherwise have. While it may be too early to render a final verdict, there is much to indicate that counterrevolutions against female emancipation are self-defeating in the long run. The eleven years of General Diyâ'u-l-Haqq's draconian antiemancipationism (1977–88) slowed down the progress of Pakistani women, but could not halt it. More than a decade of General Bashîr's equally draconian antiemancipationism (since 1989) has only strengthened the resolve of Sudanese women to forge ahead.

Many Islamists never tire of claiming that they stand for women's rights, insisting that Western statements to the contrary are wrong. And yet, developments at the end of the twentieth century make it evident that the Islamists are one of the major forces opposing female emancipation throughout the world. For example, in Kuwait they thwarted a government initiative to grant women voting rights. In December 1999, the Kuwaiti parliament narrowly defeated a motion to give women the right to vote. Of course women have been denied this right in some non-Muslim countries as well, but what is significant about the Kuwaiti case is the role of the Islamists. While several religious leaders supported the motion, Islamists opposed it on the basis of their reading of the shari`a.[5]

The year 2000 was marked by a movement against "honor killings" of women, especially in Jordan, where Prince `Alî led the protest demonstrations. The term "honor killings" refers to the murder of a young woman by her own relatives who suspect her of illicit relations with a man. Often, if not mostly, the accusation is false. Many times it is based on a rumor, but the young woman is held responsible for having spoiled the family's reputation. In some cases the young woman may have eloped with the man of her choice instead of following her parents' dictates to agree to an arranged marriage. In Pakistan, where most of these murders occur, Mahmûd Ghâzî, the director of Islamabad's International Islamic University, unabashedly defended the honor killings in a BBC interview.

EXPERIMENTS IN SEPARATE DEVELOPMENT

In terms of crimes against women, the Muslim world is second to none. This shocking state of affairs is due partly to the spreading lawlessness and chaos, perhaps most evident in Bangladesh, India, and Pakistan, the region where the bulk of the world's Muslims live (almost 400 million, more than the

---

[5] See "No Consolation for Women," a report on the debates in the Kuwaiti newspaper *Al-Watan Ad-Daulî*, November 25, 1999, pp. 3–4. Also Howard Schneider, "Kuwait at Odds on Women's Rights Issues," *Washington Post*, December 5, 1999, p. A43.

number of Arabs and Iranians combined). While it is difficult to develop precise data because of the private, familial settings in which they frequently occur, rape and other forms of abuse of women almost certainly happen here on a larger scale than in the "evil West," which Islamists stigmatize as a moral abyss. Abject poverty is a major reason for the enormous trade in human flesh that characterizes South Asia. But some of the widespread abuse of women is also due to an overemphasis on ritualism and religiosity and a commensurate neglect of the ethical dimension.

Islamist irrationality in tackling social problems has only made matters worse. The result is general despondency in the face of a moral breakdown. This is particularly noticeable in the Pakistani media, which betray profound pessimism regarding the future of their country and of Muslim society in general. The amount of crime directed against women defies the imagination, and the number of girls sold as sex slaves is probably higher than elsewhere.[6] The fact that Hindu India, Buddhist Thailand, and the Catholic Philippines have almost equal amounts of crime directed against women strongly suggests that this is a socioeconomic problem affecting large parts of today's world. But Muslims can take little comfort from the comparison; they, too, have failed miserably in

---

[6] See "8 Gangs Involved in Flesh Trade Smashed," *Pakistan Link* (Inglewood, Calif.), December 26, 1997, p. 27. According to some statistics, nearly 2,000 girls disappear from Bangladesh every year and surface as sex slaves abroad. At least the same number of Egyptian women are being married by men from richer countries, and most end up as concubines rather than as wives. The many instances of men from the Gulf states marrying girls from poor Indian families caused a furor in the media and was brought up twice before the Indian parliament, because many of these marriages are fake and the girls are used as slaves.

addressing this problem. Because of the drift into general criminality in many of these societies, many are attracted by the slogan "Islam Is the Solution," especially after the Tâlibân enforced their puritan vision, subjecting Afghan society to a virtual curfew for women.

Still, at the beginning of the third millennium, large numbers of Muslim women, if not a majority, are living incomparably freer lives than did their sisters half a century ago. In some places education is still heavily weighted in favor of males, but several countries have a surplus of highly educated women. Among the world's predominantly Muslim countries, more than half have enacted laws to promote women's rights. These laws are criticized as insufficient, but at least they are a step forward. Most of the reformed family laws stipulate a minimum age for marriage. In the case of girls it is age eighteen in Morocco and sixteen in Pakistan. Under Iran's reformed family laws, the minimum age for marriage used to be age seventeen for girls, but one of Khomeini's first acts after coming to power was to abrogate this law so that men could marry girls as young as nine years old.

As deplorable as are the various forms of continuing discrimination against women, including legal discrimination, a change for the better is underway.

The Tâlibân may practice a version of fundamentalism, but the movement is not part of the international Islamist network; it is far more atavistic. Despite its fundamentalist character, Islamism has modernist traits; it is a twentieth-century ideology based on a selective reading of the sources and their interpretation. For instance, it does not oppose female education; indeed, in some places it encourages it. But what happens after women receive their diplomas or advanced degrees? What spheres of life are appropriate for female professionals? There are a number of reasons why the emancipation of Arab and other Muslim women follows its own laws, differing from the way other Third World women emancipate themselves. In Iran, Sudan, and Pakistan, one of the reasons is that women's struggle with Islamism is not exactly the same as the conflict between religion and progress in other cultures. Here the conflict is not with a church, but with a political party or a totalitarian regime.

Muslim women have made significant advances in some professions but little in others. This is true in other cultures as well, but here the pattern differs. A fascinating development in the Islamic world is the predominance of women in journalism. The editorial staffs of several international Arab weeklies consist mainly of women. The flexibility of working hours in journalism is seen as more conducive to family obligations than, for instance, a career as pilot of a plane. The judiciary has remained largely closed to women because of prejudice against women rooted in the sharî`a; women are seen as emotionally unstable and therefore should not be judges. Among tellers in Arab banks, there have long been as many women as men, but a relatively recent development is that in the higher echelons, such as branch manager, one comes across as many women as in American or European banks.

Social pressure and the Islamist trend restrict women to a limited number of professions, usually those in which women work among women rather than among men. For their part, women try to make up for this limitation by taking over some professions as if they were female fiefs. Islamists demand gender segregation in public life, and one method of coping with their demand that women should not mix with men in the workplace is to make men feel out of place where women constitute a majority of the employees. The workplace then turns into a "women only" establishment.

This is an incipient trend, and it may be too early to draw conclusions. The decisive point is that the emancipation of Muslim women has not been blocked altogether, despite a number of setbacks, particularly in Algeria, Egypt, Jordan, Pakistan, and Afghanistan. The number of women in the workforce has increased almost everywhere. For instance, in Algeria it doubled between 1967 and 1977. Islamist attempts to reverse this trend have thus far failed. The number of girls enrolled in school has also undergone a manifold increase in most countries, even where jihâdists murdered hundreds of teachers, as in Algeria.

To sum up: Some passages of the Qur'ân appear problematic with regard to women's rights, but they are more than balanced by others that support those rights in considerable detail. As persons before God, man and woman are equal. Woman is seen neither as merely derivative from man nor as morally inferior. Eve is not portrayed as having seduced Adam; instead, Islam's holy book is explicit in emphasizing the essential oneness and equality of man and woman, as well as their dependence on one another, coupled with the idealization of harmony and mutuality rather than domination and subjugation.

However, the social order envisioned in the Qur'ân is unmistakably patriarchal. Women are called upon to respect the placement of man in the position of leadership. Given its origins in seventh-century Arabia, the elaborate outlining of women's legal rights is remarkable, and it was undoubtedly far ahead of its time in those days. It is no less true, however, that much would have to be amended in order to meet present-day standards of human rights. Such adjustment need not be difficult if the general ethical principles of the revelation are understood to be of primary importance, and the legal details as secondary.

Muslim women's struggle for equal rights is dramatic and often tragic, with many setbacks, and is still beset by great obstacles. All the same, there is discernible progress and indications that the process of emancipation has become unstoppable.

While in Saudi Arabia women fight for basic rights, such as to drive a car, in Los Angeles female Ph.D. students from Saudi Arabia plot to overthrow their government because it is not Islamist enough for their taste. Practical experience with Islamism, however, is a cure for such delusions; it is bitter and radical but effective. In Afghanistan, Algeria, Iran, Pakistan, and Sudan, the vast majority of women are adamantly opposed to the Islamists.

FEMALE CIRCUMCISION

A number of pre-Islamic practices continue in Muslim countries despite the changes brought about by Islam. Female circumcision is one of these ancient customs. The issue received publicity when a Muslim woman from West Africa asked to be granted asylum in the United States because if she returned to her native village, she would be subjected to circumcision. This and a few other cases made it appear as if female circumcision were an Islamic religious requirement.

The truth, however, is that female circumcision is practiced in several parts of Africa by followers of traditional animist religions, by many Christians, and by some Muslims too. In Sudan it used to be common among Muslims, but it has become much less so. It is widely practiced in Egypt despite the fact that the Egyptian Ministry of Health banned female circumcision in 1997.

In Sunni Islam there are four different rites, or schools, and only one of those allows female circumcision. Called the Shâfi`î school, the bulk of its adherents are found in Indonesia and Malaysia, but its major center is Al Azhar, the theological seminary in Cairo. In 1997, when some of its religious leaders argued that female circumcision was Islamic, their stand infuriated a majority of scholars who reasoned that the Prophet had discouraged this practice, which is popularly known as "Pharaonic," in other words, heathen or pagan.

A few contemporaries of the Prophet practiced female circumcision, probably because of the proximity to Egypt. Asked his opinion, Muhammad replied with dismay: "Well, if you think you must, do it, but don't cut deep!" The defenders of female circumcision construe this as an affirmative reply. Their argument is not convincing, however, because whatever the Prophet did or said is acted upon by traditionalist Muslims all over the world in minutest detail. They even aspire to cut their beards precisely as the Prophet did, even though there is no consensus regarding the correct length. However, as far as female circumcision is concerned, most Muslims learned about its existence only through the Egyptian controversy, and many do not know about it even now. When they first hear about the practice, many are left aghast, refusing to believe that such a thing truly occurs. The common reaction is a surprised: "What is there to cut in a female?" For fourteen centuries the vast majority had never heard about it, not even the masses of Shâfi`îs in Indonesia.

In a few African regions, female circumcision was introduced as an Islamic practice because those who spread Islam in these places had learned their religion in Egypt or Sudan. Some emigrants from those regions to France carry on with female circumcision, not only scandalizing the French, but also other Muslims. Moroccans find the practice incomprehensible, whereas it is normal in neighboring Senegal. Elsewhere noteworthy changes are taking place. While among Muslims the custom is waning, some Christian widows and divorcees in East Africa have themselves circumcised, believing that it will rid them of their sexual urges. The rationale that brought this practice about in the first place was, of course, the notion that circumcised girls would be immune to sexual temptation.

Female circumcision is one of several dramatic examples of how some Muslims do things in the name of Islam that other Muslims regard as the very opposite of Islamic teachings. Islam is often blamed for sanctioning the legal punishment by mutilation advocated by some traditionalists. But even most traditionalists reason that the mutilation of human beings is a grave sin, except if prescribed by the sharî`a. There is general agreement that female circumcision is an instance of barbarous mutilation, causing a feeling of shame in most Muslims.[7]

HOMOSEXUALITY

People join Islam for many reasons, some of which are mutually exclusive. As happens with converts to Christianity and other religions, people sometimes convert as a result of erroneous assumptions. For instance, quite a few European gays, among them Vincent Monteil, a renowned French Africanologist, embraced Islam because they had been impressed by its apparently greater tolerance of homosexuality. This was a misunderstanding resulting from a misperception of the distinction between the private sphere and the public sphere. The predominant Muslim attitude, anchored in the sharî`a, is that what one does in one's private life is between the individual and God. For this reason any infraction of the public sphere is punished all the more severely. For instance, the sharî`a demands capital punishment for adultery, but there must be four witnesses to the act, meaning that it is the propagation of adultery that is being punished.

---

[7] See Nawal Saadawi, *The Hidden Face of Eve: Women in the Arab World* (London: Zed Press, 1980). This widely translated book has become a classic on the question of women in present-day Islam, though the perspective is Egyptian rather than Arab or Islamic in general.

Some people convert for exactly the opposite reasons. They join Islam because they are disgusted by what they perceive to be Christianity's lax or overly accommodating attitude toward homosexuality. Both rationales for conversion miss the point, because in the final analysis the three Abrahamic religions have the same problem with homosexuality, though they react to it in widely different ways. It is telling that Muslims refer to gays as *qawm Lût* ("Lot's people"). As for the initial part of Lot's story in the Qur'an, it does not differ from the account in the Hebrew Bible:

> Lot said to his people: "Do you commit lewdness such as no people in creation committed before? You practice your lust on men in preference to women." . . . We [God] are going to bring down on the people of this township a punishment from heaven because they have been wickedly rebellious (Sûra 7:80–84).

Some Muslim societies may be fairly tolerant as far as the private sphere is concerned, but as yet there is scarcely any public discussion of the issue. As regards attempts to reconcile traditional religion with homosexuality, Jews and Christians are indubitably ahead. Muslim intellectuals have barely started to broach the issue.

Perhaps the most prominent Muslim gay in recent history was Tunku `Abdu-r-Rahmân, a prime minister of Malaysia who became secretary general of the Islamic Secretariat (Organization of Islamic Conferences) based in Saudi Arabia. His homosexuality was no secret and became widely known, but he never declared himself gay, nor did he ask for gay rights; therefore, his private life was considered an aberration rather than an abomination. In other words, his homosexuality was conveniently overlooked.[8] But when several of his favorites were given scholarships to study at Temple University in Philadelphia, the result was tragic. An African-American convert was angered because the professor of Islamic Studies, Ismâ`îl Al-Fârûqî, did not provide her with a scholarship. She persuaded another local convert that the professor had brought those gay students from Malaysia because he himself was bisexual. Having been taught that in Islam homosexuality is a crime, the convert murdered Fârûqî in 1986, and he still believes he did the right thing.

---

[8] For an in-depth study, see Khalid Durán, "Homosexuality in Islam," in *Homosexuality and World Religions*, ed. Arlene Swidler (Valley Forge, Pa.: Trinity Press International, 1993), pp. 181–198.

Epilogue: The "Battle of the Books"

In the first half of the twentieth century, intellectual life in the Arab world was primarily an Egyptian affair; Cairo was the center of publishing activity, with Beirut its only competitor. In the 1920s and 1930s the intellectual scene was dominated by liberals and reformers, among them Qâsim Amîn, Lutfî As-Sayyid, Tâhâ Husain, `Alî `Abdu-r-Râziq, M. Husain Haikal, and others whose fresh vistas scandalized traditional scholars. In the 1930s and 1940s some of these intellectual pioneers shifted their focus to more religious themes, glorifying the Islamic heritage in book after book. In retrospect this intellectual ferment came to be called the "Battle of the Books."

In the 1980s and 1990s the Arab and Muslim world witnessed another Battle of the Books, although this time of a less stimulating kind. As predicted, the Rushdî affair engendered a witch-hunt for independent writings on matters related to Islam. One did not have to be a freethinker to incur the wrath of the Islamists and their allies in the traditionalist camp. The Egyptian scholar-politician Farag Fôda was courageous and outspoken, but what he wrote and said was anything but revolutionary. All the same, he was murdered, and some Islamist preachers justified the assassination by declaring him an apostate.

259

In contrast to Fôda, another victim was a rather introvert-
ed Egyptian professor of Arabic literature, Nasr Hâmid Abû
Zaid. Threatened with murder for alleged apostasy, Abû Zaid
fled Egypt and found refuge in Holland. What he wrote in a
study of the Qur'ân was intelligent but hardly controversial.
Others had presented the same views, more or less, in several earlier publications. Scholars and writers have been assassinated or threatened with assassination in Afghanistan,
Algeria, Iran, Kuwait, Lebanon, Pakistan, Syria, Turkey,
Yemen, and the Western Diaspora, including the United
States. Few safe havens remain.

The Battle of the Books raging in much of the Arab and
Muslim world leads to the questions of how much freedom
intellectuals can exercise without risking their lives, how
much independent thinking is allowed, and what opportuni-
ties there are to express opinions freely. In short, is a Muslim
Enlightenment possible?

Many Muslim states seem to be stuck in the postcolonial
phase, unable to come into their own. The feeling of impo-
tence vis-à-vis the industrial nations of the North engenders
an attitude of intense and defensive self-affirmation, with
sporadic outbreaks of mass hysteria. In the artificially created
nation-states of the Middle East the emphasis is on national
unity, with a concomitant demand for conformity in matters
of religion.

As long as dissident opinions are not expressed and disseminated in writing, there is a fair degree of tolerance. But
open confrontations are punished, and severely, especially
when the disputes transcend local confines and are picked up

by the Western media. In such cases heresy becomes treason and is treated as collaboration with the enemy. Had Salmân Rushdî made his sacrilegious comments verbally, and only in his native milieu, few would have taken offense. At most, he would have been threatened with a sound thrashing, and his social circle might have shrunk, but his tradition-bashing would also have won him some new friends. However, the fact that he published his outrageous reflections in the form of a book, moreover in English, the language of the Great Satan, and on top of it on "enemy" territory, is considered unforgivable.

Remarkably, self-censorship is sometimes practiced even by those who suffer from it, including members of the intellectual vanguard, among them Egypt's Nobel Prize winner in literature, Nagîb Mahfûz. His most famous book was banned in Egypt, but he never raised a voice of protest. All the same, the number of those who say that this situation cannot continue has grown in recent years. Despite facing personal danger, an increasing number are speaking out in favor of freedom of expression in order to break the silence that threatens to turn the Muslim world into an intellectual cemetery. These new voices say that it should not matter to us whether propagandists for the Great Powers misuse our protests. They will assail our identity, but our identity cannot be preserved without creativity, and this includes the sphere of religious thought.

Back in 1930, Muhammad Iqbâl, the most celebrated poet and philosopher of Islam in the twentieth century, entitled his most important prose work *The Reconstruction of Religious*

Thought in Islam. In the 1980s and 1990s, the Paris-based Muhammad Arkûn, an Islamic scholar from Algeria, devoted many of his writings to the question of how to rethink Islam.[1]

What has come of those intellectual efforts? Many members of the Muslim world's intellectual elite now live in North America and Western Europe. Until his death in 1988, their leader was Fadlu-r-Rahmân, professor of Islamic Studies at the University of Chicago. As was mentioned earlier, in 1969 he was forced to leave his native Pakistan because of a book published in Britain. Candidates for the Nobel Prize in literature live in Europe; the Moroccans Idrîs Sharâ'ibî (Driss Chraibi) and Tâhir Bin Jillûn (Tahar Ben Jelloun) in France, and the Sudanese At-Tayyib Sâlih in Britain—one of his books was banned by the Islamist dictatorship in his native country.

Among the conclusions to be drawn from these experiences is that there is a precondition for Enlightenment: universal education. If most citizens were literate, many might at least cast a glance at a book before throwing it onto the pyre. In a number of Muslim states, however, the percentage of illiterates is rising rather than declining. The population in Egypt, Bangladesh, Pakistan, and other countries is increasing faster than the number of schools and teachers. In several countries the rate of illiteracy is 70 or even 80 percent. Pakistan, with a population of almost 150 million, has an admirable elite, but the many highly qualified scholars are like an island in the midst of a stormy, intellectually dead sea. Millions of illiterates, unemployed and frustrated, can be

---

[1] See Mohamed Arkoun, *Rethinking Islam* (Boulder, Colo.: Westview, 1994).

mobilized on the spur of the moment to reduce the universities to ashes. A sign from the pulpit is sufficient, not because of the pulpit's inherent power, but because people forced to idle away their time are grateful for any sign, no matter what and no matter where. One has to know the full meaning of the Algerian term *hitist*, which designates a young man leaning against a wall (*hâ'it* in Arabic, in Algeria *hît*). He stands in the street, leaning against a wall because there is nothing else he could do. He does not even have enough money for a single coffee so as to occupy a chair in the street café.

Foreigners were impressed on hearing that in Dacca, then East Pakistan, ten thousand people demonstrated against Fadlu-r-Rahmân's book *Islam* in 1968. In reality, mobilizing ten thousand demonstrators in Dacca, Karachi, or any other metropolis of the region is not much of a challenge, given the fact that there are always more than a hundred thousand people simply hanging around, hoping for something to happen. The sad thing is that the vast majority of those ten thousand demonstrators were illiterates in their own language, not to mention English. And yet they demonstrated against a book written in difficult English and printed on another continent, a book whose cover not one of them had ever seen.

In this context our concern is to counteract the common Western misunderstanding to the effect that this violence is somehow inherent in Islamic teachings or innate in Muslim peoples. Two points need to be raised to destroy these stereotypes. (1) The violent incidents mentioned above, overwhelming as they may seem, were almost exclusively the result of political intrigue rather than spontaneous outbursts of religious fervor. (2) The facility with which politicians resort to this type of hate crime is largely due to extremely deplorable human conditions. Here are some instances:

The campaign against Fadlu-r-Rahmân's book *Islam* did not come about because people read it and took offense. Rather it was a combination of petty intrigue of the most banal type, a clever political move, and perfect timing.

Fadlu-r-Rahmân, then director of Pakistan's semiofficial Islamic Research Institute, had a deputy who ought to have been very grateful to him for a number of favors. But the man wanted the director's chair. Therefore in 1968 he incited a venal politician named Maulvî Farîd Ahmad to start a campaign against the book and its author. Fadlu-r-Rahmân was a protégé of then-president Ayyûb Khân. Here was a golden opportunity for the Islamists to accuse the president, who, moreover, had fallen sick, of hostility toward Islam. The scheme worked like a perfect criminal master plan. The president had to abdicate, Fadlu-r-Rahmân was forced into exile, his deputy became director of the Islamic Research Institute, and Maulvî Farîd Ahmad, an ignorant person with nothing but drive and bravado, became a hero to the Islamists.

The story of Khomeini's *fatwa* against Rushdî is a myth created by the mullacracy in Iran. Holding their bellies with laughter, they proclaim that the West misunderstands Islam. There is no death sentence, they insist, the imam merely issued a religious ruling (*fatwa*). In his capacity as a scholar of the sacred law he could not have done otherwise but state what the law says.

In reality it was the other way around. In his last days, Khomeini was blind, his eyesight having begun to deteriorate soon after his return to Iran. Since he could not read, he spent much of his time listening to his little transistor radio, which he used to clutch especially while taking walks in the garden. In this way he listened to a journalist's interview with a seventeen-year-old high school student who said, quite innocently, that she did not consider the saint she was asked about as a role model. Khomeini immediately ordered her execution; luckily, some members of his entourage had the sentence commuted. A few days later Khomeini heard a radio report that the police in Pakistan had fired on "Muslim demonstrators," killing several of them. The demonstrators had been protesting against a blasphemous book by one Salmân Rushdî. Flaring up again, Khomeini ordered that this devil be killed. Under normal circumstances such a rash judgment has little to do with a *fatwa*, but the regime made it a principle to designate each and every little utterance of the imam a *fatwa*. In this way they arrived at the figure of twenty-five thousand Khomeini *fatwas*, an impressive figure by any standard. We do not know of anyone who could match this *fatwa* production.

Some Lebanese students at the University of California, Irvine, had connections to the pro-Iranian extremist party Hizbullah (Hezbollah). With shining eyes they explained to their teacher why the regime in Tehran was so enthralled by the Rushdî affair:

Look, we have not read the book, and we guess you
have not read it either. Forget about the contents. The
book comes handy as a means to polarize the world.
Formerly it was a polarization between Moscow and
Washington. We have to turn this into a Tehran-
Washington polarization. In order to bring this about
we have to get the largest number of Muslims on our
side. Muslims can be roused when the honor of the
Prophet is under attack, as Rushdî does in his *Satanic
Verses*. If Rushdî did not exist, we would have had to
invent him.

The case is replete with ironies. The *Satanic Verses* is not a
particularly original work, nor is it an outstanding one from
a literary viewpoint.

Neither was it particularly offensive to Iran, with the
exception of seven pages where Rushdî writes about "the
Imam and the Empress," an allegorical reference to
Khomeini. Had the imam and his entourage actually read
that part of the book, the bounty on Rushdî's head would
have been an honest expression of a totalitarian regime's
offended pride. But this was not the case. After Khomeini's
initial flare-up because of the Muslim demonstrators who
were killed, the rest was purely manipulative. The agitation
against the book served as a continuation of the circus of the
"Nest of Spies" (the 1979 takeover of the U.S. embassy and
the holding of American hostages in Tehran for over a year).

In 1985, Sudan's then-dictator, Numairî, had a seventy-
seven-year-old religious scholar publicly hanged as an

"enemy of God." The executed mystic, Mahmûd M. Tâhâ, had written many provocative books and yet was only rarely jailed. Not many people read his books, and few of them cared. However, when he led a demonstration against the civil war in Sudan and demanded an end to the enslavement of the non-Muslim South, he was arrested on charges of sedition. And yet, when Mahmûd was hanged a few days later, the charge was no longer sedition, but blasphemy. Executing such an old man, a preacher of nonviolence who had been nicknamed the "African Gandhi," would have been risky. But after Numairî declared him an apostate and blasphemer, Islamist bodies like the Muslim World League (financed by Saudi Arabia) congratulated him on the execution of the "criminal heretic."

Had Mahmûd Tâhâ not constituted a political threat to Numairî, he might have lived to a ripe old age. As usual, a regime invoked religion to rid itself of opponents. This grotesque misuse of religion recalls Dr. Samuel Johnson's famous observation that "Patriotism is the last refuge of a scoundrel." In these instances, it is religion that is the scoundrel's last refuge.

This is the sword of Damocles that dangles over political dissidents and independent theologians alike in the Muslim world. As long as medieval behavior and an authoritarian mentality prevail, the surest way of eliminating opponents is to accuse them of holding unconventional religious views. Their views rarely cause genuine disturbance among the faithful but provide a welcome opportunity for dictatorships to play the guardian of tradition and identity. The appeal to traditionalism is by no means the only effective method of gaining popular support, but it is the easiest, demanding the least effort.

The event that may be said to have ushered in the new Battle of the Books was the Egyptian parliament's 1979 ban on *Al-Futûhât Al-Makkîya* ("The Meccan Conquest"), the most important book of the famous mystic Ibn`Arabî. The ban has been seen as "a strategy by religious conservatives to enlist politicians in their ranks in order to manipulate the democratic political process and to suppress ideas they deem heretical."[2] Would that this were really the case, because it would provide better chances for an intellectual crossing of swords. Unfortunately, it is the other way round. Politicians, almost without exception, enlist religious leaders to further their designs. Thus the problem is not religious rigidity but the political culture, or the absence of a political culture

The situation says much about a government's assessment of its own performance and standing. The Egyptian government spends billions to fight terrorism, which requires an enormous army of informers and special security units in addition to a mighty police force. And yet it did not provide protection for Nasr Hâmid Abû Zaid and his wife. Bad enough that he was forced to flee, but why has he not been allowed to return? It would have sent a powerful message to the fanatics if the Egyptian government had flown him home from Holland with full honors. That act would have been the kind of signal Egyptian society needs. Such an identification

---

[2] See Th. Emil Homerin, "Ibn `Arabî in the People Assembly: Religion, Press, and Politics in Sadat's Egypt," *Middle East Journal* 40, no. 3, Summer 1986, pp. 462 f.

with the forces of progress would have been no less effective than the mammoth court cases against the terrorists returned from Afghanistan, the Balkans, and "everywhere."

Preliminary indications of a Muslim enlightenment can be found in the Maghreb (Morocco, Algeria, and Tunisia). Here the introduction of universal mandatory education has been pursued more vigorously than in Egypt or Sudan. India too has become a beacon of Muslim intellectual activity, despite the many extra hardships Muslims face in what is a largely hostile cultural environment. The secular government protects many a Muslim citizen from persecution by Islamists. Asghar `Alî Engineer, an Islamic scholar and social reformer of international renown, has several times been physically attacked by militants of his own Ismâ`îlî subsect. Were it not for the protection afforded him by the secular government of India, he would have been murdered, not because of his religious ideas but because of his social commitment and advocacy of a secular state. India is also home to such tradition-conscious institutions of liberal Islam as the Jamia Millia Islamia (National Islamic University) in Delhi with its journal *Islam and the Modern Age*, published in English and Urdu.

Under the prevailing conditions, Islamic scholars who are not merely walking encyclopedias but independent thinkers flourish best outside the traditional world of Islam. These include the Afghan Amîr Khân in Washington, D.C.; the Algerian `A'isha Al-Masîn (Aicha Lemsine) in Valladolid, Spain; the Egyptian Sharîfa (Chérifa) Magdî in Frankfurt, Germany; the Pakistani Ishtiyâq Ahmad in Stockholm, Sweden; the Sudanese Al-Bâqir `Afîf in Manchester, England; and a host of others. They are part of a long list of distinguished academicians who, in their home countries, are tourists at best, finding no support for their scholarly activities except in the West.

The problem is not so much the fetters of dogmatism but ruthless rulers who exploit Islam for their own purposes. The Islamist regimes in Iran and Sudan exploit religion in one way, Qadhâfî in another. Once democracy takes root, many will wonder how the ludicrous Battle of the Books could ever have taken place. By the turn of the millennium, democracy had finally made some strides in half a dozen Arab and Muslim countries, but state authorities have yet to assume responsibility for the safety of academicians and artists, preachers and teachers. Defense budgets will have to be cut so that education can be promoted and the masses freed from the shackles of illiteracy and semi-illiteracy.

In a treatise on *zakâ* (charity), the third of Islam's Five Pillars, M. Yûsuf Gûrâyâ, director of the `Ulamâ' Academy in Lahore, Pakistan, pleads for its use for education. According to tradition, *zakâ* is destined for *fî r-riqâb* ("those in bonds"). Today, Gûrâyâ reasons, there are scarcely any prisoners of war to be ransomed, but there are millions of people in bonds because of their illiteracy.[3] The case of an Egyptian police officer is particularly striking. He discovered a horribly sinful book and reported the find to his superiors, who raised an alarm that almost resulted in a ban on the book, which happened to be the world-famous *Arabian Nights*. The Egyptian officers had never heard of this great classic of Islamic cul-

---

[3] See Muhammad Yûsuf Gûrâyâ, *Nizâm-e zakât aor jadîd ma`âshî masâ'il* (Islamabad: Islamic Research Institute, 1983).

ture. This episode from the Battle of the Books may be anecdotal, but it is not an anecdote; it is symptomatic of the educational misery that plagues much of the Muslim world.

Education must include education in religion. The Islamist leadership, though mostly well educated in technical fields, generally lacks knowledge about religion, while the rank and file is Islamically ignorant. This historically sorry state of affairs has only worsened. The increasing Islamist extremism seems proportionate to the growing ignorance of Islam. Since this ignorance is so widespread among the masses, Islamists find it easy to present as Islamic whatever suits their purposes. Modern means of propaganda, greased with billions of petro-dollars, are used to pervert understanding and to mislead rather than educate.

Although Islamist and nationalist literature and rhetoric give much importance to the study of the national language, it is a striking phenomenon that this subject, as a field of study, ranks very low in the universities of predominantly Muslim countries. The study of Arabic and Urdu has lowly status. There is but one subject that ranks even lower: Islamiyat, the study of Islamic religion. There is good reason for the low esteem, because mostly these courses of study involve little more than rote learning of some basic facts. This "religious vacuum" has been summarized as follows:

> Religious culture is a "parasitic teaching matter": its time allocation is small; its prestige low because it is not judged by schools to be a criterion of a scholarly aptitude; the caliber of teachers is low (mostly Arabic-lan-

guage teachers who treat it in an offhand manner); the curriculum is dull, designed to have students memorize a few sacred texts and learn some acts of devotion rather than inculcate values.[4]

Devoid of any serious intellectual content, Islamic Studies is seen as useful for young women who must while away time while finding a suitable partner for marriage; indeed, it is understood to be an aid in that pursuit. A young woman holding a degree in Islamic Studies is considered to be a "good" (obedient) wife, whereas one with a degree in biology or psychology cannot be trusted.

It is one of the ironies of our time that while at Western universities Islamic Studies is a challenging subject with some prestige, in the world of Islam it is symptomatic of backwardness and underdevelopment. To elevate Islamic Studies at universities in the Muslim world by making it intellectually stimulating has been the dream of Muslim reformers since the late nineteenth century. Except for Turkey and Tunisia, these departments have rarely obtained government support or protection. The reformers have traditionally been forced to keep a low profile, if not live in hiding, but their numbers have grown. This encourages more and more of them to come out of the closet and join the Battle of the Books, a discourse now hopefully shorn of the religious demagogy and political manipulation that characterized the final decades of the twentieth century. Islam is, after all, a "book religion" for more than one reason.

---

[4] Emmanuel Sivan, *Radical Islam: Medieval Theology and Modern Politics* (New Haven: Yale University Press, 1985), p. 8.

Chronology

570 Muhammad is born in the Arabian city of Mecca.

610 Muhammad receives his first revelations and begins to condemn idol worship and immorality, warning of eternal damnation. He preaches submission (*islâm*) to the One God, Allah, and calls for a return to the message of Abraham.

622 Fleeing Mecca because of a plot to assassinate him, Muhammad settles in Medina, where he becomes head of a village community that grows into a city-state. This *hijra* (emigration) signals the beginning of Islam as a separate community. The year 622 becomes the year 1 of the Islamic (lunar) calendar.

630 Muhammad returns triumphantly to Mecca and clears the Ka`ba, the central shrine, of idols. By now the majority of Arabs have joined him.

632 Muhammad dies in Medina and is buried there. Abû Bakr, his closest Companion and father-in-law, succeeds him as leader of the community, calling himself Deputy (caliph) of the Messenger of God.

During his reign of only two years, Abû Bakr quells an

273

insurrection by Bedouin tribes and unites all Arabia under the banner of Islam.

634 Upon Abu Bakr's death, `Omar becomes caliph. During his ten-year reign, Muslims begin to conquer most of the countries neighboring Arabia, such as Iran, Iraq, Syria, Palestine, and Egypt.

638 Muslims conquer Jerusalem from the Byzantines, granting Jews and Christians religious freedom.

644 After the assassination of `Omar, `Othmân (Osman) is elected caliph. Muslims create an empire that spans most of North Africa and the Middle East. However, Muhammad's Companions are increasingly divided by bitter feuds. As the second generation takes over, the civil strife worsens. Accused of nepotism, `Othmân is assassinated in 656.

656 `Alî, Muhammad's cousin and son-in-law, becomes the fourth caliph but is immediately faced with revolts, especially by the governor of Syria, Mu`âwiya, scion of an aristocratic Meccan family that once opposed Muhammad. Because `Alî compromises with Mu`âwiya, some of his partisans desert and ultimately assassinate him. Other followers of his constitute the `Alî Party (*shî`at `Alî*), which soon develops into a sect, now known as Shi`i Islam or Shi`ism.

661 The assassination of `Alî leads to the consolidation of Mu`âwiya's rule. He makes Damascus his capital and founds the Omayyad dynasty.

711 Under the command of Târiq, a Moroccan Berber, a Muslim army crosses over into Spain and defeats the Visigoth rulers. Within a few years, Muslims conquer most of the Iberian Peninsula, largely because the Christian populace resents Catholicism, which the Visigoth kings had imposed only a century earlier. For the large Jewish community, the arrival of the Muslims means an end to the persecution they have had to endure since the conversion of the Visigoth rulers to Catholicism. The name Gibraltar derives from the Arabic *Jabal Târiq* (Mount Tariq) in memory of the conquest in 711.

732 At Poitiers, in the heart of France, a Muslim expeditionary corps is defeated by the Franks, signaling the end of northward expansion into Europe. In the new and dynamic Frankish kingdom, conditions are starkly different from those in Spain.

750 After defeating the Omayyads, the ʿAbbasids establish their own dynasty and, in 762, found Baghdad as their capital. Like the Omayyads, the ʿAbbasids are from Muhammad's tribe, the Quraish. In fact, they are his kith and kin, but their rule is marked by the Persianization of cultural life. The Muslim Empire is no longer an Arab state as it used to be under the Omayyads.

756 A lone survivor from the massacre of the Omayyads at the hands of the ʿAbbasids becomes ruler in Spain, making Córdoba his capital. Called ʿAbdu-r-Rahmân Ad-Dâkhil, he founds the western caliphate, based on a new Omayyad dynasty.

820 Shâfi`î dies. He was one of the fathers of the sharî`a and the founder of the Shâfi`î school of Islamic law.

830 Caliph Al-Ma'mûn founds an academy in Baghdad called *baitu l-hikma* ("House of Wisdom"). This is the high point of the Mu`tazila, a school of rational theologians and scientists whose movement could be called the Muslim Enlightenment.

855 Ahmad Ibn Hanbal dies; he was the founder of the Hanbalî school of Islamic law. An opponent of the rational theologians known as Mu`tazila, Ibn Hanbal may be called the first Muslim fundamentalist. Today's Islamists venerate him as a founding father of their movement.

870 Ismâ`îl Al-Bukhârî dies; he was a scholar from Bukhara (today in Uzbekistan). His *Sahîh Bukhârî* is the most famous collection of Hadîth (Muhammad's sayings), and as such the most important Islamic book after the Qur'ân. As a sign of veneration, Muslims refer to the compiler as Imâm Bukhârî.

874 The Twelfth Imam (the head of the Shi`i Muslims) disappears. Shi`is claim that he went into hiding (occultation) and will reappear at the end of time.

922 Mansûr Al-Hallâj is executed in Baghdad for having claimed to be one with God. A laborer himself, he becomes the patron saint especially of the working class. Al-Hallâj is one of the most venerated Muslim mystics.

935 Ash`arî dies; he was an Iraqi theologian who reconciled various feuding trends of thought and methodologies, producing a kind of compromise theology that becomes the basis of Islamic orthodoxy.

977 The Turkish Ghaznawid dynasty (named after the Afghan city of Ghazni) establishes itself in Afghanistan and repeatedly invades India.

1009 Caliph Al-Hakim orders the destruction of the Holy Sepulchre in Jerusalem.

1037 Ibn Sînâ (Avicenna) dies. Hailing from Khorasân (Afghanistan), he is remembered as one of the five greatest Muslim philosophers.

1099 On capturing Jerusalem, the Crusaders put the entire Muslim and Jewish population to the sword.

1111 Abû Hâmid Al-Ghazâlî dies. With his *Ihyâ' `ulûmi-d-dîn* ("The Revivification of the Sciences of Religion"), a synthesis of various trends of thought current in his time, he became the most celebrated theologian in Muslim history. Like Ash`arî before him, Ghazâlî was pivotal in the evolution and consolidation of Islamic orthodoxy. However, their achievement in reconciliation also led to intellectual stagnation, because deviations from their compromise theology came to be condemned as heresies.

1187 Saladin reconquers Jerusalem from the Crusaders and encourages Muslims and Jews to resettle the town. It is the 27th of the Islamic month of Rajab, the anniversary of Prophet Muhammad's mystical night journey to Jerusalem, from where he visited the Seven Heavens.

1191 The sûfî philosopher Suhrawardî, founder of the illuminationist school, is executed as a heretic.

1198 Ibn Rushd (Averroes) dies. An Islamic scholar in Córdoba, he had a profound influence on later Western European philosophers.

1204 Moshe Ben Maimon, known as Maimonides, dies. A Jewish philosopher in Córdoba and author of *Guide for the Perplexed*, he wrote his books in Arabic.

1240 Muhyuddîn Ibn`Arabî dies. A mystic from Murcia in Spain, he is venerated in many parts of the world as *ash-shaikhu l-akbar* (the Greatest Master).

1236 Córdoba, the capital of Western Islam, falls to the Castilians (Christians from northern Spain), followed by the fall of Seville in 1248. The Castilian victories in Andalusia lead to an exodus of tens of thousands of Muslims to North Africa, and the conversion of tens of thousands more to Catholicism.

1258 After devastating the entire eastern part of the Muslim Empire, a Mongol army under Hülägü sacks Baghdad, butchering most of the inhabitants. Nothing is left of what had been the capital of the world for four centuries. Muslims take this disaster to be the end of the world. However, much of Baghdad's elite left the city prior to the Mongol destruction. Most of them move east, with the result that Herat in Afghanistan becomes the Granada of the East, and Delhi in India a kind of New Baghdad.

1273 Rûmî (Jalâluddîn Rûmî Balkhî) dies. A sûfî poet from Balkh in Afghanistan, he spent much of his life in Konya, Turkey, where his shrine is an object of saint worship. Known as Maulana (*mevlana* in Turkish), he is a kind of patron saint to the Mevlevis, also known as the Whirling Dervishes. His famous work is the *Mathnawî*. Among sûfî philosophers it is a perennial debate as to who was greater, Rûmî or Ibn`Arabî.

1281 Seljuq Turks create the Ottoman Empire, named after its founder, `Othmân (Osman).

1328 Ibn Taimîya dies. He was a Hanbalî ("fundamentalist") scholar in Damascus and is highly venerated by today's Islamists. Profoundly antisûfî, he was a forerunner of Muhammad Ibn`Abdi-l-Wahhâb in eighteenth-century Arabia, the founder of the Wahhâbi movement that gave rise to the state of Saudi Arabia.

1406 `Abdu-r-Rahmân Ibn Khaldûn dies. A philosopher of history, he is often called the father of the science of sociology. Born in Tunis as the scion of an Andalusian family, Ibn Khaldûn worked as an administrator and teacher in several states of Spain and North Africa. His famous work is the *Muqaddima* ("Prolegomena").

1453 Under Sultan Mehmet II, the Ottoman Turks take the capital of the Byzantine Empire, Constantinople, and rename it Islampol, later changed to Istanbul. In Muslim imagery Constantinople has always been Rûm (Rome), and there is a Hadîth, a saying by the Prophet (most likely an invented one), that offers a reward to the conqueror of Rûm.

1492 Granada, the last Muslim principality on the Iberian Peninsula, is conquered by Ferdinand and Isabella, the Catholic monarchs of northern Spain. Muslims who wish to stay are forced to convert to Catholicism and given one year to learn Spanish or face expulsion. All over Spain people are prohibited from taking showers or full baths and from washing their hands and feet according to Muslim tradition. Jews have to leave too. Most of them go with the Muslims to Morocco and other North African countries, some as far as the Balkans, then part of the Ottoman Empire.

1526 The Moghul Empire is founded in India, with Delhi as its capital.

1566 Süleyman the Magnificent dies. Under him the Ottoman Empire reached its apex.

1605 The Moghul emperor Akbar dies. His reign marked the high point of the empire.

1608 The last Moriscos, descendants of Muslim converts to Catholicism, are expelled from Spain. They were severely oppressed, always suspected of continuing to practice Islam in secret. Among them are priests and nuns whose families had been Catholic for generations but were still treated as second-class citizens. Most of the Moriscos are sent to France rather than Morocco, because it is feared that they will add to Moroccan strength. They settle in Provence, where many Jewish refugees from Spain had settled as well. The Dutch philosopher Spinoza hailed from such a Spanish-Jewish family in Provence.

1744 The fundamentalist "unitarian" movement begins in Arabia. It is popularly referred to as Wahhâbî after its founder, Muhammad Ibn `Abdi-l-Wahhâb, who builds an alliance with a tribal chief, Sa`ûd, whose descendants found the state of Saudi Arabia in 1926.

1763 Shâh Waliyullâh of Delhi dies. He was a leader of Islamic revival and a proponent of the sûfî doctrine of *wah-datu-l-wujûd* ("unity of being"), which fundamentalists reject as pantheism.

1785 The Naqshbandî sûfî order leads the resistance to Russia's southward expansion into Dagestan and other Muslim lands.

1806 Temporarily occupying the hallowed places in Arabia and Iraq, Wahhâbîs destroy the tombs of saints, especially of the Shi`i imâms. Ever since, sûfîs have regarded the Wahhâbîs as their mortal enemies.

1857 In a great national uprising, Indians seek to shake off British rule. The British quell the rebellion and create the Anglo-Indian viceroyalty. The Muslims, who had ruled India for 600 years, are victimized by the British for their leading role in the uprising.

1888 Muhammad Ahmad, called the Mahdi of Sudan, dies in his capital, Omdurman. He freed his country from joint rule by the British and the Egyptians. After establishing a tyrannical regime with a narrow-minded interpretation of fundamentalist Islam, he threatened to invade Egypt and Ethiopia. The Mahdi is succeeded by a caliph, the Khalîfa Abdullâhi, who is soon defeated by the British, who occupy the entire Sudan and make it one country.

1897 Sayyid Jamâluddîn Afghânî dies in Istanbul. Of Iranian origin, he was a firebrand agitator who sought to mobilize the Muslims in several countries against their colonial masters, especially the British. Although he wrote little, his impact on intellectuals in Afghanistan, India, Egypt, Turkey, Iran, and even in Britain and France was enormous.

The first Zionist Congress convenes in Basel, Switzerland, expressing Jewish aspirations to possess a country which they can call their own.

1898 Sir Sayyid Ahmad Khân dies. He was a leader of Islamic modernism in India and founded the `Aligarh Muslim University, which produced the modern educated class of Indian Muslims that ultimately came to run the state of Pakistan. Although Ahmad Khân's liberalism is not always adhered to, for many Pakistanis he is a national father figure, lovingly referred to as "Sir Sayyid." His commentary on the Bible (Torah and New Testament), written in Urdu, is a unique contribution to interreligious understanding.

1905 Shaikh Muhammad `Abduh dies in Egypt He was a reformer who, as rector, tried to modernize Al-Azhar, Cairo's famous seminary. A translator of Western philosophical works into Arabic, `Abduh greatly stimulated intellectual life. He personified Muslim Enlightenment and inspired two generations of liberals, who referred to him as *al-ustâdh al-imâm* (the "Professor-Imâm").

1908 In India the Agha Khân leads the Ismâ`îlis back into the fold of Islam. They had been regarded as a heretical sect outside the Muslim community.

1916 Britain and France conclude a deal regarding their interests in the Middle East. The division of the region between the two colonial powers is known as the Sykes-Picot Agreement, after the British and French representatives who worked it out. Later on most people in the Near and Middle East feel deceived, realizing that what was promised to them was also promised to others.

1920 In the northern Moroccan Rif region, Muhammad Ibn `Abdi-l-Karîm Al-Khattâbî (commonly referred to as Abd el-Krim) proclaims the Islamic Republic of Er Rif, and defeats a French-Spanish army in the Battle of Anual (July 1921).

1923 Mustafa Kemal proclaims the Turkish Republic. He is given the honorific title Atatürk ("Father of Turks").

1924 The Ottoman caliphate is abolished.

1925 An Egyptian Islamic scholar, Shaikh `Alî `Abdu-r-Râziq, publishes his *Al-islâm wa usûlu l-hukm* ("Islam and the Principles of Government"), in which he describes the caliphate as an accident of history and pleads for a secularist order. Because of this treatise, he loses his job as a teacher at Al-Azhar.

1926 A conference in Mecca fails to reestablish the caliphate, thwarting King Fu'âd of Egypt's ambitions to become caliph. Instead, the Wahhâbis establish the Kingdom of Saudi Arabia and once again demolish Shi`i shrines.

1927 Abû-l-A`la Mawdûdî, an Indian journalist, publishes a series of articles on jihâd that are later reprinted as a pamphlet. Subsequently the prolific Mawdûdî becomes the chief ideologue of Islamism, voicing a new ideology modeled on the pattern of the totalitarianism then in vogue in Europe.

1928 An elementary school teacher in Egypt, Hasan Al-Bannâ, founds the Society of the Muslim Brethren, the world's first Islamist party, which soon establishes branches in Syria and other neighboring countries.

1930 Sir Muhammad Iqbâl from Kashmir publishes lectures he gave, mostly in Britain, under the title *The Reconstruction of Religious Thought in Islam*. It is one of the most important twentieth-century interpretations of Islam.

1936 General Franco, commander of the Spanish troops in the Rif (the Spanish protectorate in Northern Morocco), begins an uprising against the government in Madrid. His aim is to overthrow the left-leaning Republic. Franco wins the three-year-long civil war thanks mainly to his 20,000 Moroccan elite troops. The zeal with which they fight on the side of their colonial master amazes observers worldwide. And yet the explanation is simple. The poorly paid Muslim soldiers believe that they are fighting a *jihâd didda l-kilâb billâ dîn* ("a holy war against the godless dogs"). Clever colonial authorities made appeal to the Qur'an, according to which a Muslim is obliged to fight not only for Islam, but for Judaism and

Christianity as well, whenever they are threatened by infidels.

1938　Muhammad Iqbâl dies. He is now celebrated as the poet-philosopher of Pakistan. Iqbâl visualized himself as the third in an East-West dialogue that began with Hâfiz of Shiraz, Persia's greatest poet. Profoundly impressed by Persia's sûfî poets, Germany's Goethe wrote his *West-Östlicher Divan*, which specialists regard as his magnum opus. Iqbâl, who obtained his Ph. D. in Germany, answered with a book of Persian poetry entitled *Payâm-e Mashriq* ("Message of the East") as a continuation of the dialogue: Hâfiz-Goethe-Iqbâl.

1939　With the start of World War II, the Axis powers (Germany and Italy) present themselves to the Muslim world as liberators from the colonial yoke of Britain and France. In a secret agreement, however, they divide the Arab world between themselves. Italy is to get all of North Africa with the exception of Egypt, which is to become a German colony, along with the rest of the Arab world.

1943　In India, Abû-l-A`lâ Mawdûdî and his followers constitute the Jamâ`at-e Islâmî (Islamic Party), which is still the leading Islamist party in the subcontinent.

1945　With the end of World War II the Dutch unsuccessfully try to regain control of their colony of Indonesia, which had been conquered by the Japanese. Independent Indonesia is roughly 90 percent Muslim and thus the most populous Muslim nation in the world.

1947 India becomes independent after more than 100 years of British rule. But the subcontinent is divided into predominantly Hindu India and the Islamic Republic of Pakistan (then still including Bangladesh).

1948 The United Nations divides Palestine, until then under British administration, between Arabs and Jews. The Arab neighbor states attack the newly proclaimed State of Israel but are defeated.

1949 Hasan Al-Bannâ, the founder of the Muslim Brotherhood Party, is assassinated in Cairo, supposedly on orders of King Fârûq or his courtiers.

1953 A group of Egyptian revolutionaries, calling themselves the Free Officers, overthrow King Fârûq and abolish the monarchy.

1954 The Muslim Brethren, now a mass movement, collide with the Egyptian government under `Abdu-n-Nâsir (Nasser). Tens of thousands are jailed. Thousands of others find refuge in various Arab states, especially the Gulf countries, where they become influential and spread their fundamentalist interpretation of Islam.

1956 The Egyptian military junta headed by Jamal `Abdu-n-Nasir (Gamal Abdel Nasser) nationalizes the Suez Canal. Britain and France react by attacking Egypt. Israel, too, goes to war, penetrating deep into Sinai. The United States, however, puts strong pressure on Britain, France, and Israel to withdraw. Thus Egypt succeeds politically despite suffering military defeat.

The French protectorates of Morocco and Tunisia become independent.

Sudan becomes independent but is immediately torn by a civil war between the Arabized and Muslim north and the mainly animist and Christian south.

1962   Algeria becomes independent after a war of liberation that costs more than a million lives. For 130 years the country had been ruled as a French overseas territory.

1963 In Iran, Khomeini leads disturbances in protest against land reform and the emancipation of women. Other clerics save him from execution by promoting him to the rank of grand ayatollah (comparable to an archbishop). He spends the next fourteen years in exile in Iraq.

1966 Sayyid Qutb, the new ideologue of the Muslim Brethren, is executed in an Egyptian jail.

1967 The Six-Day War, in which Israel decisively defeats its Arab neighbors and occupies the West Bank, the Golan Heights, and the Sinai Peninsula, greatly stimulates Islamist propaganda. The Arab misfortune is said to be due to their having abandoned Islam and taken recourse to foreign ideologies, such as liberalism, nationalism, secularism, and socialism. Islamists claim that the only solution is a return to Islam, now increasingly turned into a political ideology.

1968 In their English and French publications, parties of political extremists generally referred to as Muslim fundamentalists begin to speak of themselves as Islamists. The purpose is to emphasize that Islam is not only a faith and a way of life, but a political ideology, Islamism.

1969 The first Islamic Summit Conference is held in Rabat, with the purpose of devising a joint political strategy to regain Jerusalem. This leads to the creation of the Organization of Islamic Conferences (OIC). Since most of the 40 member states join in the hope of financial rewards from Saudi Arabia, the OIC is popularly referred to as "`Alî Bâbâ and the Forty Thieves."

In Libya, Colonel Mu`ammar Al-Qadhâfî overthrows King Idrîs As-Sanûsî. At first close to the Islamists, Qadhâfi gradually drifts into the Soviet camp.

In Sudan Ja`far Numairî establishes a military dictatorship and proclaims himself field marshal. At first close to the Communists, Numairî gradually drifts into the Islamist camp, moving in a direction opposite to that of his erstwhile friend, Qadhâfî.

1971 Upon East Pakistan's opting to become the independent state of Bangladesh, Islamists commit large-scale massacres that cause the death of roughly 100,000 Hindu and Muslim secularists. Paramilitary units of the Jamâ`at-e Islamî party, such as Al-Badr, terrorize the population. Mas`ûdu-r-Rahmân (Meswoodur Rehman), a leading Islamic scholar, voices Bengali disillusionment by defining Islamism as an ideology of "looting, raping and killing." The newly independent state denies citizenship to Islamist leaders such as Prof. Ghulâm A`zam, who had fled abroad. Bangladeshis demand that he be tried as a war criminal.

Dhû-l-fiqâr `Alî (Zulfikar Ali) Bhutto, head of the Pakistan People's Party, takes over in Islamabad after winning a landslide election victory on a platform of Islamic Social Democracy. His Islamist opponents obtain barely 6 percent of the votes in elections that are universally acclaimed as free and fair.

1977 Islamist military officers headed by General Diyâ'u-l-Haqq (Zia ul-Haq) topple Bhutto and hang him two years later.

President Anwar As-Sadat surprises the world community by flying to Israel to offer peace and reconciliation. His unexpected initiative causes most Arab states to boycott Egypt.

Najîb Al-Kîlânî's book *A`dâ'u l-islâmîya* ("The Enemies of Islamism") is published in Cairo. He defines *al-islâmîya* as the Arabic rendering of "Islamism," a term that was first coined in English.

1978 Pro-Soviet military officers kill Afghanistan's "prince-president," Da'ûd, and call their takeover an April Revolution. The people reject some of the new regime's reform measures as godless and rise in revolt. A few months later nationalist students at Kabul University stage their first guerrilla attack on the garrison in Husain Kot, ushering in Afghanistan's war of liberation.

1979 Revolution breaks out in Iran. The shah flees into exile and Khomeini rises to power in Tehran, assuming the title of imam and *valiy-e faghih* ("supreme guide"). The same year Islamist ideologue Mawdûdî dies in a hospital in the much-maligned United States, where his son is a doctor.

1980 There is a general uprising against the Soviet occupation forces in Afghanistan, led by nationalist intellectuals headed by `Abdu-l-Majîd Kalakânî, who is captured and executed inside the Soviet embassy. Pakistan organizes Islamist guerrilla forces with Saudi money and weapons supplied by the CIA. Before turning against the Communists, the Islamists eliminate the "resistance of the first hour," which consists of Afghan nationalists.

With the help of the KGB and Tudeh, Iran's Communist Party, Khomeini succeeds in crushing the country's strongest political force, the Mojahedin-e Khalq (People's Mojahedin). Tens of thousands are executed, mostly tortured to death. Opposition leader Mas`ûd Rajawî (Masoud Rajavi) flees to Paris, where he founds the National Resistance Council, together with the leaders of some two dozen Iranian organizations opposed to the clerical regime in Tehran, now deridingly called the mullacracy. (In Iran *mulla*, or *mullah*, means "priest.")

1981 Egypt's President Anwar As-Sâdât is assassinated by participants in a military parade. They belong to one of the many underground Islamist groups that consider their mother party, the Muslim Brethren, too accommodationist. There are dozens of secret groups at first such as the Jamâ`atu l-Muslimîn (also called Takfîr wa Higra), but in the course of time many of them merge in the Gamâ`a Islâmîya under the leadership of Shaikh `Omar `Abdu-r-Rahmân, who eventually moves to the United States. Initially these extremist dissidents from the Muslim Brethren are called "anarcho-Islamists," but the new name that sticks is jihâdists.

1984 Jihâdist volunteers from a dozen Arab countries assemble in Pakistan, where they receive training in guerrilla warfare. Some actually join the fighting in Afghanistan. Their real aim is to prepare for the overthrow of their governments back home. These adventurers come to be known as "Arab Afghans." Prominent among them is Saudi millionaire Usâma Bin Lâdin (Osama Bin Laden).

1985 In Sudan's capital, Khartoum, Mahmûd Muhammad Tâhâ, perhaps the century's most original Islamic thinker, is publicly hanged as an "enemy of God." A lifelong advocate of nonviolence, the 77-year-old sûfî master used to be called the African Gandhi.

Islamists, who regarded him as their most potent opponent, rejoice over his death. Saudi Arabia's religious leadership congratulates the Sudanese authorities for finally having executed this "cursed heretic."

1988   Professor Fadlu-r-Rahmân (Fazlur Rahman) dies in Chicago. He was named one of the four leading Islamic scholars of the twentieth century. As director of Pakistan's semi-official Islamic Research Institute, he became the major target of Islamist opposition to the regime of liberal President Ayyûb Khân. Forced to flee his native country after the fall of Ayyûb Khân in 1969, Fazlur Rahmân became a professor at the University of Chicago.

1989 In Sudan, Islamist military officers headed by `Omar Al-Bashîr topple one of the few democratically elected governments in the Arab world. Although they outlaw political parties, in actual fact they install the National Islamic Front, an Islamist organization, in power. The head of the NIF, Dr. Hasan At-Turâbî, shows ambitions of becoming the global Islamist leader.

1990 Islamists win municipal elections in Algeria, but it soon turns out that this was a protest vote. In the national elections one year later the Islamists get 1 million fewer votes.

1992 The Algerian military stops elections which Islamists believe they could have won. The result is an armed insurrection that lasts for ten years and turns increasingly vicious, with massacres of the peasant population by the GIA (Armed Islamic Groups).

In Sarajevo Serb nationalists fire on a peace demonstration and start a campaign of ethnic cleansing that results in the death of some 200,000 persons, the ejection of some 750,000 Bosnians from their homes, and the displacement of almost 2 million people. More than 20,000 women fall victim to a systematic campaign of rape and torture, which leaves most of them mentally and physically handicapped. The perpetrators claim to be acting in defense of Christianity. British connivance and general European inaction cause anti-Western fury in much of the Muslim world.

1993 In the Sudanese capital, Khartoum, 600 delegates from sixty countries attend the Popular Arab and Islamic Conference, an alliance of Islamists, Arab nationalists, and radical leftists, such as the Palestinian Christian Nâyif Hawatma (Hawatmeh) of the Democratic Front for the Liberation of Palestine. The PAIC is the brainchild of its general secretary, Professor Hasan At-Turâbî, the ideologue of the military regime in Sudan. Former foes unite on the common platform of anti-Americanism.

1994 Because of its aggression against Bosnia, Serbia (rump Yugoslavia) is suspended from the United Nations and subjected to economic sanctions by the world community. But the Milosevic regime in Belgrade receives abundant oil supplies from Libya, via Egypt and Greece. Qadhâfî, himself subjected to economic sanctions because of Libyan sponsorship of international terrorism, now relies chiefly on Serb military advisers, experts, and security guards who take the place formerly held by East Germans and Russians.

1995 The Dayton Accord ends the fighting in Bosnia but leaves the Bosnian heartland in the hands of the aggressors, who establish a so-called Serb Republic. In Turkey, where at least 5 percent of the 60 million population is of Bosnian origin, the decimation of Bosnia leads to an increase in votes for the Islamists, who emerge as the single strongest party.

1996 In London an international group of eighty participants from all walks of life, but predominantly university professors, form an association that is to serve as an intellectual forum, educational network, and dialogue initiative of independent Muslims. Called the Ibn Khaldun Society, it is an attempt by non-Islamist Muslim academicians to come out of the closet and give a voice to the silent majority opposed to religious bigotry and political extremism.

1997 The Tâlibân (seminarists), a fundamentalist movement created by Pakistan's military intelligence, consolidate their power in Afghanistan. They are not connected to the international network of Islamist parties, who regard them as an American ploy to defame Islamism. The Tâlibân serve Islamabad as a means of extending Pakistani influence in Central Asia. But they shelter Saudi fugitive Usâma Bin Lâdin, and he organizes terrorist acts against Americans in various countries, causing both Americans and Saudis to withdraw their support for the Tâlibân.

1998   Iran intensifies its military support for the Islamist regime in Sudan, which makes a concerted effort to quell the long-standing insurrection in the south. The regime in Khartoum has the backing of China, Malaysia, and Canada. The major attraction is oil, which cannot be exploited unless the civil war is brought to an end.

1999   After twenty years of repression by one of the world's most brutal regimes, Iran experiences massive unrest, reminiscent of the uprising against the shah twenty years earlier. The clerical regime clamps down on the demonstrators with full force, while giving itself the appearance of being reform-oriented and moving toward democracy. Ironically, President Khatami, one of the architects of the Islamist regime, though surrounded by notorious warmongers and organizers of international terrorism, is welcomed in the West as a liberal.

2000   In Indonesia, now the country with the largest Muslim population in the world (close to 200 million), a liberal Islamic scholar, `Abdu-r-Rahmân Wâhid, is elected president and invites Jews and Christians to Jakarta for interreligious dialogue. In many parts of the country, however, fighting erupts between Christians and Muslims, leaving tens of thousands dead.

The Islamist regimes of Iran and Sudan are plagued by infighting. The result is a public admission of many of the crimes committed, such as the Khartoum government's complicity in attempts on the life of Egyptian President Husnî

Mubârak. The Iranian authorities admit that the number of prisoners is 600,000 (15,000 when the Islamists came to power in 1979). Under President Khatami, 700 Iranians have been executed, some having an eye gouged out before execution. Symptomatic of the increased persecution of ethnic and religious minorities under Khatami, nine Iranian Jews are sentenced for allegedly having spied for Israel. Show trials conducted over a period of many months serve to intimidate the growing opposition to Islamism.

Glossary

`âlim "Learned man," in particular a scholar of religion, though it can also mean a scientist. The plural is `ulamâ', which in English is often spelled ulema.

ayatollah "Sign of God," the title of senior religious leaders in Iran. This title, foreign to Muslims elsewhere, was created by an eighteenth-century ruler in order to raise money.

dhimmî A non-Muslim in a Muslim-dominated state. Originally it had the meaning of belonging to a protected minority, but in the course of time it acquired the meaning of a second-class citizen.

faqîh A scholar of the law (sharî`a). The term derives from fiqh, the word for Islamic jurisprudence.

halâl Permitted, in the sense of kosher

harâm Prohibited, opposite of halâl (kosher)

hijra (also spelled hijrah or hegira) The Prophet Muhammad's flight from Mecca to Medina in 622. This signals the beginning of the Islamic calendar, which is lunar.

`îd   Holiday, feast, religious celebration. The two major Muslim holidays are called `îdu-l-fitr* (breaking of the fast, at the end of the month of Ramadân), and `îdu-l-adha* (the sacrificial feast in commemoration of Abraham's readiness to sacrifice his son).

ijtihâd   "Effort," more specifically an intellectual effort. The word is related to *jihâd*, which can mean a military effort. *Ijtihâd* means to make full use of one's reason in order to arrive at an independent judgment, especially in matters for which there is no precedent in Islamic thought. As such, *ijtihâd* is the opposite of *taqlîd* (reliance on the example of the pious forebears).

imâm   Any prayer leader is called *imâm*, because he stands "in front of" the others. The term also means spiritual leader of the entire community, and as such it is used especially by Muslims of the Shi`i denomination. Their leadership has always been parallel to that of the Sunni-dominated state. The supreme leader of the Shi`is was called *imâm* in contradistinction to the *khalîfa*, the supreme leader of Sunni Muslims.

jâhilîya   "Time of ignorance," referring to pre-Islamic Arabia. It has the connotation of "dark age."

jihâd   "Effort," which can mean a moral effort in the sense of working hard for any good cause. It can also mean to fight for religious freedom. Although many Muslims object to the translation of *jihâd* as "holy war," it is not entirely wrong, though somewhat one-sided.

jizya A tax to be paid by non-Muslims under Muslim rule. Muslims pay *zakâ*, the tax stipulated by their religion. Since non-Muslims are exempt from *zakâ* but are to be protected by the Muslim-dominated state, they pay a tax of their own, the *jizya*.

khalîfa Caliph, which means "successor" or "deputy." In theology (the Qur'an) khalîfa stands for man as God's vicegerent on earth. In history the term denotes the successor or representative of God's messenger (*khalîfat rasûl-illâh*)

maghrib The word means both evening and West. Maghrib is the name of the evening prayer and also the Western part of the traditional Muslim world: Tunisia is the Near West, Algeria the Midwest, and Morocco the Far West. These countries are referred to as the Maghreb States.

masjid, masgid (*mezquita* in Spanish) Mosque

muhâjir One who leaves his home for a place where he can practice his faith without obstruction; today the term is used for (Muslim) refugees in general.

mujâhid One who strives in the path of God; in a narrower sense it denotes freedom fighters such as the Afghans in their war against the Russian invaders. The connotation is that Muslims fight a war (*jihâd*) of liberation that also implies the freedom to practice the Islamic religion. Algerians used the term in their war of liberation from French colonial rule.

Mujâhid is also a personal name, especially in Bangladesh/India/Pakistan.

Muslim (the same as Moslem) A person who submits to God, one who practices Islam, a follower of the Islamic religion. Muslim also is a personal name.

Quds "The holy one" is the common name for Jerusalem, also called *al-baitu-l-muqaddas* ("the holy house").

salâ (also spelled *salah* or *salat*) The ritual prayer which a Muslim is supposed to perform five times a day. With its minutely prescribed ritual, *salâ* is different from the nonritual prayer called *du`â*, which can be said spontaneously without requiring any prescribed form.

**sharî`a** (also spelled *shari`ah* or *shari`at*)  "The way," the name for the law of Islam as it evolved over a period of almost two centuries (7th-9th centuries) in Arabia and neighboring countries. Since the *sharî`a* also details the rituals and religious practices, thus being more than law, it is often called a "complete code of life." Parts of the *sharî`a* are strongly influenced by Judaism, in fact, the word has the same meaning as *halakha*. It is the "trodden path" that has been found to be the "right way." Thus it may be called the way to salvation.

**shî`a** (also spelled *shi`ah*) The word means "party" and was used by those who constituted the party of `Alî, the fourth caliph. Today it stands for a special confession or sect of

Muslims, the Shi`is, who constitute roughly 10 percent of all Muslims. Those belonging to the majority denomination are called Sunnis.

sûfî "Woolen," the term used for a movement of asceticism in early Islam, because they used to wear garments of coarse wool in protest against the luxurious lifestyle of the Arab rulers. Sûfî then became the name for the mystics and also for popular religion in the lands of Islam.

sunna (also spelled *sunnah* or *sunnat*) "Practice" (praxis) or "custom" and way of doing things, it could even be rendered as "behavior." More specifically the term refers to the way the Prophet Muhammad used to do things, his life as the good exemplar. Muslims also call themselves Sunnis, which is to say that they follow the Prophet in whatever he did. Shi`is, too, follow Muhammad's *sunna*, even though they are not called Sunnis.

tanzimat "Organizations," in the sense of "reorganizing" or restructuring. The term refers to a reform period in the 19th century Ottoman Empire that was characterized by a series of measures to reorganize the state.

taqlîd "Emulation" or "imitation," in the sense of following the example of the pious forebears. Rather than use their own independent judgment (*ijithâd*), believers should follow what the first generation of Muslims did.

tarîqa The "path" of the mystics (*sûfis*). Many understand this as an alternative to the *sharî`a* of the "orthodox," others hold *sharî`a* and *tarîqa* to be complementary means of arriving at the *haqîqa* ("truth," "reality").

tatbîq "Synthesis," in Arabic the word means "application" and "implementation," but in the Indian subcontinent it acquired the meaning of "synthesis" in cultural history, more precisely in Islamic thought.

Wahhabi Follower of the 17th-century Arabian reformer Muhammad Ibn `Abdi-l-Wahhab. The modern kingdom of Saudi Arabia is based on this "fundamentalist" interpretation of Islam. While the Wahhabis do not call themselves *Wahhabis* but Salafis, outside Arabia the term Wahhabi acquired a negative meaning as narrow-minded fanatic, representing an anti-intellectual brand of Islam that is hostile to culture. In recent times it has acquired the additional connotation of an imperialist outreach by self-righteous oil potentates.

walî "Friend," in the sense of "friend of God" and "saint."

Yathrib The pre-Islamic name of Medina. When the Prophet Muhammad settled there after his flight from Mecca, Yathrib came to be referred to as *madînatu-n-nabi* ("the Prophet's city"). Today it is called *al-madînatu l-munawwara* ("the illuminated city").

zakâ (also spelled *zakah* or *zakat*) The word has the connotation of "self-purification" and is mostly used together with
the word for the ritual prayer, *salâ*. *Zakâ* acquired the meaning of "charity" or "alms" and also "poor tax." At times it has
been used like a kind of property tax, though recently it has
come to resemble more the church tax levied in some
Northern European countries.

Recommended Reading

Al-Ashmawy, Muhammad Said. *Islam and the Political Order*. Washington: Council for Research in Values and Philosophy, 1994.

Arberry, A. J. *Sufism: An Account of the Mystics of Islam*. Boston: Unwin Paperbacks, 1979.

Bogle, Emory C. *Islam : Origin and Belief*. Austin: University of Texas Press, 1998.

Hick, John. *Disputed Questions in Theology and the Philosophy of Religion*. New Haven: Yale University Press, 1993. Includes a chapter on "Jews, Christians, Muslims: Do We All Worship the Same God?"

Jansen, Johannes J. G. *The Neglected Duty: The Creed of Sadat's Assassins and Islamic Resurgence in the Middle East*. New York: Macmillan, 1986.

Kramer, Martin, ed. *The Islamism Debate*. Tel Aviv: Tel Aviv University Press, 1997.

Kurzman, Charles, ed. *Liberal Islam: A Sourcebook*. New York: Oxford University Press, 1998.

Kuschel, Karl-Josef. *Abraham: Sign of Hope for Jews, Christians and Muslims*. New York: Continuum, 1995.

Lewis, Bernard. *A Middle East Mosaic: Fragments of Life, Letters and History*. New York: Random House, 2000.

Mango, Andrew. *Atatürk: The Biography of the Founder of Modern Turkey*. Woodstock, N.Y.: Overlook Press, 1999.

Mernissi, Fatima. *The Veil and the Male Elite: A Feminist Interpretation of Women's Rights in Islam*. Reading, Mass.: Perseus Books, 1991.

Miller, Judith. *God Has Ninety-nine Names: Reporting from a Militant Middle East*. New York: Touchstone Books, 1997.

Mohaddessin, Mohammad. *Islamic Fundamentalism: The New Global Threat*. Washington, D.C.: Seven Locks Press, 1993.

Muhaiyaddeen, M. R. Bawa. *The Fast of Ramadan: The Inner Heart Blossoms*. Philadelphia: Bawa Muhaiyaddeen Fellowship, 2000.

Neusner, Jacob, and Tamara Sonn. *Comparing Religions Through Law*. London: Routledge, 2000.

Pipes, Daniel. *The Rushdie Affair: The Novel, the Ayatollah, and the West.* New York: Birch Lane Press, 1990.

Poston, Larry. *Islamic Da`wah in the West: Muslim Missionary Activity and the Dynamics of Conversion to Islam.* New York: Oxford University Press, 1992.

Rodinson, Maxime. *Mohammed.* Trans. by Anne Carter. New York: Vintage Books, 1974.

Schimmel, Annemarie. *Look! This Is Love: Poems of Rumi.* Austin, Texas: Ibis Books, 1996.

Shaw, Stanford J. *Turkey and the Holocaust: Turkey's Role in Rescuing Turkish and European Jewry from Nazi Persecution, 1933–1945.* New York: New York University Press, 1993.

Swidler, Leonard, ed. *Muslims in Dialogue: The Evolution of a Dialogue.* Lewiston, N.Y.: Edwin Mellen Press, 1992.

Taha, Mahmoud Mohamed. *The Second Message of Islam.* Trans. by Abdullahi A. An-Naim. Syracuse, N.Y.: Syracuse University Press, 1987.

Tibi, Bassam. *The Challenge of Fundamentalism: Political Islam and the New World Disorder.* Berkeley: University of California Press, 1998.

Williams, John Alden. *The Word of Islam*. London: Thames & Hudson, 1994.

Wolfe, Michael. *The Hadj: An American's Pilgrimage to Mecca*. New York: Grove Press, 1995.

Wormser, Richard. *American Islam: Growing Up Muslim in America*. New York: Walker, 1994.ix

Index